The Wonderful World of Pizzas, Quiches, and Savory Pies

The Wonderful World of Pizzas,

Quiches, and Savory Pies

Anna Teresa Callen

CROWN PUBLISHERS, INC.   NEW YORK

To my husband, HAROLD CALLEN,
who, through it all, managed to retain a sense of humor,
and to my many friends, who are still talking to me,
especially MICHELLE COUSIN, ANDREA DI NOTO, MARGUERITE STEVENS,
and my niece, VIVIAN WACHSBERGER, who typed a lot.
Many thanks to MARILYN EINHORN of M. M. Einhorn Maxwell Books
for her research help, and a very special thanks to MARIAN BEHRMAN,
my wise editor, for her guidance and kindness throughout the making of this book.

The following recipes are reprinted with permission:

"Lamb Ciste" from A Taste of Ireland *by Theodora FitzGibbon, published by Houghton Mifflin Company. Copyright © 1968 by Theodora FitzGibbon. Reprinted by permission.*

"Impanata di Pesce Spada Fiammetta di Napoli Oliver" from La Grande Cucina Siciliana, *published by Moizzi Editore, S.p.a. By permission of the author. Copyright © 1976 by Fiammetta di Napoli Oliver.*

"Torta Rustica" adapted from "Savory Souffle Roll" by Jean Hewitt of November 30, 1969, the New York Times Magazine. *Copyright © 1969 by The New York Times Company. Reprinted by permission.*

Inquiries should be addressed to Crown Publishers, Inc.,
One Park Avenue, New York, New York 10016
Printed in the United States of America
Published simultaneously in Canada by General Publishing Company Limited

Library of Congress Cataloging in Publication Data
Callen, Anna Teresa.
The wonderful world of pizzas, quiches, and savory pies.
1. Cookery, International. 2. Pastry. I. Title.
TX725.A1C2   641.8′24   80-23802
ISBN: 0-517-536838

Design by Deborah Bailey Kerner

Contents

Preface

The idea of this book was born out of observation. One day at a block party in New York, I noticed how cosmopolitan the humble pizza had become. Together with the ever-present Neapolitan and Sicilian pizzas, there were luscious quiches, green speckled *spanakopitta*, stuffed pittas, dribbling tacos, and many more elaborate dishes. In short, anything more or less flat, rolled, topped, filled, or unfilled was being devoured all around me by a cheerful crowd.

So, I said to myself, why not write a book about the many faces of these specialties, which in my native Italy would go under the all-comprehensive name of *pizze* and in many other lands are called savory pies.

What exactly is a pizza?

The name itself in the Italian vernacular means *flatten*. Loosely translated into English it becomes the word *pie*: hence pizzas are pies. They are the most snackable foods ever invented. They can be taken along for lunch, a picnic, to a friend's house, to an open-air concert, and to the races. They are eaten hot, cold, sliced, torn apart, with fork and knife, and with bare hands. They require little to wash them down: a glass of cool water or soda, a goblet of wine, or a mug of beer. Whether it is plain or fancy, everybody rejoices at the appearance of a beautiful pizza or pie.

What most Americans do not realize is that there are literally hundreds of variations of this basic idea of a one-dish meal baked in, on, or even without a crust. In Naples alone, there are over thirty variations of the round, flat type of pizza. All over Italy there are hundreds of variations of *pizza rustica*, a savory pie stuffed with all kinds of delicacies.

But the idea of a savory pie is universal. In France there is the quiche, which also comes in many taste-tempting forms. The most famous is quiche Lorraine, originally baked in bread dough, and it is filled with custard and bacon baked in a crust that the French call *pâte brisée*. Gourmets also revere the famous *kulebiaka* from Russia, the *spanakopitta* from Greece, the *b'Stilla* from Morocco, and the *Iflagun* from Egypt.

Almost all are easy to make. Some can be prepared in minutes and are appropriate for informal or formal dining. A few are elegant dishes that can reveal the culinary arts at their best. Some can be eaten either cold or hot. All are suitable for any season. This book includes the best, the most delicious, the most famous, and the least famous, which may turn out to be the most interesting.

All recipes have been adapted in accordance with modern American methods and all have been kitchen-tested.

I have also kept in mind our concern with nutrition and healthier eating habits. Whenever possible some ingredients have been eliminated and substitutions suggested.

A Historical Introduction

"And as he lay and slept under a juniper tree . . . an angel touched him and said unto him, Arise and Eat. And he looked, and behold, there was a cake baken on the coals and a cruse of water at his head. And he did eat and drink . . . and went in the strength of that meat forty days and forty nights" (First Book of Kings, 19–5,6,8).

This "cake," made of some sort of grain and water, was the progenitor of bread and, if we must believe the Bible, a great source of nourishment capable of supporting a heartsick Elijah in his long journey to the mountain of God, the Horeb.

More properly called *focaccia* in the Italian version of the Book (the name, in fact, derives from the Latin word *focus*, which means hearth), the cake of Elijah makes its appearance on top of a scorching stone.

It is amazing to see how many of today's breads are of Neolithic origin: the Mexican *tortilla*, the Scottish oatcakes, the Egyptian *ta*, the Italian *piadina*, and even the journey cakes (or johnnycakes), which the American settlers had learned to make from the Indians. Many of these are still prepared and cooked in a primitive way.

Bread, in general, was easy to make and was cheap. It was the food most available to people everywhere. Sometimes it was distributed gratis by rulers and from early times breads and "cakes" were also used as payment for property or labor. When bread became scarce—because of war or other calamities— riots would erupt.

The first recorded strike in history, according to writer Giorgio Mistretta, occurred in Egypt during the reign of Ramses IX (1154–1153 B.C.) when a group of farm laborers received their ration of beer and fat but not that of bread. Enraged, they refused to work and sent a delegation to Thebes to plead for their rights. Noted in the ledger by the delegation chief is the entry: "Today we finally received the bread, but we had to give two cases of it to the flag carrier," thus establishing the bribe as an ancient institution!

Historians agree on the notion that bread, as we know it today, originated in Egypt. The Egyptians had learned about fermentation from the Mesopotamians with whom they traded regularly. The women there prepared a brew by soaking partially baked "cakes," made from sprouted dried grains, and left to ferment for a day or two. By the end of the third millennium B.C., the Egyptians were producing several kinds of beer themselves, but the discovery of yeast from the foam of beer must have been a pure accident.

By the first century, yeast was being used by other civilizations as well. Pliny the Elder, before he died in the catastrophe of Pompeii in A.D. 79, had pointed out in his writings that the breads of the Gauls and the Iberians were lighter and more digestible than the local ones because they mixed "the foam of beer" into the flour. The Romans, instead, dipped their millet flour—a rather heavy stuff—into wine.

Judging from the evidence found in the ruins of buried cities like Pompeii and Herculaneum, we see how prominent was the art of baking. A certain Publius Pauquis Proculus owned one of the richest houses in Pompeii, proving that his occupation as a baker had been quite rewarding. An old picture of a Pompeian bakery shows an oven containing a large number of round loaves ready to be eaten. Unfortunately, the wrath of Vesuvius had stilled them into stones for posterity. A statue in the Museo Archeologico in Naples called "Il Placentario" (The "Cake" Vendor) again bears witness to the importance of baking.

Over the years, people, especially the poor, decided to improve on bread—not out of a desire to make it fancier but just to vary it. They started by adding a few seeds, some relishes, a sprinkling of herbs. The unsavory little "cake" of the plebes, thus adorned, was called a *moletum* by the Romans and later on *pizza* (meaning "flatten") by the Neapolitans.

Professor John Ades of Southern Illinois University traces the origins of pizza to Virgil (70–19 B.C.). In Book VII of the *Aeneid*, Virgil writes:

Aeneas and his chiefs and captains . . . place cakes of meal alone
The sword beneath the viands . . . and they crown the wheaten base with
fruits of the field . . . (They) turn their teeth upon the slender cakes
to profane with hand and jaw the fateful circle of crust.

The "circle of crust" is undoubtedly a pizza. But why does he call it "fateful"? Because the eating of this food reminded Aeneas of a similar meal in the land from which he was running. The repetition of such a meal in the land he had just reached was an indication that his destiny to found a new nation was about to be fulfilled.

One cannot help but muse over the coincidence of Virgil's adopted residence. After living in Rome for a while, he spent most of his mature life in Campania, mainly in Nola and Naples, a city commonly associated with pizza. He is buried there on the green hill of Posillipo, in a sumptuous mausoleum with glass windows that have a magic way of catching, for a few seconds, the last rays of the sun over the incandescent bay of Naples.

I agree with Waverly Root's statement in his book *The Food of Italy* that pizza, as we eat it today, is the sole invention of the Neapolitan people. Even before *pizza al pomidoro* (with tomato) appeared on the face of the earth, the Neapolitans were already improving their circle of crust with lard, oil, herbs, and when available, cheese. They were also the first to adopt the tomato brought back by Columbus's sailors from Peru. The Italian saying *Vale un Perú* (it has the value of Peru), to define something of great value, had its origin in those days. Neapolitan women concocted the delicious *pizza al pomidoro* among clouds of flour, slapping of dough, squashing of tomatoes, by passing to each other, door to door, the variations they found most appealing. Pizza was the special food with which they greeted the return of an overworked husband, rekindled the smile of a hungry child, consoled an afflicted friend—a true treat and an easily affordable one.

By the sixteenth century pizza had come out of these Neapolitan hovels, mainly those of Spaccanapoli, the anthill hole of the city. At that time the Tavern of the Cerriglio was a hangout for the Spanish soldiers of the Viceroy. They flocked there to feast on the specialty of the house—pizza.

One century later, pizza had already become fit for nobility. Ferdinand IV, King of Naples, in his summer palace of Capodimonte, allowed his cook to bake a few pizzas in the ovens in which his father, Charles III, had had his famous porcelain fired. Pizza had become a favorite dish of the king's wife, Maria Carolina.

In 1889 another pizza was royally emblazoned with the name of a queen, Margherita. This pizza was the same version that today Americans devour coast to coast without knowing that it was once fit for a queen. It is the pizza on which an inventive Neapolitan *pizzaiolo*, Raffaele Esposito, placed the first slice of mozzarella. The story, well documented, notes that when Esposito was summoned to the palace to prepare some of his famous pizzas, he made three different kinds. The queen declared all of them delicious but favored the pizza with mozzarella. Raffaele was delighted. He had decorated this particular one with a patriotic theme in mind, to honor the queen. The ingredients were the colors of the Italian flag: tomato for red, the mozzarella for white, and bright basil leaves for green.

Pizza was now ready to cross mountains and seas. Today one can find it in the most diversified places of the world.

Even famous chefs started to pay attention to this circle of dough and adapted it to their own taste and fantasy. Antonin Carême, chef par excellence, designed monumental *pizze rustiche* and savory pies, as one can witness from old cookbooks and prints. Pellegrino Artusi in his erudite cookbook *L'Arte di Mangiar Bene*, on which our Italian mothers were raised, does not think *pizza alla Napoletana* elegant enough for his concept of "The Art of Eating Well," so he adds sugar to it, eliminates the tomato, but keeps the name. On the other hand, his *pizze rustiche*, called sometimes appropriately, *pasticci* or *tortini*, are masterpieces.

Thus, the *focacce*, pizzas, and savory pies of the past, made by housewives and innkeepers to improve on bread and preserve meats, cheese, and vegetables, were refashioned by famous chefs. The dough, transformed and refined, became *pâte brisée*, or short and puff pastry. Stuffings were minced, combined with creamy sauces, and flavored with delicate spices. In short, the convenience food of such humble origins had become fit for the banquet table of the world.

How to Begin

Doughs and Pastries

CRUSTY-WRAP DOUGH

2½ packages active dry yeast
lukewarm water (105° to 115°F.)
3 cups all-purpose flour
salt

2 eggs
1 tablespoon lard, softened
1 tablespoon olive oil

Dissolve yeast in lukewarm water. Let stand for 10 minutes. In a mixing bowl combine flour and salt. Make a well in the center, add the eggs, beat a little, then add the lard and oil. Start blending the flour into the egg mixture. Gather into a ball. Turn dough out on a floured board. Knead the dough for about 10 minutes. Gather dough into a ball and place it in a lightly oiled bowl. Set the bowl in a warm place, cover, and let rise for 1 hour, or until doubled in bulk.

Punch dough down, knead a little, shape into a ball, and let rise again for about 1 hour. At this point dough is ready to use.

FOCACCIA AND PIZZA DOUGH
ONE RECTANGULAR FOCACCIA,
9 x 12 INCHES,
OR TWO 12-INCH PIZZAS

2 packages active dry yeast
1 cup lukewarm water (105° to
    115°F.)

3½ cups all-purpose flour
1½ teaspoons salt
3 tablespoons olive oil

Dissolve yeast in lukewarm water. Let stand for 10 minutes. In a mixing bowl combine flour and salt. Make a well in the center and pour in the oil and the yeast mixture. Beat the flour into the liquid and gather the mixture into a ball. Turn dough out on a floured board. Knead and slap the dough for about 15 minutes. While kneading, add a little more flour if necessary. Dough must be smooth, elastic, and not sticky. Gather dough into a ball and place it in a lightly oiled bowl. Set the bowl in a warm place, cover, and let rise for about 1 hour, or until doubled in bulk.

Punch dough down and knead a little. Shape into a ball and let rise again for about 1 hour. At this point dough is ready to use.

NOTE: After the first rising, dough can be punched down and refrigerated or frozen. If frozen, thaw in refrigerator overnight.

The following basic recipes can be used for pastry in many crostate, quiches, tarts, and *other savory pies, covered or uncovered. They can be made in a food processor as well (see p. 8), and can be frozen.*

PÂTE BRISÉE I
ONE 9-INCH 1-CRUST PIE
OR 6 SMALL TARTS

1½ cups all-purpose flour
¾ teaspoon salt
4 ounces (1 stick) butter, chilled, cut
    into pieces

¼ cup ice water

In a mixing bowl combine flour and salt. Add the butter and work with knives or a pastry blender (fingers will soften the butter too much) until mixture resembles coarse meal.

Pour in water a little at a time while mixing with a fork. You may not need all the water. Gather dough into a ball, wrap in a plastic wrap, and chill for 20 minutes, or until ready to use.

PÂTE BRISÉE II

*ONE 9-INCH 2-CRUST PIE
OR SIX SMALL 2-CRUST PIES*

2 cups all-purpose flour
½ teaspoon salt
4 ounces (1 stick) butter or
    margarine, chilled, cut into
    pieces

2 eggs, lightly beaten
1 tablespoon lemon juice
1 tablespoon ice water, if necessary

In a mixing bowl combine flour and salt. Add the butter or margarine, and work with knives or a pastry blender (fingers will soften fat too much) until mixture resembles coarse meal.

Make a well in the center and add eggs and lemon juice. Blend in the flour. If dough is too dry, add the water. Gather dough into a ball. Wrap in plastic wrap and chill for 20 minutes, or until ready to use.

WHEATEN EGG DOUGH

TWO 9-INCH 1-CRUST PIES

Especially suitable for meats and game pies.

1 cup all-purpose flour
½ cup whole-wheat flour
½ teaspoon salt
4 ounces (1 stick) butter, or 4
    ounces lard or vegetable
    shortening

1 egg, lightly beaten
3 tablespoons milk

In a mixing bowl combine both flours and the salt. Add butter or other fat and work with knives or a pastry blender (fingers will soften fat too much) until mixture resembles coarse meal.

Make a well in the center and add the egg and milk. Blend in the flour and gather dough into a ball. Turn dough out on a lightly floured pastry board and knead very lightly for a few minutes. Wrap in plastic wrap and chill for 20 minutes, or until ready to use.

AMERICAN PIECRUST
Lou-Ann Pilkington's Recipe

ONE 10-INCH 1-CRUST PIE

1½ cups flour
½ cup vegetable shortening, chilled
1 teaspoon salt

¼ cup cold water
1 egg (optional)
1 tablespoon white vinegar

Place flour in a mixing bowl. Chop shortening into flour. Add salt. Add cold water, a little at a time, and mix with a fork after each addition. Add egg, if used, and the vinegar. Turn dough out on a floured board and knead gently for a few minutes. Gather into a ball and chill for 30 minutes, or longer.

On a floured board, gently roll dough into a circle, turning over once or twice while rolling; this will prevent shrinkage of dough while cooking.

This dough is good also as a topping for casseroles and for turnovers or individual tarts.

Food Processor Method
For Piecrusts

Use steel blade; place flour, salt, and fat in the bowl of the processor. Turn machine on and off until mixture resembles coarse meal. Add liquids (water, juices, milk) through the feed tube and stop processing as soon as a ball of dough forms on the blade. You may not need all the liquid listed in the recipe, or you may need just a little more.

Wrap dough in plastic wrap and chill or freeze.

PASTA FROLLA SEMPLICE, FOOD PROCESSOR METHOD

ONE 12-INCH 2-CRUST PIE

3 cups all-purpose flour
½ cup instantized flour
2 ounces (½ stick) butter
4 tablespoons lard or vegetable
    shortening

1 egg
1 tablespoon sugar
pinch of salt
½ cup milk
water

Before starting, fit the steel blade in your food processor. In the bowl of the processor, place both flours and both fats. Turn machine on and off until mixture resembles coarse meal. Add remaining ingredients and milk, process until a ball of dough forms on the blades. If necessary, add a little water.

Wrap dough in plastic wrap and chill until ready to use.

This dough is particularly good with cheese pies and fish pies.

SHORT PASTRY

TWO 9-INCH 1-CRUST PIES
OR EIGHT 4-INCH TARTS

1¾ cups all-purpose flour
1 teaspoon salt
6 tablespoons chilled lard or
    vegetable shortening, cut into
    pieces

¼ cup ice water

In a mixing bowl combine flour and salt. Add the lard or shortening and work with knives or a pastry blender (fingers will soften fat too much) until mixture resembles coarse meal.

Pour in water, a little at a time, while mixing with a fork. You may not need all the water. Gather dough into a ball, wrap in plastic wrap, and chill for 20 minutes, or until ready to use.

VERY SHORT PASTRY

TWO 9-INCH 1-CRUST PIES

2 cups all-purpose flour
1 teaspoon salt
8 tablespoons chilled lard or
      vegetable shortening, cut into
      pieces
1 egg, lightly beaten
1 tablespoon cream or milk

In a mixing bowl combine flour and salt. Add the lard or vegetable shortening, and work with knives or a pastry blender (fingers will soften fat too much) until mixture resembles coarse meal.

Make a well in the center and add the egg and cream or milk. Mix with a fork and gather dough into a ball. Wrap in plastic wrap and chill for 20 minutes, or until ready to use.

These are particularly good for turnovers, knishes, stuffed fritters, and other small pastries.

CREAM CHEESE PASTRY

*14 TO 16 TURNOVERS
OR TWO 9-INCH 1-CRUST PIES*

8 ounces cream cheese, at room
      temperature
8 ounces (2 sticks) butter, at room
      temperature

¼ cup heavy cream
1 teaspoon salt
2 cups flour

In a mixing bowl beat cream cheese and butter until light and fluffy. Add heavy cream and salt; mix by hand. Add flour gradually and gather dough into a ball. Do not overhandle.

Wrap dough and refrigerate for at least 1 hour.

This dough can be prepared a few days ahead. It can be frozen. Defrost at bottom of refrigerator.

PUFF SHELL DOUGH
Pasta Bigne or Pâte à Choux

ONE 10-INCH SAVORY PIE
OR 20 TO 30 PUFFS

2 ounces (½ stick) butter
⅔ cup water
½ teaspoon salt

1 cup all-purpose flour
4 large eggs

Place butter, water, and salt in a saucepan. Bring to a boil, then reduce heat. As soon as butter has melted, add flour all at once, and stir vigorously with a wooden spoon until a dough forms and starts to come away from the sides of the pan. Beat the dough for 1 or 2 minutes and remove from heat. Cool.

Add 1 egg at a time to the dough and mix well until mixture is very thick, smooth, and shiny. This last part can be done in the bowl of a food processor.

This dough can be refrigerated for 1 to 2 days.

CLASSIC PUFF PASTRY
Pâte Feuilletée

3 BATCHES, ENOUGH FOR
3 MEDIUM-SIZE PIES

Nicolas Malgieri, former pastry chef at Windows on the World, the famous New York restaurant, has been the only one, at least for me, able to take the mystery out of puff pastry. Usually, the instructions are so involved that one loses heart before even trying. "No need," says Mr. Malgieri, "for all that chilling and wrapping of ingredients and equipment. Just be patient and work as fast as possible."

I wrote the following recipe while watching him perform at the New School for Social Research Culinary Department, and I hope it sounds as uncomplicated as Nicolas showed it to be.

This recipe takes a lot of time because the "turns," or folding and rolling of the dough, and the rest periods in between are necessary. Fortunately one can start the recipe 2 or 3 days in advance. The dough can be frozen for up to 4 months, to be thawed overnight at the bottom of the refrigerator, before using it. The scraps of finished dough can be reused; if possible, it is better not to roll scraps, for the dough will rise unevenly. Pat scraps together with a rolling pin, or use for small pastries.

1 cup ice water, approximately   4½ cups all-purpose flour
½ teaspoon salt   1¼ pounds (5 sticks) butter, chilled

Combine water and salt, stir, and set aside. Reserve ½ cup of the flour. Place remaining flour in a mixing bowl. Cut 1 stick of butter into small pieces directly into the bowl with the flour. Toss lightly with fingers. Slowly add just enough salted water to gather mixture into a soft dough. Form into a ball, wrap, and chill.

Place remaining butter sticks on a pastry board and pat with a rolling pin to make the butter blend together. Knead remaining flour into the butter, working quickly and thoroughly until no lumps remain and butter is softer but still firm. Form into a square block and set aside.

Place the chilled dough on the board. Cut a large cross at the top, opening up the ball of dough into a cloverleaf-shaped square with 4 "ears." Sprinkle lightly with flour and roll a little to flatten dough and the 4 "ears" to ½-inch thickness. Moisten dough with water. Place the butter block in the middle of the cloverleaf. Fold each "ear" over to form a package. Pat the package with the rolling pin to flatten it and roll into an even rectangle. Fold the rectangle into 3 parts and roll out again into an even rectangle like the first one; this is called a turn. Repeat the rolling and folding once more. Press 2 fingers into the dough to indicate that you have made 2 turns. Wrap and chill for 2 hours. The dough requires 5 or 6 turns in all with a rest period of at least 2 hours after each turn. At every "turn" press fingers into dough to mark how many "turns" dough has received.

As a rule this dough must be baked in a 425°F. oven.

QUICK PUFF PASTRY

ONE 10-INCH 2-CRUST PIE
OR 24 TURNOVERS

3½ cups instantized flour   1 cup plus 1 tablespoon cold water
2 teaspoons salt   14 ounces (3½ sticks) butter, diced

Combine flour and salt in a mixing bowl. Add water, a little at a time, and blend with an electric mixer at low speed to make a stiff dough. Add butter and continue mixing at low speed for 10 to 15 seconds. Gather the mixture into a ball, flatten top, wrap, and place in freezer for 10 minutes.

Proceed as in previous recipe until you have completed 4 turns. Chill overnight.

Next day give the dough 1 more turn before using. Chill a finished pie for 30 minutes before baking.

The following recipes are ideal for those preparations using brioche dough. The first one is made by hand and it is especially good for topping pot pies. The second, made in a food processor, never fails when filled or wrapped around food.

All brioche doughs can be prepared in advance and frozen well.

BRIOCHE DOUGH I

ONE 10-INCH 2-CRUST PIE

1 package active dry yeast
½ cup lukewarm water (105° to 115°F.)
2 ounces (½ stick) sweet butter, at room temperature

1 teaspoon sugar
3 eggs, at room temperature
2 teaspoons salt
3½ cups all-purpose flour

Dissolve yeast in lukewarm water. Let stand for 10 minutes. In a mixing bowl beat the butter until light and fluffy. Add the sugar. Beat in the eggs, the salt, and 1 cup flour. Add the yeast mixture. While continuing to beat, gradually add 2 more cups of flour.

Turn dough out on a floured board and knead until smooth, using remaining flour when necessary. Gather dough into a ball and place in a buttered bowl. Cover and set in a warm place to rise for 1½ hours.

Punch dough down, cover, and refrigerate. Place a weight on top of cover. Keep in refrigerator for at least 6 hours, or overnight. At this point the dough is ready to use.

Dough can be refrigerated for 24 hours or frozen.

BRIOCHE DOUGH II, FOOD PROCESSOR METHOD

ONE 9-INCH 2-CRUST PIE

1 package active dry yeast
½ cup lukewarm water (105° to
    115°F.)
4 ounces (1 stick) sweet butter, at
    room temperature

1 tablespoon sugar
3 eggs, at room temperature
1 teaspoon salt
2¾ cups all-purpose flour

Dissolve yeast in lukewarm water. Let stand for 10 minutes. Place butter and sugar in the bowl of a food processor fitted with the steel blade. Process while adding 1 egg at a time. Blend well. Add the salt, half of the flour, and the yeast mixture. Process until flour disappears. Reserve ¼ cup flour. Add remaining flour to the bowl and process until well blended. Dough will be soft and rather sticky.

Lightly oil a bowl and transfer the dough to it. Cover and let rise at room temperature for 1½ hours.

Punch down dough, cover, and place in refrigerator overnight.

Next day turn dough out on a floured board and knead for a few minutes, adding reserved flour if necessary. Gather dough into a ball and place in a lightly oiled bowl to rise for about 1½ hours.

This dough is excellent for all *en croûte* dishes.

AUSTRIAN STRUDEL PASTRY

2 STRUDEL STRIPS

This is the classic Viennese strudel pastry, which can be used for either sweet or savory pastries.

2 cups all-purpose flour
pinch of salt
1 teaspoon oil or butter, at room
    temperature

½ cup warm water

On a pastry board sift flour and salt together. Make a well in the center of the flour and add the oil or butter and the water. Mix in the flour and gather into a ball. Knead dough well, until smooth and elastic. You will need to sprinkle flour on the board while kneading, but use as little as possible.

Shape dough into a ball, brush it with a little oil, cover with a bowl, and let it rest for at least 45 minutes, away from drafts, before using it.

If you do not have a large table, divide the dough into 2 parts. Roll the dough as thin as possible with rolling pin and stretch it with the help of your fingers. Do not worry if dough tears. You can patch it up or ignore the hole. With practice this will become easier. The sheet should be paper-thin. (Many prefer to roll this dough on a well-floured linen cloth. It is a good idea to secure edges of cloth underneath table with tape.) Discard ends, which remain too thick.

Lightly oil the rolled dough or brush with melted butter, and let it rest for 10 minutes before filling.

HOT-WATER RAISED PASTRY

1 LARGE COVERED MOLDED PIE

4 cups sifted all-purpose flour
¾ teaspoon salt
pinch of ground mace

1 egg, lightly beaten
½ cup plus 2 tablespoons water
½ pound lard, cut into pieces

Butter and flour a mold. In a mixing bowl combine flour, salt, and mace. Add egg and mix. Bring the water and lard to a boil and immediately pour this into the mixing bowl. Stir quickly together with flour to make a ball. Turn out on a lightly floured board and knead quickly and briefly until smooth. Let the dough rest for a few minutes, but do not let it get too cool.

Pull off one third of the dough for the lid, wrap this portion, and reserve in a warm place. Pat the remaining dough by hand into a flat disc large enough to cover the bottom of the prepared mold. Drop dough into the mold and gently but quickly pat and stretch the dough up the sides of the mold. Let some dough hang over the edge. Add prepared filling as recommended in the recipe.

Roll out the dough for the lid and place it on the filled pie.

VARIATION: For individual pies use 3 cups cake flour and 1 cup water. Do not use egg. Other ingredients remain the same. This proportion will line 4 individual 7-ounce tins (like tuna tins). A good method of preparing empty cans is to discard top, cut bottom all around, but leave a little segment attached, like a hinge. When the pie is baked, the hinge can be cut and with the bottom you can push the cooked and cooled pie out of the tin.

Sauces

SUGO FINTO
Tomato Sauce

2 CUPS SAUCE

¼ cup olive oil
1 ounce (2 tablespoons) butter
1 small onion, chopped
1 small carrot, chopped
1 celery rib, chopped

1 parsley sprig, minced
2 cups canned tomato sauce
1 basil leaf or pinch of dried basil
salt and pepper

Pour the oil into a saucepan and add 1 tablespoon butter. Combine all chopped vegetables and add to saucepan. Cook over medium heat, stirring, for about 10 minutes. Add parsley, tomato sauce, basil, and salt and pepper to taste. Bring to a boil, cover, and cook over medium-low heat for 30 minutes. Remove from heat and add remaining butter. Stir.

NOTE: Sugo finto, literally fake sauce, is the name given to a tomato sauce made without meat.

PESTO
Basil and Garlic Sauce

1 CUP SAUCE

4 cups loosely packed basil leaves,
    washed and dried
4 or 5 garlic cloves
¼ cup olive oil

1 tablespoon pine nuts (pignoli)
1 tablespoon butter
pinch of salt

Place everything in the bowl of a food processor fitted with the steel blade, or in a blender. Process to a very fine purée.
    Pesto can be frozen.

SUGO ALLA MARINARA
Marinara Sauce

2 CUPS SAUCE

¼ cup olive oil
1 garlic clove
2 parsley sprigs
1 basil leaf or pinch of dried basil,
    or pinch of orégano

2 cups canned tomato sauce
salt and pepper

Place all ingredients in a saucepan. Bring to a boil, cover, and simmer for 15 minutes. Strain the sauce.

BÉCHAMEL SAUCE

1 CUP SAUCE

1 tablespoon butter
1 tablespoon flour
1 cup milk

pinch of salt
pinch of white pepper

Melt the butter in a saucepan. Add flour and let froth together. Cook for a few minutes, stirring with a wooden spoon. Remove from heat. Add the milk, a little at a time, stirring constantly until sauce liquefies. Set saucepan over medium heat and cook, stirring constantly, until sauce thickens and reaches the boiling point. Let the sauce puff once or twice. Remove from heat and add salt and pepper.

NOTE: If recipe calls for a thicker béchamel, add more flour at the beginning.

MORNAY SAUCE. Add 3 to 6 tablespoons coarsely grated Swiss cheese, or a combination of Swiss and Parmesan, to 1 cup of hot béchamel. Stir until cheese is melted and well combined.

TARRAGON SAUCE

1¼ CUPS SAUCE

1 cup dry wine
4 tablespoons chopped fresh
    tarragon
5 tablespoons minced fresh parsley
3 tablespoons minced shallots or
    green onions

1 cup Béchamel Sauce (p. 17)
1 tablespoon butter, at room
    temperature

Pour the wine into a saucepan. Add 3 tablespoons of the tarragon, 1 table-spoon of the parsley, and the shallots or green onions. Bring to a boil and reduce infusion to 3 to 4 tablespoons.

Strain, pressing as much juice out of herbs as possible. Combine strained infusion with béchamel sauce. Heat sauce and simmer for a few minutes. Remove from the heat. Stir in remaining herbs and the butter.

NOTE: If fresh tarragon is not available, use 1½ tablespoons dried tarragon with the wine and ¼ teaspoon dried tarragon in the béchamel.

Chervil can be used instead of tarragon to make chervil sauce.

MADEIRA SAUCE

2 TO 2½ CUPS SAUCE

¼ cup oil
4 or 5 fresh mushrooms, sliced
2 celery ribs, cut into 2-inch pieces
2 medium-size carrots, cut into
    2-inch pieces
1 medium-size onion

¼ cup all-purpose flour
1¼ cups beef broth
¾ cup dry Madeira wine
1 bay leaf
¾ cup water

Spoon 2 tablespoons oil into a 3-quart pan. Add mushrooms and cook over medium-high heat until tender, about 5 minutes. With a slotted spoon, remove mushrooms to a small bowl. Pour 2 tablespoons more oil into the same skillet. Add celery, carrots, and onion, and cook until all vegetables are soft, about 20 minutes. Add flour and cook, stirring frequently, until flour is lightly browned. Gradually stir in beef broth, the Madeira, bay leaf, and water; heat to boiling. Reduce heat to low; simmer uncovered for 15 minutes. With a slotted spoon, remove vegetables and bay leaf; discard them. Return cooked mushrooms to sauce, and heat through.

CHICKEN BROTH OR STOCK

1 stewing chicken (fowl), cleaned and fat taken out	1 carrot, scraped
	1 parsley sprig
1 onion	10 peppercorns
2 cloves	1 teaspoon salt
1 celery rib	

In a stockpot, or heavy casserole, place the chicken, the onion with the 2 cloves stuck into it, all the remaining ingredients, and enough water to come up 3 inches above vegetables and meat. Bring to a boil and simmer for 2 to 2½ hours.

Strain broth before using.

NOTE: Beef broth or stock is prepared exactly the same way. Use 3 to 4 pounds of stewing beef, bones included. Ask your butcher to give you a marrowbone and some veal bones. These are particularly good when one needs a more gelatinous type of stock.

Although this is not technically a sauce, I have included it here for convenience.

DUXELLES

1 CUP DUXELLES

½ pound mushrooms, minced	salt and pepper
1 tablespoon butter	3 tablespoons Marsala wine
1 tablespoon oil	3 tablespoons beef or chicken stock
2 tablespoons minced shallot	(optional)

Place mushrooms in the middle of a linen towel, wrap towel around them to make a ball, and twist to extract as much liquid as possible from mushrooms. Do this on top of a bowl to save the juices, which can be used in soups or stews. Place butter and oil in a skillet, heat, and add shallot. Sauté shallot until golden. Add mushrooms and continue to sauté, stirring occasionally, until mushrooms are lightly browned. Season with salt and pepper. Add wine, and stock if used. Continue to cook over low heat until liquids are evaporated. When cooled, store in refrigerator, or freeze.

Cooking Hints

To test the freshness of yeast, add a little sugar when dissolving it in water. If the mixture doesn't bubble within 10 minutes, the yeast is dead. Yeast and water alone do not bubble without sugar.

Bread dough must be "worked" well. Kneading and slapping on the pastry board is the best method for good texture.

Risen dough needs little kneading. After shaping *focacce, pizze,* etc., let dough stand at room temperature for 10 to 15 minutes before baking.

When refrigerating yeast dough overnight, punch dough to deflate it and put a weight on it to prevent rising. It can also be frozen, well-wrapped in plastic wrap.

While making dough, yeast dough included, if you suddenly have to go out, do not panic. Just refrigerate it.

Yeast dough is better when stretched by hands. When ready to shape, do not cut with a knife, just break.

Pizza crusts should not be more than ½ inch thick or they will not come out thin and crusty, as they should.

Always drain vegetables well before topping pizzas.

Add mozzarella or other melting cheeses 5 to 10 minutes before taking pizza out of the oven. Cheese will dry out otherwise. It is a good idea to dribble a little oil over cut-up mozzarella. This step will prevent cheese from drying when added to a pizza.

Add seafood at the last 5 minutes to avoid toughness in the fish.

Bake all pizzas at a high temperature—400° to 450°F.

Pierce bottoms and sides of pastry-lined pans before filling. This is necessary for *pâte brisée* if not prebaked. Crust will bubble and puff up unevenly if this is not done.

When prebaking *pâte brisée* cover pastry with aluminum foil and fill with beans or rice to prevent dough bubbling unevenly. Store "baked" beans in a jar to reuse for the same purpose.

Pâte brisée, short pastry, and piecrusts in general will have a more tender texture if 1 tablespoon butter is substituted for part of lard or vegetable shortening.

When possible, reserve 1 to 2 tablespoons of beaten egg when working eggs into dough or filling. You can use this quantity to make egg wash. Just add 1 or 2 tablespoons of water or milk to dilute egg. (The French name of this egg wash is *dorure.)* Leftover egg mixture can be frozen for up to 3 months.

Prosciutto is excellent and more flavorful than ham. When a recipe calls for chopped prosciutto, ask your grocer to sell you a *culetto* (an end piece); it is less expensive and it works very well for stuffings.

When a recipe calls for peeled tomatoes, just place the tomatoes in a bowl and pour boiling water on them. Let cool a little, just enough to handle; lift out of the boiling water, as you don't want them to cook. You will find tomatoes easy to peel this way.

Peel peppers by charring the skin over a gas flame or in a broiler, or baking them in a hot oven until skin blisters.

When deep-frying, purify the hot oil by first adding a piece of bread soaked in vinegar. Bread should float immediately in hot oil; if it sinks to the bottom of the frying kettle, oil is not ready. However, by the time the bread browns, the oil will be of the right temperature. Fried food will keep nice and crisp for 30 to 45 minutes in a switched-off oven, or in an oven with a pilot light.

If pies have been refrigerated, bring them to room temperature before serving. If warming is called for, be sure to follow instructions. As a rule place in a preheated 350°F. oven for about 30 minutes.

Spinach is used often in these recipes. Keep in mind that 1¼ pounds of fresh spinach will yield 1 cup of squeezed cooked spinach.

When making stock or broth, freeze some of the strained liquid in ice-cube trays. You will have your own bouillon cubes when needed.

When quantities for salt and pepper and herbs and spices are omitted, it means "to your own taste."

When type of wine is not specified, it means to your own taste, white or red, but preferably dry. Of course in countries where drinking wine is not the custom, there is no mention of it.

Leftover dough can be frozen or used for little biscuits.

Leftover fillings, if cooked, can be used in sauces, or to dress pasta or rice. If uncooked (egg, vegetables, cheeses), it can be used in omelets, mixed in scrambled eggs, or to stuff vegetables.

$\mathcal{I}taly$

taly holds a special place in this book. Ada Boni, the doyenne of Italian food connoisseurs, lists about a hundred recipes for *focacce, pizze, crostate, calzoni, frittelle*, etc., in her book *Il Talismano della Felicità* under the general name of *pizze rustiche*. But Italy has many more varieties.

Italians love pizzas with a passion. They eat them at every hour of the day: for breakfast, with the 11 A.M. aperitivo, as a snack in the afternoon, and as an entrée for supper.

It is a ritual to go to a pizzeria after a show in the wee hours of the night when Italian theaters close their doors.

Some pizzas are traditionally made for holidays. Anchovy pizza is eaten for lunch on the day before Christmas, the *torta pasqualina* and *fiadone* at Easter. There is no picnic without a *pizza rustica* in a basket, and no party without a selection of *pizzette*.

Among the long and varied lists of *pizze* there are many that can be served as an entrée or a main dish. Most of them can be prepared in advance, served cold, or easily reheated. Many are much better if made a day in advance.

An added bonus, in these days of rising prices, is that *pizza rustica* can inspire an imaginative cook to use leftovers and present them at the dinner table without apologies.

FOCACCE AND PIZZE

What is the difference between *focacce* and *pizze*? Not much really. In the North of Italy a pizza, unless the dish is one of the classic Neapolitan kind, is more often called *focaccia*. *Focaccia* per se is rather unadorned: a sprinkling of salt and a few drops of olive oil make the condiment. It is eaten like bread or split and filled like a sandwich.

Focacce and flat pizzas (let's make a distinction here because *pizze rustiche* sometimes are monumental, layered, and stuffed with a variety of foods) are basically made of bread dough, but not necessarily so, as in the case of *castagnaccio* which is made with chestnut flour, and *gattò* which is usually made with potatoes.

FOCACCIA DEL FORNAIO
Baker's Focaccia

SERVES 15

If you go to a bakery in Italy early in the morning, you will find fresh, warm *focacce* which you can buy by the piece. These golden slabs of flattened dough, finger marked with little wells into which a drop of oil and a grain of salt always come to rest and melt during the baking, are cooked before the regular bread, to test the heat of the oven. Oil and salt are the usual condiment for a basic *focaccia* like this one.

1 batch of *focaccia* and Pizza Dough   olive oil
    (p. 6), ready to use   Kosher or rock salt

Preheat oven to 400°F. Lightly oil a baking sheet 10 x 15 inches. Flatten dough with hands and place it on the sheet. With oiled fingers, or a rolling pin, stretch the dough into a ¾-inch-thick rectangle the size of the baking sheet. Press fingers into dough and make little wells about 2 inches apart all over the dough. Dribble oil on the dough and sprinkle it with salt. Let it rest for 15 to 20 minutes.

Bake for 20 to 25 minutes, or until golden.

NOTE: In some parts of Italy, fennel seeds or herbs such as basil, orégano, etc., are sprinkled all over the *focaccia.*

In Apulia, the southern region forming the spur and the heel of the Italian boot, the *puddica* (a local *focaccia)* is prepared as usual, but after the dough is flattened, a mixture of tomato, garlic, oil, salt, and orégano, is pushed into the wells instead of being spread all over.

FOCACCIA DEL MIETITORE (Reaper's Focaccia). Split a baker's *focaccia* and fill with a combination of yellow, red, and green bell peppers, roasted, peeled, cut into strips, and dressed with olive oil, minced garlic, and parsley, and sliced mozzarella cheese.

FOCACCIA DELLA VIGILIA (Christmas Eve Focaccia). This is a specialty from the Abruzzi, traditionally eaten for lunch the day before Christmas, instead of the customary middle-of-the-day meal.

Make wells in the *focaccia* dough and press pieces of anchovy into them. Dribble with oil and sprinkle with pepper.

FOCACCIA DI CASTELLANETA
Castellaneta's Focaccia

SERVES 16

A specialty from Apulia. Castellaneta is famous for its beautiful twelfth-century cathedral.

¼ cup olive oil	6 anchovy fillets, chopped
2 leeks, trimmed and sliced	salt and pepper
2 pounds Italian broccoli, tender parts only	1 baker's focaccia (p. 24), already cooked

Pour the oil into a skillet, heat slightly, and add leeks; cook for 5 minutes. Add broccoli, cover skillet, reduce heat, and cook for 10 minutes. Check broccoli, stir, and add a little water, if necessary, to prevent burning. Add anchovies and salt and pepper to taste. Cook for 5 minutes longer and remove from heat.

Split *focaccia* into halves, fill with vegetables, and serve.

WINE: Bianco di Locorotondo, Apulia

PIADINA

Emilia-Romagna is considered one of the greatest eating regions of Italy. The land, fertilized by the Po River as it flows toward the Adriatic Sea, is rich and prosperous. On its arrival at the sea, the Po settles serenely into a large delta which is famous for the best eels and *capitoni* (a special kind of eel, very fat in comparison to the usual, long thin eel, and a specialty for Christmas Eve) of Italy. The Adriatic coast, with its resort towns of Rimini, Riccione, Cattolica, is a mecca for fish lovers.

Bologna, the capital, has earned the sobriquet of *la grassa*, the fat one. And yet its women are some of the slimmest, most elegant, and good looking of Italy.

Parma, a town beloved by artists and writers like Stendhal and Boccaccio, who even mentions its famous cheese in the *Decameron*, produces one of the best hams of Italy, prosciutto di Parma, which goes very well with *piadine*.

Giovanni Pascoli, the poet on whom Italian children are nurtured, called *piadina* "the bread, actually the national food of Romagna." In its simplicity, *piadina* is indeed the best accompaniment for the exquisite salami, cotechini, hams, and cheeses on which the people of this region dote.

The *piadina* is cooked in a special pan called *testo*. Since I do not have one, I improvise with an iron skillet turned upside down on the heat. When the skillet is scorchingly hot, I cook the *piadina* on it. Of course, one can try the ancient method of the stones. After all, this food is the direct descendant of Elijah's "cake"! But, jokes aside, my method works very well.

It is great fun to make *piadine* in the open air. The skillet can be put directly on the charcoal or a wood fire. Have a tray of sliced salami, prosciutto, ham, and cheese ready. Pass the *piadine* around as soon as they are cooked, and let everyone top his own with the meat of his choice.

PIADINA ROMAGNOLA

10 TO 12 PIADINE

4 cups all-purpose flour
½ teaspoon baking soda
salt
⅓ cup lard or vegetable shortening,
    melted and cooled

⅓ cup milk
warm water

In a mixing bowl combine dry ingredients. Make a well in the center and pour in the melted fat, milk, and enough water to obtain a consistent dough. Turn dough out on a pastry board and knead for 5 minutes. Shape a piece of dough into a ball the size of an egg. Flatten the dough into a circle 1/16 inch thick. Sprinkle with flour to prevent sticking. Repeat with the next ball. Place the *piadine* one on top of another until you have all of them ready. Keep covered with a napkin.

Place an iron skillet upside down on the heat. Let it get very hot. Dribble a drop of water on the skillet; if it skips and dries immediately, skillet is ready. Place 1 *piadina* at a time on the skillet. Pierce with a fork while cooking. Let it get brown at the bottom, turn, and cook the other side. *Piadine* are done in 5 minutes. Keep cooked *piadine* hot.

Leftover *piadine* can be reheated in the oven. Just sprinkle them with a little water.

TIGELLE MONTANARE

ABOUT 24 TIGELLE

This preparation takes its name from the fireproof round discs with which *tigelle* were cooked, on the hearth, amid flaming chestnut leaves. A waffle grill will do as well if one doesn't mind getting a crust which is a trifle thicker than it should be. I make mine in a *pizzelle* machine, but another solution, and a good one, is to fry them. After the *tigelle* are cooked, they are coated with a spread called *battuto*. It is fun to make *tigelle* in the presence of guests and let them eat as soon as they are made.

3 packages active dry yeast
1 cup lukewarm water (105° to
    115°F.)
3 tablespoons lard or vegetable
    shortening

4 cups all-purpose flour
salt and pepper

Dissolve yeast in lukewarm water and let stand for 10 minutes. Melt lard and cool. In a mixing bowl combine flour with salt and pepper to taste. Make a well in the center and pour in the yeast mixture and the lard. Beat in the flour. Turn dough out on a floured board. Knead the dough for about 15 minutes, until smooth and soft. Place it in a floured bowl and set in a warm place to rise for about 1 hour.

If *tigelle* are to be cooked in a waffle iron or *pizzelle* machine, pull a piece of dough the size of an egg from the prepared batch and cook as you would a waffle or a *pizzella*.

To fry them: Roll dough into a very thin sheet, less than ⅛ inch thick, and cut into 4-inch rounds. Deep-fry in hot oil, drain, and keep warm.

BATTUTO

¼ pound prosciutto	2 garlic cloves
1 teaspoon rosemary (better if fresh)	2 tablespoons lard or vegetable shortening

Chop all *battuto* ingredients together. Use a blender or a food processor, since the mixture should be very creamy and smooth, so that it can spread easily on the *tigelle*. Place *tigelle* and *battuto* on a serving tray and let everyone help themselves, or cut *tigelle* into halves, spread one half with *battuto*, and top with other half to make little sandwiches.

NOTE: *Pizzelle* machines are sold in Italian specialty shops and some department stores.

CASTAGNACCIO FIORENTINO
Chestnut-Flour Pie

16 SQUARE PIECES

Castagnaccio is, in a way, considered the pizza of Florence. If the Ligurians are famous for their *farinata*, so are the Tuscans for their *castagnaccio*. Sold by street vendors, it is eaten in the middle of the afternoon with a frothy *cappuccino* or an aromatic cup of tea.

Recipes for *castagnaccio* are found in many old books, going back to the Renaissance. This is one of them.

1 pound chestnut flour (see Note)
salt
2 tablespoons oil
2½ cups water

2 tablespoons raisins
2 tablespoons pine nuts (pignoli)
2 tablespoons chopped walnuts

In a mixing bowl combine chestnut flour and salt. Add oil and water, a little at a time, to obtain a rather liquid batter.

Preheat oven to 375°F. Oil a baking sheet 15 x 10 inches, and pour the batter on it. Arrange raisins, pine nuts, and walnuts over the top. Bake for 45 to 50 minutes, or until quite brown and crunchy. The top should crack slightly.

Serve at room temperature.

NOTE: Chestnut flour is sold in Italian specialty shops or health-food stores.

FARINATA DI CECI
Chick-Pea Pie

16 PIECES

This type of *focaccia* is found all along the coastal arch of the Italian and French rivieras. It is sold mostly in open-air markets by street vendors and in wine taverns as a snack and as a buffer for heavy drinking.

The condiment varies somewhat according to the town. In some places minced onions or rosemary are sprinkled on top of the *farinata* before it is baked. In San Remo, the *farinata* is very thin and crisp, as it is in Nice, where it is called *socca*.

1 pound chick-pea flour (see Note)
3 cups water
¼ cup oil

salt
freshly ground pepper

Place chick-pea flour in an earthenware or china bowl and add the water, a little at a time, stirring with a whisk to prevent lumping. Set mixture aside for at least 4 hours or longer. Keep in a cool place.

When ready to cook, preheat oven to 450°F. Coat a baking sheet 15 x 10 inches with 1 tablespoon oil. Set pan aside.

Remove foam formed on the top of the chick-pea mixture. Pour in remaining oil, and salt and pepper to taste. Stir well. The mixture should have the consistency of a pancake batter. If too thick, add more water. Pour mixture onto the prepared baking sheet. Bake until top becomes nicely brown, in 10 to 15 minutes. For extra crispness, place under a broiler for the last 5 minutes.

Grind pepper on the *farinata*. Cut into diamonds or squares, and serve hot.

NOTE: Chick-pea flour is sold in Italian specialty shops or health-food stores.

PIZZA CLASSICA ALLA NAPOLETANA
Classic Neapolitan Pizza

SERVES 8

As I pointed out in the Introduction, according to Waverly Root, the noted American food writer, pizza with tomatoes is the invention of the Neapolitans. He says, "the antiquity of pizza as a Neapolitan dish is firmly established," and nobody can dispute that. The Neapolitans spread the fame of their beloved pizza to the four winds, making more conquests than the legions of Caesar.

A Neapolitan will tell you that one can live with a piece of bread, a tomato, and a little oil. True! You will very often see Italian children at snack time biting into a slab of thick bread smeared with olive oil and topped with a few slices of fresh red tomatoes. It takes only another step and a little inventiveness to go from this simple repast to a succulent pizza.

DOUGH
1 batch of Pizza Dough (p. 6),
    ready to use

TOPPING
3 tablespoons olive oil   pinch of orégano
4 or 5 ripe pear-shaped tomatoes, salt
    peeled and seeded   1 garlic clove, minced

Preheat oven to 425°F. Lightly oil a 12-inch pizza pan. Flatten the dough and place it in the prepared pan. With oiled fingers stretch the dough toward the rim of pan, pushing to form a ½-inch rim all around. In a small bowl combine the oil, tomatoes, orégano, salt to taste, and garlic. Spread this mixture on top of prepared dough. Bake for 25 to 30 minutes, until rim gets crusty and brown.

Cut into wedges and serve.

VARIATIONS OF CLASSIC NEAPOLITAN PIZZA

NOTE: As a rule, cheese and seafood are added during the last 5 to 10 minutes of cooking, unless otherwise specified.

alle cozze (with mussels). Add 1 pound shelled mussels during the last 5 to 10 minutes.

Margherita or *della Regina* (Margherita or of the Queen). Substitute basil for orégano, preferably fresh basil. Add sliced or diced mozzarella cheese. Use no garlic.

alla Romana. Add anchovies, in fillets or coarsely chopped, and a pinch of pepper. Finish with sliced mozzarella and a sprinkling of grated Parmesan cheese.

alla Siciliana. Add chopped onions and anchovies. Finish with shredded caciocavallo or provolone cheese.

alla Ligure (Ligurian style). Substitute rosemary for orégano and add a handful of pitted black olives.

antica alla Frattese (ancient, from Fratta). Omit tomato. Just top pizza with a mixture of grated cheese and oil (2 to 3 tablespoons of each) and a pinch of pepper. This is also called *pizza bianca,* "white pizza," and dates back to the classic Neapolitan pizza, before tomatoes were discovered.

all'ortolana (kitchen-garden style). Substitute roasted and peeled red, yellow, and green peppers, cut into strips, for the tomatoes. Add a handful of pitted green olives.

alla Siracusana (Syracuse style). Use no tomatoes. Top with fried eggplants, mozzarella slices, orégano, peppers, green olives, and a few spoons of tomato sauce.

all'Amalfitana (Amalfi style). Use no tomatoes. Top with ½ pound uncooked, fresh small sardines, heads removed, and dressed with a mixture of olive oil, salt, pepper, and 1 garlic clove, minced.

con gli occhi (with the eyes). Add tomato slices, oil, anchovies, 2 tablespoons Parmesan cheese, and pepper, and cook for 15 minutes. Add 3 tablespoons shredded mozzarella, and cook for 5 minutes more. Break 4 eggs on top of the pizza, add salt, and continue cooking until eggs are done, 5 to 8 minutes.

della luna (of the moon). With fingers spread oil on pizza, nothing else. Cook for 20 minutes and top with ¼ cup pesto.

quattro stagioni (four seasons). With a knife score prepared uncooked pizza in 4 sections. Top each section with the following condiments:
   pitted black olives and chopped anchovies; dribble with oil;
   pickled artichokes in oil;
   sautéed mushrooms;
   raw mussels or clams tossed in olive oil and minced garlic; add these
      during the last 5 minutes of cooking.

Or substitute the condiment of any one section with one of these:
   tomato fillets and diced mozzarella cheese;
   prosciutto strips and diced mozzarella cheese;
   chopped onions, Gruyère cheese, and ham;
   sautéed onions and zucchini, or eggplants, and orégano.

PIZZA DI ZUCCHINE
Zucchini and Cheese Pizza

SERVES 8

This is one of the many pies without a crust.

3 eggs
3 cups grated zucchini or summer
   squash, drained and squeezed
⅓ cup all-purpose flour, or more if
   needed
2 slices of prosciutto or bacon,
   chopped
salt and pepper
¼ cup mozzarella cheese, shredded

¾ cup smoked mozzarella cheese,
   shredded
12 black olives, pitted and sliced
3 scallions, chopped
pinch of orégano
pinch of basil
3 tomatoes, sliced thin

Preheat oven to 450°F. Butter a 12-inch pizza or quiche pan. Beat eggs well in a mixing bowl. Add zucchini, flour, and prosciutto or bacon; stir well.

Add salt and pepper to taste. Spread mixture in prepared pan and bake for 15 minutes. Remove from oven and reduce temperature to 350°F.

Combine all the mozzarella, olives, and scallions. Scatter this mixture evenly on the zucchini. Sprinkle with orégano and basil, arrange the tomato slices on top, and bake for 20 to 30 minutes longer.

Serve hot or cold.

PIZZE RUSTICHE AND TORTE RUSTICHE

Pizze rustiche and *torte rustiche* are savory pies *par excellence;* the names can be used interchangeably. The former is heard more in the South and the latter in the North. In general, when we Italians say pizza we mean a savory pie, but there are also sweet pizzas, and in that case one must say *pizza dolce,* which indicates a cake. The same happens with *torta,* which is a cake unless it is followed by the word *rustica,* and then we know that it is a savory pie.

In the following recipes, there is sometimes no indication of the number of portions the dish can serve, since the pies can be cut into small or large pieces. For instance, bite-sized pieces are more appropriate for cocktail parties, larger pieces for a lunch or dinner.

FIADONE VILLESE

SERVES 8

Fiadone is the Abruzzese *pizza rustica,* which is traditional for Easter. The name is of barbaric origin, late Latin from Germanic tribes, and it means *focaccia* or pizza. There is another region of Italy using this name—the Trentino-Alto Adige in the North. There *fiadoni* (they prefer the plural) are sweets shaped in the form of turnovers.

This recipe was given to me by a very famous professional chef, Antonio Stanziani, the recipient of the "Golden Oscar" from the Accadèmia Italiana della Cucina and the Director of the Chef's School of Villa Santa Maria, one of the oldest in the world.

Stanziani, an ebullient and enthusiastic man, is unusually modest. When I told him that I would name this recipe for him, he declared with the gusto of an opera performer, *"Giammai!* (never). This is *fiadone villese,* a specialty of

Villa Santa Maria. It belongs to the people, every family here makes it for the Easter season!" Well, he may be right in a way, but nobody has his expertise and, if we consider the uncontrollable Italian need to personalize a recipe, this is an Antonio Stanziani specialty.

DOUGH

3 eggs
2 teaspoons baking powder
¼ cup olive oil

3½ cups all-purpose flour
⅓ cup milk
1 tablespoon water or milk

FILLING

6 small eggs
1 tablespoon baking powder
1 pound pecorino Romano or Sardo
    cheese, grated

pepper
nutmeg

In a mixing bowl, beat the eggs. Remove 2 tablespoons of egg to a cup to use later for egg wash. Add baking powder and oil to eggs. Beat, blending in the flour and adding the milk gradually. Turn dough out on a lightly floured board and knead until smooth. Gather into a ball and set aside.

Preheat oven to 350°F. Butter a 12-inch pie pan. In a mixing bowl beat the 6 eggs until frothy. Add remaining filling ingredients, and mix well.

Divide dough into 2 parts. Roll one piece at a time into a round sheet as thin as possible. Cut first sheet with a toothed wheel into a 14½-inch circle and line the prepared pan with it. Let the edge of the dough hang over the side of the pan all around. Pour filling into dough. Cut second sheet into a 13-inch circle and cover the filling.

Add 1 tablespoon water or milk to the reserved beaten egg in the cup. With this egg wash paint a rim on the top of the dough all around the outer edge. Fold overhanging dough in and press to seal. Flute decoratively. Paint with remaining egg mixture. Pierce top with a toothpick. Bake for 1 hour, or until nice and golden.

Serve at room temperature.

WINE: Mr. Stanziani recommends a good glass of Abruzzese *vino cotto*, which is not easily found in the United States. As an alternative, a good dry Marsala or a dry port will do nicely.

PIZZA ALL'ANDREA

ONE 12-INCH PIZZA

This pizza, a specialty from Liguria, was supposedly invented by the Doge Andrea Doria. Throughout the centuries the name has changed a little. From *pizza all'Andrea* it became *pizzalandrea,* and now, in Ligurian dialect, is just *pissadella.* Along the coast, though, it appears under a different name—*Sardaneira.* Personally, I think this must have been what it was called before the Doge made it famous. *Sardaneira* comes from the word sardine, which gives this pizza its distinctive taste.

DOUGH

1 package active dry yeast

¼ cup lukewarm milk (105° to 115°F.)

1¾ cups all-purpose flour

salt

2 tablespoons olive oil

¼ cup warm water

TOPPING

3 tablespoons olive oil

1 onion, sliced

1 pound ripe pear-shaped tomatoes, or 8 ounces canned peeled tomatoes

2 teaspoons tomato paste

2 fresh basil leaves, or pinch of dried basil

5 ounces canned sardines, coarsely chopped

2 garlic cloves, slivered

20 black olives, pitted and halved

Dissolve yeast in lukewarm milk and set in a warm place. In a mixing bowl, combine flour and salt. Make a well in the middle and add oil and the yeast mixture. Beat in the flour and add water, a little at a time, only enough to obtain a soft, smooth dough. Turn dough out on a floured board and knead for about 15 minutes. Gather dough into a ball, place in a slightly oiled bowl, cover with a napkin, and set in a warm place to rise for about 2 hours.

When dough is about ready to be used, preheat oven to 400°F. In a saucepan heat the 3 tablespoons olive oil. Add the onion slices and cook over medium heat until soft and translucent. Do not let onion get brown. If fresh tomatoes are used, pour boiling water on them, then peel, seed, and chop. If canned tomatoes are used, drain, remove seeds, and chop. Add tomatoes to onion, together with tomato paste and basil. Cook, uncovered, over medium heat for about 15 minutes, until juices evaporate. However, do not let the mixture get too dry. Add sardines and cook briefly, just to heat through.

Oil a 12-inch pizza pan. Stretch the risen dough with your fingers and place in the pan. Continue stretching until dough covers the entire surface of the pan. Push dough against the rim to make an edge so sauce will not run out. Pour sauce over the dough. Scatter the garlic pieces, together with olives, all over the top. Bake for 20 to 25 minutes, until rim is brown and crusty.

PIZZA UMBRA DI PASQUA ALLA CECILIA
Easter Umbrian Pizza alla Cecilia

TWO 8-INCH ROUND PIZZAS

Cecilia was the nanny who raised my three cousins, Gianna, Franca, and Adriana. She wasn't at all the refined English type, although my aunt tried to transform her into one. She came from the mountains of Foligno, in Umbria, a town famous for its chimney sweepers. It took a week of bathing and grooming to eliminate the smell of goats from Cecilia. She always looked awkward in starched white collars and bonnet, pushing an elegant British pram. The war and the growth of the girls cured all that. For the rest of her life with us, she was dressed normally, with our discarded dresses and new shoes; ours didn't fit. We adored her. Never humble, but extremely patient and good natured, she loved the summer best, when our dispersed families would converge on grandmother's house in the country. There she could revert to her old ways and tend the chickens, rabbits, and pigeons. My father and uncle always took her around when buying animals for the farm as she knew which ones were the best.

I was the oldest of the girls and the first one to get married. It is customary in Italy for relatives and close friends to give silver objects at weddings. Cecilia was very upset when I forbade her to buy me silver spoons but asked for a deluxe edition of *Il Talismano della Felicità (The Talisman of Happiness)* by Ada Boni, which is the bible of Italian cooking. She, of course, obliged. To this day I cannot read the inscription on the book written in my cousin's handwriting (Cecilia didn't trust her own) without feeling a knot in my throat. It reads *Alla Signorina Teri* (my nickname) *con affetto* (To Miss Teri with affection). There is an addition, which I remember she insisted on. Between *Alla* and *Signorina* another word is inserted—*Cara* (beloved).

This pizza comes from Cecilia's goat land, and it carries the sweetness of the hills of Umbria so loved by Giotto and Saint Francis.

3 packages active dry yeast	1 teaspoon ground cinnamon
½ cup lukewarm water (105° to 115°F.)	4 eggs
	1 cup ricotta cheese
butter and flour for baking dishes	salt
3½ cups all-purpose flour	grated rind of 1 lemon

Dissolve yeast in lukewarm water and set aside in a warm place. Butter and flour 2 soufflé dishes or charlotte molds, 8 to 9 inches in diameter; set aside.

In a mixing bowl combine 3½ cups flour and the cinnamon. Make a well in the center and break the eggs into it; beat with a fork. Add ricotta, salt to taste, and lemon rind. Blend in the flour and add the yeast mixture. Gather into a bowl and turn onto a floured board. Knead until dough is smooth and velvety. Add more flour when necessary, by sprinkling the board and pushing excess flour aside. Divide dough into 2 parts and place in the prepared dishes, which should not be more than half full. Let the pizzas rest, covered with a napkin and away from drafts but not in a warm spot, for at least 10 hours, or overnight.

Bake in a preheated 375°F. oven for about 1 hour. Insert a skewer to test for doneness; if it comes out clean the pizzas are cooked. This dish can be eaten either as a snack or as a dessert.

WINE: Orvieto Abboccato, well chilled

ERBAZZONE DI REGGIO EMILIA
Grass Pie from Reggio Emilia

SERVES 6

The name *erbazzone* comes from the word *erba*, meaning grass in Italian. And indeed when you cut the pie it looks as though it's filled with grass.

Many kinds of green leafy vegetables can be used, for example, spinach, chicory, and escarole. This recipe uses Swiss chard, which makes a more delicate *erbazzone*.

In Lombardy this pie is called *scarpazzon* (old big shoe)—funny name, and they do not even use a crust. The filling, plus a few additions, is simply baked in a casserole.

DOUGH

3 cups all-purpose flour
1 teaspoon salt
4 tablespoons lard or vegetable
　　shortening at room temperature

warm water
oil for pan

FILLING

2 pounds Swiss chard
¼ pound bacon
2 garlic cloves, sliced
3 parsley sprigs
3 leeks, green included, washed and
　　chopped

¾ cup grated Parmesan cheese
1 egg, slightly beaten
salt and pepper

In a mixing bowl, combine flour and salt. Make a well in the center and add softened fat and enough water to make a soft dough. Gather into a ball and chill, wrapped in wax paper, for 30 minutes.

Wash and trim Swiss chard and cook in very little water. Drain, squeeze out as much moisture as possible, and keep aside in a colander.

Chop together bacon, garlic, and parsley to the consistency of a cream; reserve 1 tablespoon, and place the mixture in a skillet. Set skillet over medium heat and add leeks. Cook until mixture is lightly colored. Stir often. Remove from heat, add Parmesan, egg, and salt and pepper to taste. Mix thoroughly.

Oil a 9-inch pie pan. Preheat oven to 375°F.

Roll out two-thirds of the chilled dough into a circle large enough to line the bottom and sides of prepared pan; let dough hang over the edge. Pour green mixture into shell and smooth top. Roll remaining dough into a second circle. Place over filling and trim excess dough with scissors. Fold overhanging dough over the top and pinch edges all around to seal pie. Spread the reserved bacon mixture on top of the pie. Pierce with fork and bake for about 45 minutes.

Serve warm or at room temperature.

WINE: Chilled Lambrusco

CROSTATA DI CARCIOFI E FORMAGGIO
Artichoke and Cheese Pie

SERVES 6 TO 8

This is, perhaps, my favorite *crostata*. It is easy to make and even people who do not care for artichokes love it. The subtle delicacy of the flavor is better tasted when the *crostata* is left to cool for 15 minutes.

DOUGH

butter for pan

1 batch of Pâte Brisée II (p. 7)

FILLING

1 ounce (2 tablespoons) butter

1 tablespoon oil

1 package (9 ounces) frozen artichoke hearts, defrosted and quartered, or 8 small fresh artichokes, tough leaves removed, sliced

salt and pepper

¼ cup grated Parmesan cheese

¼ pound Edam or Gouda cheese, diced

¼ pound Bel Paese cheese, diced

¼ pound mozzarella cheese, diced

½ cup heavy cream

In a skillet heat butter and oil and sauté artichokes over medium heat for a few minutes. If fresh artichokes are used they will need more cooking time and you might need to add a little water. Add salt and pepper to taste. Cool.

Preheat oven to 375°F. Butter a 9- to 10-inch pie or quiche pan.

On a floured board, roll out dough into a circle large enough to cover bottom and sides of prepared pan. Fit dough into the pan, and trim excess dough with scissors. Flute edges all around and pierce bottom and sides of the dough with a fork. Arrange cooked artichokes in prepared pastry, sprinkle with Parmesan, scatter the other diced cheeses around, and pour heavy cream evenly over all. Grate a touch of pepper over the top. Bake for about 40 minutes.

WINE: Tocai del Friule

CROSTATA DI POMODORI
Tomato Pie

DOUGH

butter for pan

1 batch of Pâte Brisée II (p. 7)

FILLING

6 tablespoons oil
1 pound onions, sliced (6 cups)
pinch of thyme
2 tablespoons minced parsley
2 tablespoons bread crumbs
1 egg

1 tablespoon milk
2 tablespoons grated Parmesan
 cheese
salt and pepper
3 firm medium-size tomatoes
pinch of basil

Pour oil into a skillet. Add onions, cover, and cook over low heat until onions are soft and translucent, about 45 minutes. Add thyme, parsley, and bread crumbs. Cook for 5 more minutes, stirring, and remove from heat. In a mixing bowl beat the egg with the milk. Add the onion mixture, the Parmesan, and salt and pepper to taste. Mix well.

Preheat oven to 350°F. Butter a 9-inch pie or quiche pan.

On a floured board, roll out the dough into a circle large enough to cover bottom and sides of pan. Fit dough into the pan, and trim excess dough with scissors. Flute edges and pierce bottom and sides of the dough with a fork. Pour onion mixture into the pastry and smooth the top. Plunge tomatoes into boiling water for 1 minute. Peel and cut into halves. Gently squeeze out liquid and seeds, sprinkle with basil. Place 5 tomato halves, cut side down, in a circle on top of the filling, and the remaining halves in the center. Bake for 45 minutes.

Serve warm.

CROSTATA DI PEPERONI (Pepper Pie). Substitute rosemary for thyme; omit tomatoes. Fill the pie with ¾ cup each of green and red peppers, skinned, chopped, and blended into the onion mixture. Proceed as in the basic recipe.

PIZZA RUSTICA AMORE

SERVES 6 TO 8

This is my cousin Gianna's wonderful adaptation of a classic Neapolitan specialty. The green used in the filling is escarole. The pizza is usually filled with a layer of small heads of escarole stuffed with the other ingredients of the filling. However, in this recipe all ingredients are mixed together.

DOUGH

2 cups all-purpose flour

salt

1 egg (optional)

1 tablespoon olive oil

¼ cup wine

FILLING

2 pounds curly escarole, green parts only

¼ cup olive oil

salt and pepper

2 anchovies, chopped

10 pitted green olives, chopped

10 pitted black olives, chopped

1 tablespoon capers, minced

2 tablespoons pine nuts (pignoli)

2 tablespoons raisins

In a mixing bowl combine flour and salt. Make a well in the center and add the egg, if used, the oil, and wine. Beat the flour into the liquid and gather into a soft but consistent dough. Make a ball and set aside to rest.

Trim and wash escarole and blanch in boiling water. Drain. Heat the oil in a skillet and add escarole. Cook over medium heat, stirring often, until escarole is tender and moisture has evaporated. Add all other ingredients and cook briefly.

Preheat oven to 375°F. Oil a 9-inch springform pan. Roll out two-thirds of the dough into a circle large enough to line the bottom and sides of prepared pan. Fit dough into pan, leaving ¾ inch extra to overhang the rim of the pan. Fill dough with escarole mixture. Roll out remaining dough into a second circle, place over filling, and trim excess dough with scissors. Pinch edges together to seal the pizza well. Pierce top with fork. Bake for 30 to 40 minutes, until nice and golden.

WINE: Ravello Bianco

TORTA PASQUALINA
Easter Pie

SERVES 16

The queen of *torte* and *pizze rustiche*, and undoubtedly the most famous in Italy, comes from Liguria. It is a traditional Easter specialty and the main attraction of Easter Monday, a national holiday in Italy, celebrated with a lavish picnic. According to traditions the *torta* should be made with 33 layers of dough to honor Christ who was thirty-three years old when he died. (For practical purposes this *torta* is made with only 10 layers of dough.) The filling of *erbette* (spring greens) with whole raw eggs baked in it symbolizes the rebirth of nature after winter.

DOUGH

3 cups flour

salt

2 tablespoons olive oil

1 cup water

FILLING

1 pound Swiss chard

10 small fresh artichokes, or 1 package (9 ounces) frozen artichokes, defrosted

lemon juice

1 ounce (2 tablespoons) butter, plus 2 ounces (½ stick) chilled butter

1 tablespoon oil, plus oil for brushing on baking pan and dough

1 garlic clove

1 tablespoon minced fresh parsley

3 tablespoons dried mushrooms, soaked

salt and pepper

marjoram

2 pounds ricotta cheese, drained

2 tablespoons flour

¼ cup heavy cream

12 small eggs

¾ cup grated Parmesan cheese

In a mixing bowl combine flour and salt. Make a well in the center and add the oil and enough water to make a consistent dough. You may not need the entire cup of water. If dough should come out too soft, add a little more flour. Turn dough out on a floured board and knead for 10 minutes. Gather into a ball and set aside, covered, for at least 30 minutes.

Wash and trim Swiss chard, breaking the stalks and removing fibers as you would do with celery. Cook in a little boiling water until wilted and tender. Drain well. Squeeze out as much water as possible and chop very fine. Place in a colander and reserve. Wash artichokes (if fresh), discard tough outer leaves, trim tops, and quarter them. Soak pieces in water and lemon juice to prevent discoloration while preparing all of them.

Heat 1 ounce butter and 1 tablespoon oil in a skillet. Drain artichokes and add, together with the garlic clove. Cook over medium heat, stirring often, until artichokes are tender. Add parsley during the last 5 minutes. Remove artichokes with a slotted spoon. Slice or coarsely chop artichokes and place in a mixing bowl. Discard garlic.

Drain mushrooms and add to skillet in which artichokes were cooked. Sauté briefly. Remove with a slotted spoon, chop, and add to mixing bowl. Put the drained Swiss chard in the same skillet and sauté briefly. Add to the bowl, and mix all vegetables together. Add salt and pepper to taste and a pinch of marjoram.

In a separate mixing bowl place ricotta, flour, and cream. Mix. Add 4 eggs, one at a time, mixing after each addition. Add ½ cup Parmesan and all the vegetables. Mix well and taste for seasoning.

Preheat oven to 400°F. Oil a 14-inch springform pan. Cut the reserved dough into 10 pieces and shape each piece into a ball. Keep dough covered while rolling out one piece at a time as thin and round as possible and large enough to cover bottom and sides of prepared pan. Line the pan with 1 sheet of the dough. Brush with oil. Add 4 more sheets, placing them one on top of the other, and brush each one with oil. Add a fifth sheet of dough but do not brush it. Add the filling and smooth the top. With the back of a wet spoon, using a circular motion, make 8 wells in the filling. Break 1 egg into each well. Top each egg with a sliver of chilled butter and a sprinkling of Parmesan. Roll out the remaining dough into circles and top the pie, brushing each circle with oil. Trim excess dough with scissors and pinch edges together to seal the pie. Decorate with scraps of dough, if you wish. Pierce the top with a toothpick, being careful not to break the eggs inside. Bake for 10 minutes. Reduce heat to 375°F. and bake for 40 minutes longer. Brush with oil several times toward the end.

Serve at room temperature.

NOTE: Spinach can be substituted for Swiss chard, but the flavor is different.

TORTA DI ZUCCA
Savory Pumpkin Pie

SERVES 10 TO 12

Pumpkin, or *zucca*, is considered peasant food in Italy, so much so that it is rare to find it on menus of restaurants or even country inns. No Italian would go out to eat *zucca*. But apart from the fact that most peasant dishes are delightfully tasty, *zucca* can be prepared in many delicate and elegant ways. This *torta*, gay and colorful in appearance, is as good as it looks. A specialty from Liguria, at one time it was only made on farms and cooked in open-air ovens. It was a seasonal dish that went with the harvest of autumn. Not knowing how the traditional one tasted, we can be particularly pleased with this homemade version because the American pumpkin is a queen.

DOUGH

3½ cups flour

¾ teaspoon salt

6 tablespoons olive oil

water

FILLING

1 small yellow pumpkin, 2½ to 3
   pounds

1 pound Swiss chard

1 large onion

coarse salt

4 eggs

5 tablespoons grated Parmesan
   cheese

marjoram

nutmeg

salt and pepper

5 tablespoons olive oil

bread crumbs (optional)

Combine flour and salt in a mixing bowl. Make a well in the center, and add the olive oil and enough water to make a soft but consistent dough. Turn dough onto a floured board and knead for about 10 minutes. Gather into a ball, cover, and let the dough rest for 30 minutes.

Peel pumpkin, remove seeds, and chop the pulp. Wash and trim Swiss chard, and chop the onion. Place pumpkin in a colander, sprinkle with coarse salt, and let it stand for 30 minutes. This will soften the pumpkin flesh. Place Swiss chard in another colander and sprinkle it also with coarse salt. Place chopped onion in a scrap of cheesecloth and tie securely.

Bring 4 cups of water to a boil and add the onion bundle. After 5 minutes, add the Swiss chard. Cook just until greens are wilted. Drain both. Beat the eggs in a mixing bowl. Remove 2 tablespoons of egg to a cup and reserve for egg wash. Chop the blanched Swiss chard and add it to the bowl with the eggs. Unwrap the onion and add it and all other filling ingredients except bread crumbs. Mix well and set aside.

Preheat oven to 375°F. Oil a 12-inch cake pan. Divide prepared dough into 4 parts. Roll 1 piece at a time into a very thin circle (⅛ inch thick, or less) large enough to line bottom and sides of prepared pan leaving 1 inch extra to hang over the side of the pan. Line prepared pan with 1 circle of dough and brush it with oil. Top with a second circle. Pour in filling, and smooth the top. Cover with the third circle of dough, brush it with oil, and top with the last circle of dough. Trim excess dough with scissors, and pinch edges all around to seal. Combine reserved beaten egg with 1 tablespoon water or milk, and paint the top of the dough. Pierce with a fork in several places. Bake for 1 hour.

CRESPELLONA ALLA SILVANA GONELLA
Shellfish Crêpe Pie

SERVES 8

This is a *torta rustica* made with crêpes, *crespelle* in Italian, named after my friend Silvana who prepares it for me when I visit her in Milan.

CRESPELLE

5 eggs	salt
3 tablespoons flour	butter
¾ cup water	

FILLING

1 pound cooked shrimps, lobster, or crabmeat, or a mixture of all 3	1 jigger (3 tablespoons) sherry
2 cups Béchamel Sauce (p. 17)	2 tablespoons shredded Gruyère cheese
nutmeg	

In a mixing bowl beat the eggs. Stir in remaining *crespelle* ingredients except butter. Set aside while preparing filling.

Heat a crêpe pan or 7-inch skillet. Use a piece of paper towel to rub some butter on the bottom and sides of pan. Wipe lightly with a clean paper towel. Heat the pan and make very thin crêpes, turning each one once. Set aside. You should have about 16 crêpes.

Place cooked shellfish in a mixing bowl. Add 1 cup béchamel sauce, nutmeg to taste, and 1 tablespoon sherry; mix well.

Preheat oven to 400°F. Butter a 10-inch baking dish or casserole. Line the bottom of the casserole with a layer of crêpes, overlapping them in a circular fashion. Spread some of the shellfish mixture over. Continue layering until mixture is finished, giving the dish a cupola shape. Finish with 1 layer of crêpes.

Add remaining 2 tablespoons sherry and the Gruyère to remaining béchamel sauce. Mix and pour on top of the *crespellona*. Bake until the top starts to color and the cheese has melted, 15 to 20 minutes.

Serve hot.

IMPANATA DI PESCE SPADA FIAMMETTA DI NAPOLI OLIVER
Swordfish Pie alla Fiammetta

SERVES 8

Fiammetta is a friend of mine and a talented artist. She is also the author of an excellent cookbook called *La Grande Cucina Siciliana (The Great Sicilian Cuisine)* from which this recipe comes. It is a specialty of Messina.

DOUGH

1 batch of Pasta Frolla Semplice
  (p. 9)

FILLING

2 pounds fresh swordfish, cut into
  thin slices like cutlets
flour
½ cup oil
salt
1 onion, chopped
1 carrot, chopped
1 celery rib, chopped
1 parsley sprig, minced

6 ripe tomatoes, peeled, seeded,
  drained, and chopped
1 fresh basil leaf, or pinch of dried
  basil
1 tablespoon capers
1 tablespoon raisins
10 black olives, pitted and sliced
2 ounces caciocavallo cheese,
  shredded

Dust the slices of swordfish with flour. Heat 6 tablespoons of the oil in a frying pan. Sauté fish, a batch at a time, for a few minutes on each side. Remove slices to a dish; sprinkle very lightly with salt. Set aside.

Discard oil in which fish was cooked, if any remains. Wipe out skillet with a paper towel. Add remaining oil; heat. Add onion, carrot, and celery; cook over medium heat for 10 minutes. Add parsley, tomatoes, and basil; cover, and cook until vegetables are tender and sauce thickens, about 45 minutes. If at the end of that time there is too much liquid, remove lid and let it evaporate. Sauce should not be too dry. During the last 5 minutes of cooking, add the capers, raisins, and olives.

Preheat oven to 400°F. Generously grease a 10-inch springform pan. Set aside. On a floured board roll out two-thirds of the dough to a 12-inch circle ¼ inch thick. Fit circle into prepared pan. Let extra dough overhang the rim of the pan. Pierce the bottom of dough with a fork. Arrange a layer of swordfish in the dough-lined pan. Pour half of the sauce over and scatter half of the cheese on top. Repeat. Roll remaining dough into a circle and cover pie. Fold the overhanging dough in; smooth nicely with hands. Pierce dough with a fork to allow steam to escape. Reduce oven temperature to 375°F. Bake the pie for 45 minutes, until top is lightly colored.

Let pie rest for 10 to 15 minutes before slicing. It is also excellent cold.

VARIATION: In some other parts of Sicily the fish, cut into small pieces, is cooked in the sauce during the last 5 to 10 minutes. The *impanata* is layered with this mixture; then one adds a layer of zucchini, cut into strips, dipped into egg and flour, and deep-fried; a layer of dough, another layer of sauce and fish mixture, another layer of fried zucchini; finally the *impanata* is topped with dough. No cheese is used in this version.

WINE: Etna Bianco, well chilled

BABÀ RUSTICO ANNA SERAFINI
Savory Babà Anna Serafini

SERVES 8 TO 10

Anna is a Bolognese lady and a dear friend who cooks with the buoyant tradition of her native city. I had this *babà* for the first time on a balmy summer afternoon sitting on her green terrace, sipping a glass or two of Sangiovese di Romagna. The conversation, led by Dr. Serafini, Anna's husband, a learned and amusing raconteur, sparkled with optimistic thinking about the sad state of the world (which we were trying to solve), and that of Italy in particular.

In New York I make this *babà* when I want to share a special bottle of wine with friends. Sunday afternoon is my favorite time. If the group lingers after the *babà* is finished, I make a big salad and serve it with a basket of pears and a nice round of Bel Paese or Brie. Prosecco di Conegliano, a sparkling white wine, is my favorite for this occasion. A good pot of espresso is the appropriate ending to such a reunion; it will sober up the boiling spirits and send everybody home.

2½ packages active dry yeast
½ cup lukewarm milk (105° to 115°F.)
1 teaspoon sugar
2 eggs, separated
1 extra egg white
4 ounces (1 stick) butter, melted and cooled

1½ cups flour
1 teaspoon salt
2 tablespoons grated Parmesan cheese
¼ pound Fontina cheese, diced
3 slices of mortadella, chopped
pepper

Butter and flour a decorative 8½-inch springform pan. Set aside. Combine yeast, milk, and sugar, and set in a warm place.

In a mixing bowl beat the egg yolks and butter together. Gradually add the flour, salt, and yeast mixture. Add the cheeses and mortadella. Mix well. Beat the egg whites until stiff and fold into the dough. Add a good pinch of freshly grated pepper. Pour mixture into the prepared pan and set it in a warm place, covered with a napkin, for about 2 hours. This dough doesn't rise too much.

Preheat oven to 375°F. Bake the *babà* for 40 minutes, or until a skewer inserted in the center comes out clean.

Cool before unmolding. Serve at room temperature.

GATTÒ SANTA CHIARA
Savory Pie Santa Chiara

TWO 8-INCH ROUND PIES

Gattò, minus the accent, means tomcat in Italian. How to explain the use of this name for a pie? Easy. Since the appellative is used mostly in Naples and usually for certain types of savory pies resembling cakes, it must be a relic of the years of French domination. The Neapolitans, who are well known for their teasing attitude, transformed the French word *gâteau* (cake) into *gattò*. Sometimes they even write the word without the accent on top of the "o," creating quite a confusion.

This recipe comes from the famous monastery of Santa Chiara in Naples. The Clarisse nuns used to prepare it for special occasions. The monastery, apart from its architectural beauty, is also famous for a marvelous Neapolitan song, of the same name, which expresses all the sorrow and sense of loss endured by this indomitable race of people during the last war, when the monastery was almost destroyed by bombs.

lard or shortening for pans	½ teaspoon pepper
flour for pans	½ cup melted lard or vegetable
3 small potatoes	shortening
3½ cups all-purpose flour	4 eggs, at room temperature
3 packages active dry yeast	8 ounces mozzarella cheese, diced
lukewarm water (105° to 115°F.)	½ pound prosciutto, in 1 slice, diced
1 teaspoon salt	

Grease and flour 2 soufflé dishes or charlotte molds, 8 to 9 inches in diameter, with lard or shortening, and set aside. Boil the potatoes and cool them.

In a mixing bowl place 4 or 5 tablespoons of flour, the yeast, and enough lukewarm water to gather the mixture into a soft ball. Cover with a napkin and set in a warm place for about 15 minutes.

Peel and mash potatoes. Place in a mixing bowl; add salt, remaining flour, and the pepper. Make a well in the center and add the melted fat and the eggs. Beat for 5 minutes and start blending in the flour. Add the yeast mixture and gather dough into a ball. Turn dough out on a floured board and knead, slapping the dough around for 15 minutes. Add more flour when necessary. The dough should be soft, elastic, and not sticky. Continue kneading while adding, a little at a time, the mozzarella and the prosciutto. Add more flour whenever necessary.

Divide the dough into 2 parts and place in the prepared dishes. They should not be more than half full, but if they are, build a collar around the dish with aluminum foil to prevent spilling. Set dishes in a warm place, cover with a napkin, and let rise for 1 hour, or until doubled in bulk.

Preheat oven to 375°F. Bake the pies for 45 minutes, or until a skewer inserted in the *gattò* comes out clean.

Let rest for 10 minutes before unmolding. Serve at room temperature.

GATTÒ DI PATATE GIANNA AMORE
Potato Pie Gianna Amore

SERVES 12

This *gattò* is a recipe from my cousin Gianna, an excellent and inventive cook. She lives with her beautiful husband and children in Campania, that part of Italy so loved by Virgil. She has been able to blend the traditions of her Abruzzese origins with those of the land of her choice.

4 pounds baking potatoes	4 ounces smoked mozzarella cheese
4 ounces (1 stick) butter, plus butter	¼ pound prosciutto, in 1 slice, diced
for pan and for dotting on top	bread crumbs
⅔ cup grated Parmesan cheese	2 eggs
1 cup milk	1 tablespoon minced fresh parsley
8 ounces mozzarella cheese	salt and pepper

Boil potatoes. Peel and mash them. Add 4 ounces butter and the Parmesan. Mix well. Add milk. Cut the plain mozzarella into thin slices; dice the smoked mozzarella. Add diced mozzarella and prosciutto to the potato mixture.

Preheat oven to 375°F. Butter a 12-inch cake pan; sprinkle with bread crumbs. Beat eggs. Add parsley and salt and pepper to taste, and pour into potato mixture. Spoon half of the mixture into prepared pan; smooth top. Arrange the mozzarella slices in a layer on top. Add remaining potato mixture and sprinkle with more bread crumbs. Dot with butter. Bake for 45 to 50 minutes.

Cool for 15 minutes before slicing. This *gattò* reheats well.

CROSTATA ELEGANTE DI VERDURE
Elegant Green Pie

SERVES 6 TO 8

DOUGH

butter for pan

1 batch of Pâte Brisée I (p. 6)

PANADE

¼ cup small pastina or any kind of broken spaghetti, noodles, etc., broken into small pieces, or ¼ cup rice

boiling salted water

Cook pastina or rice in boiling salted water until well done. Drain and use as recommended.

FILLING

2 large eggs

5 tablespoons grated Parmesan cheese

1 cup Panade

2 tablespoons minced fresh parsley

4 ounces mozzarella cheese, shredded

2 tablespoons chopped prosciutto

2 shallots, chopped and sautéed in butter

2 cups cooked greens (escarole, endive, Italian broccoli, or a mixture of these)

2 tablespoons tomato purée

2 tablespoons cream

1 ounce (2 tablespoons) Marsala wine or sherry

pinch of grated nutmeg

salt and pepper

In a mixing bowl beat eggs and Parmesan cheese together. Add all other filling ingredients and mix well. Preheat oven to 400°F. Butter a 9-inch pie pan.

Roll out dough to a circle large enough to line bottom and sides of pan. Fit dough into pan. Trim excess dough with scissors, leaving ½-inch extra overhanging edge of pan. Pierce bottom and sides of dough with a fork. Pour filling into prepared pastry. Make a lattice top with remaining dough. Turn in overhanging dough all around and pinch in a decorative fashion. Bake for 10 minutes. Reduce heat to 350°F. and bake for 40 minutes longer.

Cool for 15 minutes before slicing. This dish can also be served at room temperature.

PIZZA RUSTICA DI PASQUA JO INZERILLO
Easter Savory Pie Jo Inzerillo

SERVES 12

This recipe was given to me by Jo Inzerillo, a dear friend who, in her capacity as assistant director of the Italian Government Tourist Office of New York, has never lost her enthusiasm in assisting me. When I cannot find the place where and when a certain Italian traditional event occurs, such as the making of a thousand-egg omelet the week before Lent, Jo tells me that it is in Ponti, a small town in the North of Italy!

This *pizza rustica* is a treasured family recipe that Jo generously wanted to share with me and my readers. It is, in my opinion and that of others who have tried it, the most delicious pizza of its kind. The slightly sweet crust blends perfectly with the salty taste of the prosciutto and the smoky flavor of the provola cheese. The addition of sugar is of course a legacy of the Arab domination in the South of Italy and Sicily where Jo's family originates. The custom of combining sugar with savory, which carried through the Renaissance, is practically lost now. The selectively tasty dishes that remain are those in which the subtle blending of spices and condiments has been refined to perfection through the years.

DOUGH

3 cups all-purpose flour
¾ cup sugar
6 egg yolks, beaten well
salt

¾ cup lard or vegetable shortening,
    melted and cooled
¼ cup ice water

FILLING

8 large eggs
3 tablespoons grated pecorino
    Romano cheese
pinch of salt
1 teaspoon pepper

2½ pounds ricotta cheese, drained
¾ pound smoked provola or
    mozzarella cheese, diced
½ pound prosciutto, chopped

In a mixing bowl combine flour and sugar. Make a well in the center and add egg yolks. Add salt and lard, and start blending in the flour while adding enough of the water to make a soft dough. Gather into a ball, wrap, and chill.

Beat the whole eggs for the filling in a mixing bowl. Add the grated cheese and salt and pepper, and beat. Add ricotta and mix until filling reaches the consistency of a smooth cream. Add remaining ingredients and stir to combine mixture well.

Preheat oven to 350°F. Butter a 12-inch cake pan. Roll out two-thirds of the dough into a circle ⅛ inch thick and large enough to line the bottom and sides of the prepared pan and to overhang the edge a little. Fit dough into the pan and pierce the bottom. Pour filling in and smooth top. Roll out remaining dough into a circle to cover filling. Run a wet finger over the dough all around the edge of pan. Fold in overhanging dough and enclose pizza well. Trimming is not necessary. Pizza is turned upside down in the unmolding, which gives it a smooth, fine look. Bake for about 2 hours.

Cool pizza. Turn upside down on a serving dish. Serve at room temperature.

SFOGLIATA RUSTICA ALLA PERUGINA
Pizza Perugia Style

SERVES 6 TO 8

DOUGH

3 cups all-purpose flour
1½ packages active dry yeast
lukewarm water (105° to 115°F.)
salt
2 ounces (½ stick) butter, at room temperature, plus butter for pan

warm milk
1 egg, beaten with 1 tablespoon milk, for egg wash

FILLING

¼ pound Gruyère cheese, shredded
¼ pound prosciutto, chopped

1 egg, beaten

In a small bowl combine 4 tablespoons flour, the yeast, and enough lukewarm water to make a small ball of dough. Cover and set aside in a warm spot for 15 minutes.

In a mixing bowl combine remaining flour and salt. Make a well in the center, add the butter and chop, beating in some of the flour. Add the yeast mixture and enough warm milk to make a soft but consistent dough. Gather dough into a ball, place in a buttered bowl, cover, and set in a warm place to rise for about 2 hours.

Butter a 10-inch pie pan. In a bowl combine Gruyère and prosciutto. Add the egg and mix well. Turn dough out on a floured board and knead a little. Divide dough into 2 parts. Roll one piece at a time into a very thin (⅛ inch or less) rectangular sheet. Leave the sheet uncovered on the board to rest for 30 minutes.

Leave 1 inch of the dough on a long side of the rectangle without filling. Place a thin "ribbon" of filling beside this bare strip. Fold the dough over and enclose the filling. Repeat with a second "ribbon" along the filled strip. Fold this over and enclose the 2 ribbons together. Coil, like a sausage, along the edge of the prepared pan. Repeat with remaining dough and filling until all is used and pan is full. You may or may not have a hole in the middle of the coil. Pierce tops with a fork. Set in a warm place for 30 minutes. Preheat oven to 375°F.

Brush dough with egg wash. Bake for 45 to 50 minutes until nicely brown. Serve warm.

WINE: Orvieto, well chilled

PIZZA RICCA DI GRANONE "CASA MIA"
Rich Cornmeal Pie "My Home"

SERVES 8

This pizza is also known by the amusing name of *polenta maritata*, married polenta. In Abruzzo, the region where I come from, every household has its own version. It was a favorite meal in my home for cold winter nights. With it, my mother always served a minestrone, a salad, and a light dessert of fruits. My father's choice of wine was a Chianti Classico from Tuscany, and he would have finished the entire *fiasco* (a straw-covered bottle) if mother had permitted it.

Granone is the name given in some parts of Abruzzo to cornmeal. It literally means "big wheat." In other areas, it is called *farina gialla,* yellow flour. A more basic pizza made with cornmeal and traditionally eaten with green leafy vegetables is called *pizza gialla,* yellow pizza.

3 sweet Italian sausages	2 tablespoons olive oil, plus oil for
3⅓ cups milk	pan
1 cup yellow cornmeal (polenta)	6 eggs, separated
4 tablespoons grated Parmesan	8 ounces mozzarella cheese, diced
cheese, plus enough additional	1 cup Tomato Sauce (p. 16)
to sprinkle on topping	1 cup Béchamel Sauce (p. 17)

Place sausages in a skillet, pierce them with a fork, cover with water, and cook covered until water is completely evaporated. Sauté sausages by turning them in their own rendered fat, once or twice, until brown. Remove sausages to a dish. Reserve 2 tablespoons of the fat. When sausages are cool, slice into very thin rounds.

Bring the milk to a boil. Add cornmeal in a steady stream, stirring constantly to prevent lumping. Cook over medium heat for 10 to 15 minutes. Add the 2 tablespoons sausage fat, remove cornmeal from heat, and add the Parmesan and 2 tablespoons olive oil. Set aside.

Preheat oven to 375°F. Oil a 12-inch pie pan that can be brought to the table. (I use a glass one.) Set aside.

Add the egg yolks to the cornmeal mixture one at a time, beating after each addition. Beat the egg whites until stiff and fold into cornmeal mixture. Spoon one-third of cornmeal into the prepared pie pan; smooth the top. Arrange half of the sliced sausages in one layer on pie. Scatter half of the diced mozzarella over the top. Combine half of the tomato sauce with the béchamel sauce. Pour some on the sausage-mozzarella layer. Spoon on another layer of cornmeal mixture and top with remaining sausages, mozzarella, and béchamel-tomato sauce. Finish with another layer of cornmeal mixture and top with remaining tomato sauce. Sprinkle with additional Parmesan. Bake for 45 minutes.

Let rest for 10 to 15 minutes before cutting. This pizza reheats very well. It is also good at room temperature.

PITTA ALLA CALABRESE
Calabrian Meat and Cheese Pie

SERVES 8

The word *pitta* is a dialect form of pizza, used in some regions of the South like Calabria and Lucania. It is the echo of another civilization, that of Greece, which at one time had colonized most of the South of Italy.

In the regions of Apulia, Lucania, and Calabria the meat supply is poor. People have lamb occasionally, and once a year a pig is killed for the use of the family. But very often the only parts of the pig eaten fresh are the odd ones. The rest will be preserved in the form of prosciutti, salami, and sausages for which these regions are justly famous, to last until the next *maialatura*, the slaughter of the pig. The odd parts of the pig are treated with reverence, too, because the people know how tasty they are and what wonderful dishes can be concocted out of a pig snout. Of course, many of these parts are used to fill delicious savory pies, which are unlike any others in the rest of Italy.

A classic *pitta alla Calabrese* owes its chewy, succulent flavor to a layer of tasty *frittole*, a mixture of pieces of snout, ears, cheeks, and feet of the pig, diced, cooked in lard, and perfumed with a touch of spices. A *pitta* is rustic fare, but delicious.

DOUGH

3 cups all-purpose flour
2½ packages active dry yeast
lukewarm water (105° to 115°F.)
salt

2 eggs
1 tablespoon lard, softened, lard for pan and top of dough
1 tablespoon olive oil

FILLING

½ pound chicken giblets
4 pig's feet, each cut into 4 pieces
1 large carrot
1 bay leaf
1 tablespoon lard
1 large onion
salt and pepper

allspice
cloves
8 ounces ricotta cheese, drained
¼ pound capocollo, sliced thin
¼ pound provolone cheese, sliced thin
2 hard-cooked eggs, sliced

In a small bowl combine half of the flour and the yeast. Add ¾ cup lukewarm water to make a very soft dough. Cover the bowl and set in a warm place to rise for 1 hour, or until doubled in bulk.

Place the giblets, pig's feet, carrot, bay leaf, and lard in a heavy pot. Cut a cross at the bottom of the onion and bury it in the middle of the mixture. Add enough water barely to cover the meat and vegetables. Season with salt, pepper, allspice, and cloves. Place on low heat and cook, covered, for about 1 hour. At this point all meat should be cooked and water evaporated. If not, uncover the pot and let the water boil away.

Sauté the mixture in the fat accumulated at the bottom for about 10 minutes. Be careful not to burn the mixture, which should be only lightly browned. Remove from heat and cool.

In a mixing bowl combine remaining flour and salt. Make a well in the center and add the yeast mixture, the eggs, lard, and oil. Beat until liquids are well amalgamated and lard has melted. Start mixing in the flour and add some water to make a soft dough. Turn dough out on a floured board and knead for about 15 minutes. Gather into a ball, cover with a napkin, and set in a warm place.

Discard bay leaf from cooled meat mixture. Remove vegetables and purée them in a food processor or blender. Set aside. Dice the giblets. Bone pig's feet, dice the meat, and combine with giblets. Set aside.

Grease a 10-inch pie pan with lard. Divide dough into 2 parts. Roll out, or stretch with hands, into 2 circles large enough to line the prepared pan. Fit 1 circle into pan, stretching with fingers, and let extra dough overhang the rim of the pan. Pour in half of the ricotta and smooth the top. Spoon some of the vegetable purée on the ricotta. Cover with a layer of capocollo, then a layer of provolone, and scatter the diced meat mixture all over. Arrange the sliced eggs on top. Cover with another layer of provolone and another of ca-pocollo. Pour on remaining ricotta and top with a few tablespoons of the vegetable purée. Cover with remaining circle of dough. Fold in overhanging edge of dough and pinch edges all around to seal *pitta* well. Brush top with a little bit of melted lard, pierce top, and let the pie rest for about 20 minutes.

Preheat oven to 375°F. Bake the *pitta* for 45 minutes, until top is nice and golden.

NOTE: Leftover filling can be mixed together and used to dress pasta or rice.

WINE: Aglianico del Vulture

BRIOCHE SALATA ALLA FOGGIANA
Sweetbread Brioche Foggia Style

SERVES 8

DOUGH

2 packages active dry yeast

2 teaspoons sugar

½ cup lukewarm water (105° to 115°F.)

3 cups all-purpose flour

3 eggs, lightly beaten

4 ounces (1 stick) butter, melted and cooled

pinch of salt

FILLING

1 ounce (2 tablespoons) butter, plus 1 tablespoon melted butter

1 cup blanched sweetbreads or brains, cubed (see instructions that follow)

1 cup cooked peas

1 ounce (2 tablespoons) Marsala wine

2 tablespoons chopped prosciutto

4 ounces mozzarella cheese, chopped

2 cups Béchamel Sauce (p. 17)

nutmeg

salt and pepper

Dissolve yeast and sugar in the water and set aside. Place the flour in a mixing bowl. Make a well in the center. Remove 2 tablespoons of the beaten egg to a cup and reserve for egg wash. Pour the rest of the eggs into the well. Blend in some of the flour, add the melted butter, the salt, and the yeast mixture, and continue to blend in the flour. Turn dough out on a floured board and knead until soft and smooth, about 15 minutes. Gather into a ball, place in a buttered bowl, cover, and set in a warm place to rise for about 2 hours.

Melt 1 ounce butter in a skillet and sauté the sweetbreads or brains until lightly colored. Remove them with a slotted spoon, chop coarsely, and place in a mixing bowl. Add peas to the skillet and cook briefly just to heat through. Remove with a slotted spoon and add to sweetbreads or brains. Add the Marsala to the skillet; over heat scrape up the brown particles clinging to the skillet. Cook for a few minutes, then add to the bowl together with the prosciutto and mozzarella. Add the béchamel and all the seasoning to taste. Stir all ingredients well.

Butter a soufflé dish 8 inches in diameter and set aside. Roll out two-thirds of the brioche dough into a circle large enough to line bottom and sides of the prepared soufflé dish. Fit dough into the dish and let extra dough overhang the rim of the dish. Fill brioche with sweetbread or brain mixture. Roll remaining dough into a circle and cover filling. Trim excess dough with scissors. Turn in overhanging dough and pinch edges all around to seal brioche well. Cut a cross, not too deeply, into the top of the brioche. Cover the dish and set in a warm place to rise for about 1 hour.

Preheat oven to 375°F. Add 2 tablespoons water to reserved egg and paint top of brioche. Bake for 1 hour. Brush with melted butter 2 or 3 times during the last 10 minutes.

BASIC PREPARATION OF SWEETBREADS

Soak sweetbreads in running cold water for 20 minutes; or let them soak for 4 hours, changing the water several times until the water no longer shows any color. Put soaked sweetbreads in a large saucepan with 4 cups water, 1 tablespoon salt, and 1 tablespoon lemon juice. Bring water to a boil, then simmer sweetbreads for 20 minutes. Drain, and cool in very cold water for 15 minutes. Remove sinews, blood vessels, and membranes. Place sweetbreads between 2 plates and weight them (to flatten them and firm the texture) for 1 hour.

NOTE: Brains are treated in the same way.

PASTICCIO DI LEPRE
Hare Pie

I have mentioned Pellegrino Artusi in the historical introduction. I consider him the Craig Claiborne of the nineteenth century. His cookbook *L'Arte di Mangiar Bene* (the Art of Eating Well) has been translated into English under the title *Italianissimo*. A witty, knowledgeable chef and raconteur, Artusi also wrote a biography of Ugo Foscolo, the Italian poet, a fact which endears this inspired man to me immensely.

This recipe is one of his famous *pasticci*, gems of Italian cuisine.

DOUGH

2 cups all-purpose flour
salt
2 teaspoons sugar
2 ounces (½ stick) butter, plus
    butter for mold

1 tablespoon vinegar
2 egg yolks
water

FILLING

1 hare, dressed
1 ounce (2 tablespoons) butter
1 tablespoon oil
½ pound prosciutto, in 1 slice
broth or bouillon
½ cup Béchamel Sauce (p. 17)

½ pound lean veal, ground twice
2 eggs
2 truffles, diced (optional)
salt and pepper
¼ pound tongue, cut into strips
4 slices of prosciutto, cut very thin

MARINADE

¼ onion
½ carrot
½ celery rib, cut into pieces
2 parsley sprigs

2 bay leaves
salt and pepper
Marsala wine

The day before serving: Cut out from the fleshy parts of the hare 2 fillets as large as possible; place them in a bowl. Cut hare into pieces and add to bowl. Add all the ingredients of the marinade and enough Marsala wine to cover all. Chill overnight.

The day of serving: Place the butter and the oil in a heavy pot large enough to contain the cut-up hare. Cut all the fat from the large slice of prosciutto. Dice the fat and add to the pot. Heat the pot. Cut the rest of that slice of prosciutto into strips and set aside. Drain the meat from the marinade. Strain marinade and discard solids. Add the pieces of hare to the pot and brown them over high heat, adding the strained marinade, a little at a time. Reduce heat and continue cooking until hare is done. You may need more liquid; if so, use broth or bouillon. Cool.

When cool enough to handle, separate the meat from the bones. Discard bones. Cut the large fillets into 8 strips each and set aside. Place remaining meat in the bowl of a food processor fitted with the steel blade, or in a blender, and add a little Marsala wine or broth. Purée the meat; the purée should not be dry. Transfer it to a mixing bowl. Add the béchamel, the ground veal, the eggs, and half of the fresh truffles, if used. Add salt and pepper to taste.

Prepare the dough. In a mixing bowl combine flour, salt, and sugar. Make a well in the center and chop the butter into it. Add vinegar and egg yolks. Beat in the flour mixture and, if necessary, add a little water while gathering dough into a ball. Wrap and chill.

Butter a 12-inch springform pan or oval pâté mold. Preheat oven to 375°F. On a floured board roll out two-thirds of the dough to a sheet ¼ inch thick and large enough to line bottom and sides of the pan or mold. Fit the dough into the pan. Spread one-third of the filling on the bottom of the dough. Arrange some of the diced truffle, if used, and some of the hare fillets and strips of prosciutto and tongue on top. Make another layer of filling. Repeat with remaining ingredients, finishing with filling. Cover with the thin slices of prosciutto. Press the filling down.

Roll out the rest of the dough to fit the top of the pan, and cover the filling. Pinch the edges all around to seal well. Make a hole in the center to let steam escape. Set the pan or mold on a baking sheet to prevent dripping. Bake in the preheated oven for 45 minutes.

Serve cold.

WINE: Barolo

CROSTATA ALLA FINANZIERA
Pie, Financier Style

SERVES 6 TO 8

Finanziera (financier) is a sauce made with chicken gizzards, hearts, livers, cocks' combs, etc. In Florence it is called *cibrèo*. *Cibrèo* was one of Caterina de' Medici's favorite condiments. In this *finanziera*, only the ingredients available on the American market are used, therefore no cocks' combs.

DOUGH

butter for pan

1 batch of Pâte Brisée II (p. 7)

FILLING

12 ounces chicken gizzards and
    hearts
1 small onion
2 cloves
1 small carrot, cut into 4 pieces
1 celery rib, cut into 4 pieces
1 parsley sprig
1 bay leaf
salt and pepper
2 ounces (½ stick) butter
1 tablespoon oil

1 onion, thinly sliced
2 cups sliced mushrooms
3 tablespoons white wine
12 ounces chicken livers
1 ounce (2 tablespoons) dry
    Madeira
1 cup broth (from gizzards and
    hearts)
1 tablespoon flour
3 tablespoons heavy cream
nutmeg

Butter a 12-inch pie pan. On a floured board roll out dough to a circle large enough to line bottom and sides of pan. Fit dough into pan, and trim excess dough with scissors. Flute edges. Cover dough with aluminum foil and fill with beans or rice. Bake for 15 minutes. Remove foil and beans or rice. Set piecrust aside.

Place the gizzards and hearts in a saucepan. Add the onion stuck with the cloves, the carrot, celery, parsley, bay leaf, and salt and pepper to taste. Cover with water and cook until gizzards and hearts are tender. Set aside to cool.

Heat 1 tablespoon butter and 1 tablespoon oil in a skillet. Add the onion and mushrooms and cook over medium heat until mushroom liquid has evaporated. Add white wine and salt and pepper to taste. Cook for 10 minutes. Remove from heat. Pour any remaining liquid from the skillet into a measuring cup and reserve. Turn vegetables into a mixing bowl. Return skillet to heat and add 2 tablespoons butter. Quickly sauté chicken livers in it. Add Madeira and season with salt and pepper. Cook briefly and remove from heat. Pour any remaining liquid into the measuring cup. Chop the livers coarsely and add to mixing bowl with vegetables. Preheat oven to 375°F.

Drain gizzards and hearts. Chop meats coarsely and add these, too, to mixing bowl. Add enough broth from gizzards and hearts to the reserved liquid to make 1 cup. In a saucepan melt remaining tablespoon of butter and add the flour. Cook until butter and flour froth together; remove from heat. Add the cup of broth and cook and stir until sauce liquefies. Put back over medium heat and cook until sauce thickens. Add heavy cream and nutmeg to taste. Add half of this sauce to mixing bowl. Combine ingredients well. Pour the mixture into the partly baked piecrust. Smooth the top and pour remaining sauce over all. Bake for 25 to 30 minutes, until filling is set and bubbly. Do not let it dry.

Serve warm.

CROSTATINE. Make individual small tarts and fill as described in the basic recipe.

WINE: Vernaccia di San Gimignano

TORTA MIRANDA ALLA PADOVANA
Torta, Padua Style

SERVES 6 TO 8

The smoked pork in this *torta* smacks of Austrian origins. Since the recipe comes from Padua, it must be a legacy from the Austro-Hungarian domination over that region before 1914. In Italy, smoked meats are found mostly in the North.

DOUGH

2 batches of Short Pastry (p. 9) or
　　Very Short Pastry (p. 10)

FILLING

2 tablespoons oil, plus oil for pan
2 onions, thinly sliced
2 pounds fresh spinach, washed and
　　trimmed, or 2 packages (10
　　ounces each) frozen spinach

1 pound smoked pork, diced
8 ounces ricotta cheese, drained
allspice
4 eggs, lightly beaten
salt and pepper

Heat the oil in a skillet. Add the onions, cover, and cook over very low heat, shaking the pan once in a while, for about 15 minutes. Cook spinach in the water clinging to the leaves until wilted. Drain, squeeze out as much water as possible, and chop. In a mixing bowl combine pork, ricotta, allspice to taste, and eggs. Add spinach and onions. Mix well. Taste for seasoning and add salt and pepper.

Preheat oven to 425°F. Oil a 9-inch pie pan. Roll out half of the pastry into a circle large enough to line bottom and sides of prepared pan. Fit dough into pan, and press dough with fingers. Brush bottom and sides with a little oil. Pour in filling. Roll out remaining pastry and cover the pie. Trim excess pastry with scissors. Fold and pinch edges all around to seal pie. Decorate pie with scraps of dough if you wish. Make a hole in the center to permit steam to escape. Bake for 40 minutes, or until top is nice and golden.

Serve at room temperature. This pie can be reheated. Also, it freezes well.

WINE: Cerasuolo del Piave

CALZONI AND PANZEROTTI

Calzoni and *panzerotti* are savory pastries similar to turnovers. Italians eat them as snacks with the *aperitivo* and at afternoon teas. In the United States I serve them with drinks, and often at lunch. *Calzoni* are usually made with a yeast dough and baked. *Panzerotti* are usually made with unrisen dough, and fried. In some regions the opposite happens. The Italians are happily divided even on the subject of gastronomy.

CALZONE SEMPLICE
Simple Calzone

10 TO 12 PIECES

DOUGH

1 batch of Pizza Dough (p. 6), ready to use

oil

1 egg, beaten with 2 tablespoons water

FILLING

1 pound mozzarella cheese, diced

¼ pound salame, chopped

On a floured board roll out dough to a sheet ¼ inch thick. Cut into 4-inch rounds. Brush each round with oil.

Put an equal amount of mozzarella and salame on each round. Brush edge of rounds with beaten egg. Fold dough over filling to form a crescent. Press edges to seal. Place *calzone* on cookie sheets and brush each one with oil. Let stand for about 30 minutes.

Meanwhile preheat oven to 400°F. Bake turnovers for 10 minutes. Reduce heat to 375°F. and bake for 10 to 15 minutes longer, or until golden brown.

CALZONI DI RAVENNA. Use cotechino instead of regular salame.

PANZEROTTI ALLA BARESE. Omit salame; add ½ pound ripe tomatoes, peeled, seeded, and cut into thin wedges.

PANZEROTTI DI QUARESIMA (Lenten Panzerotti). Use 2 cups Béchamel Sauce (p. 17) and 7 ounces canned anchovies, minced. Mix and fill *panzerotti*.

PANZEROTTI ALL'ELVIRA LIMENTANI

ABOUT 30 PIECES

Elvira is a Roman friend of mine who lives in New York. It is at her parties that I have savored these *panzerotti*, which are light and delicious.

DOUGH

2 cups all-purpose flour
pinch of salt
pinch of sugar
4 ounces (1 stick) butter, cut into
    pieces

1½ ounces (3 tablespoons)
    margarine
approximately ⅔ cup water

FILLING

4 eggs
4 tablespoons grated Parmesan
    cheese
nutmeg

pepper
1 cup chopped mozzarella cheese
¼ pound prosciutto, in 1 slice, or
    salame, chopped

In a mixing bowl combine flour, salt, and sugar. Make a well in the center and add butter and margarine. Work with a pastry blender or 2 knives until mixture resembles coarse meal. Add water, a little at a time, when gathering the dough into a ball. You might not need all the water. Cover and set aside.

Break the eggs into a mixing bowl and beat until frothy. Add the Parmesan cheese, nutmeg, pepper, mozzarella, and prosciutto or salame. Filling should be rather soft. If not, add another egg or a few spoons of cream.

On a floured board roll out dough to a sheet ⅛ inch thick. Cut out 4-inch circles. Place 1 tablespoon of the filling on each circle. Fold dough over filling to form a crescent. Press edges to seal. Deep-fry until golden brown.

Serve hot.

PANZEROTTI ALLA CIOCIARA. Use Gruyère cheese instead of mozzarella, ham instead of prosciutto. Use only 2 eggs and add 1 tablespoon grated Parmesan cheese.

WINE: Castelli Romani

CAVICIUNETTI DI RICOTTA ALL'AGNONE
Savory Pastries from Agnone

ABOUT 30 PIECES

Agnone is a charming town in Molise, famous for its industry of bronze bells.

DOUGH

1 pound all-purpose flour
8 tablespoons lard or vegetable
    shortening, cut into pieces

2 eggs
juice of 1 lemon
oil for deep-frying

FILLING

3 cups ricotta cheese, drained
¼ pound prosciutto, chopped
2 egg yolks

¼ cup minced fresh parsley
salt and pepper

Place the flour in a mixing bowl. Make a well in the center, add the fat, and chop it. Break the eggs into the well and beat a little, blending in the flour while adding the lemon juice. Gather the mixture into a ball, cover, and chill.

In a mixing bowl combine ricotta and prosciutto. Add remaining filling ingredients and mix well.

On a floured board roll out the dough as thin as possible. Cut into 3-inch circles. Place 1 tablespoon of the prepared filling on each circle. Fold dough over to form a crescent and press edges to seal. Deep-fry until golden brown.

Serve hot.

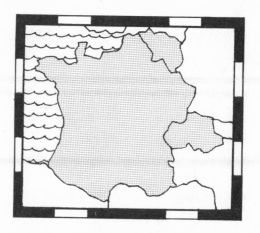

France
and Her Neighbors
France · Switzerland · Belgium

From a simple cooking, chiefly spit-roasting and grilling of fish, meat, and game, practiced by the Gauls, the French had developed an elaborate cuisine by the time of Charlemagne. At the end of the sixteenth century a cook named Saupiquet worked out the method of making puff pastry, with ultimately hundreds of layers of flour and butter. By the Middle Ages French pastry makers had their own "union," as did the bakers of bread, whose role has continued to be important in all the centuries since. A simple bread dough was the original crust of quiche Lorraine, but later short pastry became popular, and countless varieties of quiche, an open custard tart, were developed. Also many pastries were invented, to be wrapped around fish, meats, vegetables, and cheeses.

While the elaborate classic cuisine seems so typically French, there still exists a simpler and heartier home cooking, which varies according to region and climate. The *pissaladière* of Provence and the Riviera is closely related to the pizza, and the quiche to the *crostata*, yet the combination of the ingredients and the beauty of the presentation make them uniquely French.

France's neighbors, Belgium to the Northeast and Switzerland to the East, share many similar dishes. In Belgium they make good use of two special vegetables—endive and chicory—and of their delicious hams.

Switzerland also shares the cooking styles of Germany and Italy, since it has German-speaking and Italian-speaking areas. This gives an enormous variety to its food. One common denominator is Swiss cheese, not only Emmenthaler, the cheese with the holes, but Gruyère and many others, all adding delicious flavor as well as nutritive value to pies and tarts.

PISSALADIÈRE

(F R A N C E)
SERVES 8 TO 10

Pissaladière, a specialty of Nice, is made with yeast bread dough, usually baked on a baking tray. It is very much like an Italian pizza. In other parts of France, it is more like a quiche, with a pastry made of *pâte brisée*. The topping, with its mixture of onions, olives, anchovies, and herbs, contains the essence of the Mediterranean in its flavor and color.

DOUGH
oil for pan

1 batch of Pizza Dough (p. 6)

TOPPING
2 pounds onions, chopped
4 tablespoons oil
1 bouquet garni made with 1 small
 bay leaf, 1 clove, 3 parsley
 sprigs, 2 garlic cloves, pinch of
 thyme, all tied in cheesecloth

salt and pepper
14 tinned anchovies, skin and bones
 removed
24 pitted black olives
olive oil

Lightly oil a 12-inch pizza pan. Flatten dough and place it in the pan. With oiled fingers, stretch the dough toward edge of pan and push up to form a ½-inch rim all around.

Place onions, oil, and bouquet garni in a saucepan. Cover and cook over very low heat, stirring occasionally, for about 1 hour. Add salt and pepper to taste. Taste for flavor, let the sauce cool. Discard bouquet garni.

Preheat oven to 400°F. Spread the sauce on top of the dough. Arrange the anchovies and olives in a decorative fashion, and dribble some olive oil all over the *pissaladière*. Bake for 20 to 25 minutes, or until rim is brown and top is nice and bubbly.

WINE: Côtes de Provence

TARTE À L'OIGNON   (F R A N C E)
Onion Tart

SERVES 10 TO 12

DOUGH

2¼ cups all-purpose flour

1½ teaspoons salt

3½ ounces (1 stick less 1 tablespoon) butter, chilled, plus butter for pan

2 tablespoons oil

ice water

FILLING

2 ounces (½ stick) butter

1 tablespoon oil

2 pounds onions, thinly sliced

1 tablespoon sherry

5 tablespoons flour

pinch of ground allspice

2 eggs

2 cups heavy cream

2 tablespoons caraway seeds

salt and pepper

Sift flour and salt together in a mixing bowl. Chop in the butter, add the oil, and blend ingredients, adding as much water as necessary to make a soft, smooth dough. Wrap dough in foil and chill for at least 1 hour.

Heat butter and oil in a skillet. Add onions, stir, and set over very low heat, covered, until onions are almost puréed, about 1 hour. Toward the end of the cooking add the sherry. While onions cook, preheat oven to 375°F. Butter a 12-inch pizza or quiche pan.

Roll out the dough to a circle large enough to cover bottom and sides of prepared pan. Pat the dough into the pan at the bottom and up the sides to make a rim. Pierce bottom of the dough with a fork. Line dough with aluminum foil, fill with beans or rice, and bake for 10 to 15 minutes. Remove from oven; remove foil and beans or rice. Cool.

When onions are cooked, sprinkle in the flour, and stir and cook the mixture for about 5 minutes. Add the allspice, stir, and cool. Beat the eggs in a bowl until frothy. Beat in the cream and add the caraway seeds and salt and pepper to taste. Stir in the onion mixture and pour all into the prepared dough-lined pan. Bake the tart in the preheated oven for 40 to 45 minutes, or until top is set and nicely browned.

NOTE: Red onions can be used instead of yellow ones.

WINE: Sylvaner

GOUGÈRE BOURGUIGNONNE   *(FRANCE)*
Burgundy Cheese Pastry
                                                          SERVES 6 TO 8

⅔ cup water
½ teaspoon salt
3 ounces (¾ stick) butter, cut into
    pieces
1 cup plus 1 tablespoon flour
¼ pound Gruyère cheese, half
    grated, half diced

4 eggs
1 teaspoon pepper
1 egg yolk, mixed with 2
    tablespoons water

Preheat oven to 375°F. Butter a 10-inch springform pan. Pour water into a heavy saucepan and add salt and butter. Bring to a boil over medium heat, and add the flour all at once. Stir vigorously with a wooden spoon until a dough forms. Mash the dough against the sides and bottom of saucepan for a few minutes. Remove pan from heat. Stir in the *grated* Gruyère cheese and cool.

Add eggs, one at a time, stirring well after each addition; the batter should be smooth and shiny. Stir in the *diced* Gruyère and add the pepper. With a large spoon, drop mounds of batter into the pan around the edge, leaving a bare space in the middle about 3 inches across. The mounds will swell in baking and join to make a ring. Brush with egg-yolk wash. Bake for 40 to 50 minutes, until puffed and nicely colored.

Serve warm.

WINE: a red Burgundy

BEIGNET À FROMAGE
Cheese Puff

(FRANCE)

SERVES 8

DOUGH

1 pound all-purpose flour

⅔ cup flat beer

2 eggs, separated

1 tablespoon oil

salt

nutmeg

butter for pan

FILLING

1¼ pounds Gruyère cheese,
    cut into ¾-inch slices

pepper

nutmeg

oil for deep frying

5 eggs

salt

Place the flour in a mixing bowl, make a well in the center, and pour in the beer. Mix a little of the flour into the beer, then add the egg yolks, oil, and salt and nutmeg to taste. Beat the liquid mixture while blending in the flour. This is easier to do with an electric mixer. The dough will be thin, like a batter. Beat the egg whites until stiff and gently fold them into the batter. Refrigerate for 1 hour.

Sprinkle the sliced Gruyère with pepper and nutmeg. Set aside.

Preheat oven to 375°F. Butter a 9-inch soufflé dish. Dip the cheese slices into the prepared batter and fry in hot oil. Drain on paper towels. Arrange the slices of fried cheese in overlapping circles in the soufflé dish. Beat the 5 eggs until frothy, and add salt. Pour eggs on the fried cheese slices. Bake for 20 to 25 minutes, until top is puffed and nicely colored.

Serve immediately.

WINE: Côtes du Rhône

QUICHE AUX CHAMPIGNONS
Mushroom Quiche

(F R A N C E)

SERVES 8

DOUGH

butter for pan
1 batch of Pâte Brisée I (p. 6),
    chilled

FILLING

2 ounces (½ stick) butter
1½ pounds onions, thinly sliced
¾ cup uncooked rice
3 cups chicken broth or bouillon
salt and pepper

¼ cup heavy cream
nutmeg
1½ pounds mushrooms, sliced
⅓ cup sherry or port
¼ cup grated Gruyère cheese

Melt 1 ounce of the butter in a heavy saucepan. Add the onions, cover, and cook over very low heat for about 25 minutes. Add the rice and the broth with salt and pepper to taste. Bring to a boil, cover, and cook over low heat until rice is very tender and liquid is absorbed.

Force the mixture through a food mill. Return the purée to the pan and add the cream. Reheat, stirring, until mixture starts to puff. Add a dash of nutmeg. Remove from heat.

Melt remaining butter in a skillet and sauté the mushrooms. Add the sherry and cook until liquid evaporates. Season with salt and pepper. Set aside.

Preheat oven to 375°F. Butter an 11-inch quiche pan. On a floured board roll out the chilled dough into a circle large enough to cover bottom and sides of prepared pan. Fit dough into the pan, and trim excess dough with scissors. Cover dough with aluminum foil and fill with beans or rice. Bake for 15 minutes. Remove foil and beans or rice. Spread the mushrooms on the bottom of the partly baked pastry. Top with the rice mixture. Sprinkle with the grated Gruyère. Bake for 15 to 20 minutes, or until cheese melts.

WINE: Saint-Estèphe

ZWIEBELWÄHE
Onion and Cheese Tart

(SWITZERLAND)

SERVES 8

This is the pizza of Switzerland and as popular there as its sister in Italy.

DOUGH

1 tablespoon butter for pan, softened

1 batch of Short Pastry (p. 9)

FILLING

2 tablespoons vegetable oil

1 cup finely chopped onion

½ pound imported Swiss
   Emmenthaler cheese, coarsely
   grated

2 eggs

½ cup light cream

½ cup heavy cream

½ cup milk

¼ teaspoon salt

⅛ teaspoon grated nutmeg

Spread the tablespoon of softened butter over the bottom and sides of a 12-inch pizza pan. On a lightly floured board roll out the dough into a circle large enough to line the bottom and sides of the prepared pan. Fit the dough into the pan. Roll the pin over the rim of the pan to trim excess dough. Preheat oven to 400°F. Cover bottom of dough with aluminum foil and fill with beans or rice. Bake on the middle shelf of the oven for 10 minutes. Remove the foil and filling. Return the pan to the oven for 10 minutes, or until pastry begins to brown. Remove it from the oven and cool before using.

Reduce oven temperature to 350°F. Heat the oil in a heavy skillet over moderate heat. Add the onion and cook, stirring frequently, for about 5 minutes, or until onion is soft and transparent but not brown. Scatter half of the cheese in the baked pastry and spoon onion over the cheese. Spread with the remaining cheese. Beat the eggs, creams, milk, salt, and nutmeg together; pour the mixture evenly over the cheese. Bake in the upper third of the oven for 10 minutes. Increase the heat to 425°F. and bake for 15 minutes longer, or until the filling has puffed and browned and a knife inserted in the center comes out clean.

Serve hot or at room temperature.

WINE: Swiss Johannisberg

TARTE À POIS
Dotted Tart

(SWITZERLAND)

SERVES 6 TO 8

The funny name comes from my Swiss friend Marguerite Vartany. *À pois* means "with little balls or dots."

DOUGH

10-inch baked tart crust made with
Pâte Brisée I (p. 6)

FILLING

⅔ cup diced Swiss Emmenthaler
cheese

3 eggs

2 cups light cream

1 cup frozen peas, defrosted

1 tablespoon melted butter

salt and pepper

pinch of grated nutmeg

pinch of dried tarragon

1 cup grated Swiss Emmenthaler
cheese

Preheat oven to 350°F. Arrange the *diced* Swiss cheese at the bottom of the baked tart crust. Set aside. Beat eggs and cream together in a mixing bowl. Add all remaining ingredients. Pour into prepared crust. Bake for 15 to 20 minutes, or until custard is set and slightly colored.

Cool before slicing.

WINE: Neufchâtel

QUICHE DE HOMARD
Lobster Quiche

(FRANCE)

SERVES 8

DOUGH

butter for pan

1 batch of Pâte Brisée II (p. 7)

FILLING

1½ cups diced lobster meat

2 tablespoons minced fresh parsley

2 tablespoons vermouth

salt and pepper

5 eggs

1½ cups milk

pinch of cayenne pepper

paprika

Preheat oven to 400°F. Butter a 12-inch quiche pan. On a floured board, roll out the dough into a circle large enough to line the bottom and sides of the prepared pan. Fit the dough into pan. In a mixing bowl, combine lobster meat, parsley, vermouth, and salt and pepper to taste. Break the eggs into another mixing bowl. Dip a brush into the egg white portion and paint the bottom of pastry to prevent sogginess. Pour lobster mixture into pastry and set aside.

Beat the eggs. Add milk, salt to taste, and cayenne. Pour over the lobster. Sprinkle with paprika. Bake for 10 minutes. Reduce heat to 350°F. and continue baking for 20 to 30 minutes longer, or until top is set and rim of pastry is slightly brown.

WINE: Muscadet

BRIOCHE À L'OPPIO   *(FRANCE)*
Brioche Oppio Style

SERVES 8

Oppio, a small village, perches on a hill overlooking the sunny fields sloping toward Nice.

DOUGH
butter for pan
1 batch of Brioche Dough I (p. 13)   egg wash

FILLING

1 pound fish fillets, e.g., flounder, red snapper, striped bass	1 pound mushrooms, sliced thin
4 egg whites	salt and pepper
1 ounce (2 tablespoons) butter	1 cup cream
1 tablespoon oil	1 cup cooked mussels (see Note)
2 shallots, sliced	1 cup cooked small shrimps
1 carrot, diced	10 ounces tomatoes, peeled, seeded, and diced

Purée the fish fillets in a food processor or blender, then transfer to a mixing bowl. Add the egg whites, one at a time, beating with an electric mixer. Set aside.

Heat the butter and oil in a skillet. Cook the shallots, carrot, and mushrooms over moderate heat. Season with salt and pepper. Remove with a slotted spoon before vegetables start to color. Cool.

Beat 1 cup of cream into the fish mixture. Fold in the cooked vegetables. Butter a meat-loaf pan and set aside.

On a floured board, roll the brioche dough into a rectangle large enough to line bottom and sides of prepared pan. Let enough dough hang over the edges to cover brioche. Spoon in one layer of the fish mixture. Arrange half of the mussels and half of the shrimps over it, and dot with half of the tomatoes. Repeat as before and finish with the fish mixture. Enclose the brioche securely with the overhanging dough. Decorate with scraps of dough. Paint top with egg wash and set brioche aside for about 30 minutes to let the dough rise.

Preheat oven to 375°F. Paint top again with egg wash before baking. Bake for 35 to 40 minutes.

Slice and serve.

NOTE: Place mussels in a skillet, set over medium heat. As soon as shells start to open, remove them with a slotted spoon. Pluck mollusks out; discard shells.

WINE: Entre-Deux-Mers

TARTE AUX CREVETTES *(FRANCE)*
Shrimp Tart

SERVES 8

DOUGH

butter for pan

1 batch of Very Short Pastry (p. 10)

FILLING

1½ pounds raw shrimps, shelled and deveined

½ pound fillet of sole or flounder

2 eggs

salt and pepper

1 cup heavy cream

pinch of pepper

pinch of grated nutmeg

1 tablespoon minced fresh parsley

1 ounce (2 tablespoons) sherry

3 tablespoons grated Parmesan cheese

Preheat oven to 375°F. Butter a 10-inch pie pan. On a floured board, roll out the dough into a circle large enough to line the bottom and sides of the prepared pan. Fit the dough into pan. Pierce bottom of the dough with a fork. Set aside.

Cut the shrimps and the fish into pieces. Place the shrimps and fish in the bowl of a food processor fitted with the steel blade, or in a blender. Chop with 3 or 4 on and off turns until coarse. Transfer fish to a mixing bowl and add other ingredients except Parmesan cheese. Mix well. Spoon mixture into the pastry-lined pan. Smooth top and sprinkle with Parmesan. Bake for 30 to 35 minutes, or until top is nice and golden. Serve immediately.

NOTE: Sometimes a quiche will exude some liquid on top. If this happens, soak up gently with paper towels.

WINE: Entre-Deux-Mers

TARTE AUX CREVETTES ET AUX ARTICHAUTS
Shrimp and Artichoke Tart   *(B E L G I U M)*

SERVES 6 TO 8

DOUGH
10-inch baked tart crust made with
    Pâte Brisée I (p. 6)

FILLING

1 package (9 ounces) frozen artichokes	1 ounce (2 tablespoons) butter
	¼ pound fresh mushrooms, sliced
1 pound small shrimps, cooked, shelled, and deveined	2 tablespoons sherry
	1 teaspoon Worcestershire sauce

THICK BÉCHAMEL SAUCE

2 ounces (½ stick) butter	¾ cup heavy cream
4 tablespoons flour	pinch of paprika
¾ cup milk	salt and pepper

Prepare béchamel sauce: Melt butter in a pan, add flour, cook briefly, and remove from heat. Gradually add milk and cream, stirring constantly, until sauce liquefies. Cook over medium heat until sauce thickens and starts to bubble. Add seasoning to taste and set aside, stirring occasionally to prevent formation of a skin on the top.

Cook artichokes according to package directions, and drain thoroughly. Preheat oven to 375°F.

Cut artichokes into quarters and scatter at the bottom of the tart crust. Cut shrimps into 2 or 3 pieces and scatter on top of artichokes. Melt the butter in a skillet and cook mushrooms in it until they have released all their moisture. Add sherry and Worcestershire sauce, cook briefly, and add to the tart. Pour béchamel sauce in and smooth top with a spatula. Bake for 30 to 35 minutes, until set and nicely browned.

TOURTIÈRE D'HUÎTRES ET DES POIREAUX
AU MADÈRE   (F R A N C E)
Oyster and Leek Pie with Madeira

SERVES 4 TO 6

DOUGH

½ batch of Short Pastry (p. 9)   1 egg yolk

FILLING

2 ounces (½ stick) butter   2 tablespoons flour
2 cups thinly sliced potatoes   1 jigger (3 tablespoons) Madeira
3 dozen shucked oysters, drained   wine
milk   1 jigger (3 tablespoons) white wine
1 slice of bacon, ¼ inch thick, diced   salt and pepper
2 or 3 leeks, white part only, sliced   cayenne pepper
    thin

Preheat oven to 425°F. Butter a 9-inch pie dish with 1 tablespoon of the butter. Cook potatoes in salted water until tender. Drain. Transfer to a mixing bowl. Melt 1 ounce butter in a skillet. Add oysters and cook over medium heat until oysters begin to curl around the edges. Remove oysters with a slotted spoon to the bowl containing potatoes. Pour liquid from skillet into a measuring cup. Add enough milk to make 1 cup of liquid.

Melt 1 tablespoon butter in a saucepan. Add bacon and sauté for a few minutes. Add leeks and sauté, stirring frequently, until leeks start to color. Add the 1 cup reserved liquid, and simmer slowly until leeks are tender. Place flour in a cup or small bowl and dissolve with Madeira and white wine. Slowly add wine mixture to the pan of leeks, and cook until sauce thickens. Combine leeks with potatoes and oysters. Season to taste with salt, pepper, and a dash of cayenne. Turn into the prepared pie dish.

Roll out dough to fit pie dish. Place over filling and fasten and crimp rim of dough to the dish. Cut a hole in the center to allow steam to escape. Beat egg yolk with 2 tablespoons cold water. Paint top of pastry with this egg wash. Bake for 40 to 50 minutes, or until top is nice and golden.

WINE: Pouilly-Fumé

QUICHE D'ESCARGOTS
Snail Quiche

(F R A N C E)

SERVES 6 TO 8

DOUGH

butter for pan

1 batch of Very Short Pastry (p. 10)

FILLING

1 ounce (2 tablespoons) butter

1 shallot, minced

1 garlic clove, minced

24 cooked snails (if canned, drain)

1½ cups heavy cream

salt and pepper

4 eggs

nutmeg

1 tablespoon minced fresh parsley

Preheat oven to 375°F. Butter a 9- to 10-inch quiche pan. On a lightly floured board, roll out the dough into a circle large enough to line bottom and sides of prepared pan. Fit the dough into the pan. Cover dough with aluminum foil and fill with rice or beans. Bake for 15 minutes. Remove foil and rice or beans. Continue baking the piecrust for 10 minutes longer. Remove from oven and set aside.

Melt the butter in a skillet. Add shallot and garlic. Cook over medium heat until vegetables are soft. Add snails, cook for 1 minute, then add ¼ cup cream, and salt and pepper to taste. Remove from heat and cool.

Beat the eggs in a mixing bowl, add remaining cream. Season with salt and pepper, add nutmeg to taste, and the snail mixture. Pour into the baked pastry. Scatter minced parsley all over. Bake until top is set, for 25 to 30 minutes.

WINE: Fleurie

TOURTE PAYSANNE
Country Chicken Pie

(F R A N C E)

SERVES 10

DOUGH

4 cups all-purpose flour

1 teaspoon salt

¾ pound (3 sticks) butter, cut into
  pieces

6 tablespoons water

2 eggs

1 tablespoon heavy cream

pinch of pepper

FILLING

1 chicken, 3½ to 4 pounds

¾ cup Madeira wine

1 pound boned shoulder of pork,
  cubed

5 chicken livers

2 eggs, lightly beaten

salt and pepper

3 or 4 slices of bacon, blanched

¼ pound canned pâté de foie gras,
  cut into strips

1 truffle, julienned (optional)

Remove the skin of the chicken and reserve for another use; it will make an excellent galantine. Remove as much meat as possible from the bones of the chicken. Cut the breast meat into strips and the dark meat into chunks. Place meat in a bowl, cover with Madeira, and chill for 5 or 6 hours, or overnight.

Combine flour and salt in a mixing bowl. Add the butter and mix with a pastry blender or fingers until mixture resembles coarse meal. Add water, eggs, cream, and pepper, and gather the dough into a bowl. Chill for about 2 hours, or overnight.

Lift out the white meat strips from the Madeira and set aside. Coarsely chop the pork meat and the dark meat of the chicken. Chop the chicken livers similarly. Place together in a mixing bowl and add the Madeira in which chicken soaked. Reserve 2 tablespoons of the egg in a cup for egg wash. Add remaining egg to the chopped meat, with salt and pepper to taste. Toss to mix all ingredients together.

Preheat oven to 350°F. Butter a meat-loaf pan (9 x 5 x 3 inches) and set aside. Roll out the dough to a sheet as thin as possible, about ¼ inch thick, and line the bottom and sides of the prepared pan. Let dough overhang the rim all around. Cover the bottom with the blanched bacon slices. Spread half of the chopped meat mixture over bacon. Arrange the strips of chicken, the pâté de foie gras, and the truffle on this layer, pushing some of the strips down with fingers. Spoon in remaining meat mixture. Fold in the overhanging dough to enclose the *tourte* completely. Dampen the edges of the dough and press to seal. Press the top of the *tourte* down a little, to firm the inside and flatten top. Make 2 slits in the top and insert a funnel in each one to permit steam to escape while dish cooks.

Add 2 tablespoons water to reserved egg and paint top of pastry with a brush. With the point of knife, delicately design a lattice without piercing the dough. Bake for about 30 minutes. Reduce heat to 300°F., loosely cover top with a buttered sheet of aluminum foil, and bake for 45 minutes longer.

Unmold and let cool for 15 minutes before slicing.

WINE: Bergerac

QUICHE LORRAINE   (F R A N C E)

SERVES 6

DOUGH

butter for pan   1 batch of Pâte Brisée I (p. 6)

FILLING

5 eggs   1½ cups heavy cream, warm
salt and pepper   6 slices of bacon, sautéed in butter
nutmeg

Preheat oven to 425°F. Butter a 9-inch quiche pan and reserve. On a floured board, roll out chilled dough into a circle large enough to line bottom and sides of prepared pan. Fit the dough into the pan and trim excess dough with scissors. Pierce bottom of the dough with a fork. Chill.

Beat the eggs in a mixing bowl. While beating, add salt, pepper, and nutmeg to taste, and the cream. Set aside.

Bake the pastry for 8 minutes. Remove from oven and arrange the bacon strips over the bottom. Pour the egg mixture over and bake for 10 minutes. Reduce temperature to 350°F. and continue baking until top is set, 15 to 20 minutes.

WINE: Vin Gris de Lorraine

QUICHE AUX ENDIVES   *(B E L G I U M)*
Endive Quiche

SERVES 6

DOUGH

butter for pan   1 batch of Pâte Brisée I (p. 6)

FILLING

6 heads of Belgian endive, trimmed   1 cup grated Gruyère cheese
    and washed   crumbled
2½ tablespoons lemon juice   3 eggs
¼ teaspoon salt   1 cup light cream
1 cup light cream   1 cup grated Gruyère cheese

Preheat oven to 375°F. Butter a 9-inch quiche or tart pan. Leave endives whole. Cut a cross on the root end of each one. Pour lemon juice into a saucepan, add salt and boiling water, and bring again to a boil. Add endives and simmer for 5 minutes. Drain endives thoroughly. Cut them into ½-inch slices, and reserve in a colander.

On a floured board roll out the dough into a circle large enough to line bottom and sides of prepared pan. Fit dough into the pan, pierce bottom with a fork, trim excess dough with scissors, and flute edges all around. Scatter the crumbled bacon on the bottom of the dough. Arrange endives in a layer on top of bacon. In a mixing bowl, beat the eggs and cream well. Add the grated cheese, mix, and pour over endives. Bake for 35 to 40 minutes, or until custard is set.

Cool slightly and serve.

QUICHE AUX ASPERGES (Asparagus Quiche). Substitute asparagus for endives.

WINE: Vouvray

TOURTE D'AGNEAU
Lamb Pie

(F R A N C E)

DOUGH

butter for pan

1 batch of Wheaten Egg Dough
(p. 7)

FILLING

1 ounce (2 tablespoons) butter

¼ cup oil

1 onion, sliced

1 carrot, diced

1 celery rib, chopped

1 parsley sprig, chopped

1 pound boned shoulder of lamb,
cubed

½ pound mixed veal and pork,
ground

salt and pepper

pinch of ground allspice

1 jigger (1½ ounces) Armagnac

1 teaspoon tomato paste

4 or 5 pear-shaped tomatoes,
skinned, seeded, and chopped

2 eggs, slightly beaten

2 to 3 ounces pâté de foie gras, cut
into strips

1 truffle, diced (optional)

Place 1 tablespoon butter and 2 tablespoons oil in a skillet. Heat, and add all vegetables. Cook over low heat until vegetables are almost tender. With a slotted spoon, remove vegetables to a mixing bowl.

Put the remaining butter and oil into the same skillet and heat. Sauté cubed lamb for about 20 minutes, stirring often. Add the ground meat and continue cooking until all meat loses its pink color. Add salt and pepper to taste and allspice. Pour Armagnac into the meat and let it evaporate. Add tomato paste and tomatoes. Cook over low heat, covered, for 10 to 15 minutes, or longer. Combine meats with vegetables in the mixing bowl. Add the eggs; mix well.

Preheat oven to 375°F. Butter a 12-inch pie pan. On a lightly floured board, roll out two-thirds of the dough into a circle large enough to line bottom and sides of prepared pan. Fit the dough into the pan. Trim excess dough with scissors, but leave 1 inch of the dough hanging over the edge of the pan.

Pour half of the meat mixture into the dough-lined pan and smooth with a spatula. Arrange the strips of foie gras over this and scatter the diced truffle on top. Pour in remaining meat mixture and smooth top. Roll out remaining dough and cover pie. Trim excess dough with scissors. Fold overhanging dough over the top layer, and seal pie all around in a decorative fashion. Bake for 45 minutes.

WINE: Bordeaux Rouge

POUNTI   *(FRANCE)*
Prune and Ham Pie
SERVES 6 TO 8

This pie, not well known even in France, is a specialty from Auvergne. The surrounding region, dominated by the scenic volcanic mountains, is famous for its medicinal waters. It was here that the rebellious Gallic leader Vercingetorix was subdued by Caesar.

If the natural beauty, a sense of history, and the restorative powers of the water are not enough to entice a visitor to Auvergne, a wedge of *pounti* will.

4 or 5 dried prunes	2 tablespoons minced parsley
2 packages active dry yeast	½ teaspoon minced chervil
pinch of sugar	¼ teaspoon minced tarragon
3 tablespoons lukewarm milk (105° to 115°F.)	½ cup flour
	4 eggs, lightly beaten
¾ cup minced ham	salt and pepper
½ cup minced salt pork	¼ cup milk, if necessary
2 onions, minced	2 tablespoons oil
⅓ cup minced beet greens or spinach	

Place prunes in a pan, cover with water, and simmer for 20 minutes. Let stand for 30 minutes. Drain, reserve water, and keep it warm. Pit the prunes, chop them, and set aside.

Preheat oven to 350°F. Combine yeast, sugar, 3 tablespoons milk, and ¼ cup water from prunes. In a mixing bowl combine all the other ingredients but ¼ cup milk and the oil. Add the reserved prunes and the yeast mixture. If batter is too thick add a little more milk.

Heat the oil in a 10-inch ovenproof skillet. Pour the batter into it and cook for 1 minute. Transfer the skillet to the oven and bake for 30 to 40 minutes.

WINE: Beaujolais

TOURTE SAVOYARD   *(F R A N C E)*
Savoy Pork Pie

In Savoy a special sausage is used for this pie. It is a *cervelas truffé*, containing truffles. Since it is not easy to find it in this country, I have devised this adaptation.

DOUGH

1 batch of Brioche Dough II (p. 14)   1 egg yolk mixed with
2 tablespoons milk

FILLING

1½ pounds shoulder of pork, boned   1 garlic clove, minced
and cubed   ½ teaspoon *quatre-épices* (see Note)
¼ pound fresh pork fat, diced   2 tablespoons very fine unflavored
(optional)   bread crumbs
salt   1 truffle, fresh or canned, diced
½ teaspoon crushed peppercorns   (optional)
1 tablespoon minced fresh parsley   oil

BROTH

1 onion   1 carrot
2 cloves   1 parsley sprig
1 celery rib   2 bay leaves

The day before serving: If shoulder of pork contains enough fat, eliminate extra fat. Coarsely chop the pork meat in a food processor fitted with the steel blade. Remove to a mixing bowl and add all other filling ingredients except oil. Mix with wet hands to combine ingredients well. Pat into the shape of a large sausage, 3 inches in diameter. Soak a double layer of cheesecloth in cold water, spread it flat, and oil it lightly with a brush. Place the sausage on the cheesecloth, wrap, and secure it at both ends with strings. Refrigerate overnight.

Make the broth: Stick the cloves into the onion and put in a saucepan large enough to hold the sausage. Add remaining broth ingredients. Add the sausage and cover with water. Bring broth to a boil, then reduce to a simmer and cook for 45 minutes. Let sausage cool in its own broth. Remove the cheesecloth.

Preheat oven to 425°F. Roll out the brioche dough to a rectangle large enough to enclose sausage. Brush the surface of the brioche with the egg yolk mixed with milk; this is a *dorure* (egg wash). Place sausage on dough and brush sausage all over with *dorure*. Wrap sausage with the dough, enclosing it completely. Place the package on a buttered baking sheet and brush again with *dorure*, taking care that the mixture does not run into the baking sheet, which would cause the *tourte* to stick to the pan. Make 2 small holes on top of the dough to allow steam to escape. Bake the *tourte* for 25 to 30 minutes.

Serve hot.

NOTE: Quatre-épices is a combination of 4 spices. To make your own combine 5 tablespoons ground cloves, 3 tablespoons ground ginger, 3 tablespoons grated nutmeg, and 3 tablespoons pepper. Use it by the pinch.

WINE: Beaujolais

L'OREILLER DE LA BELLE AURORE *(F R A N C E)*
Beautiful Aurora's Pillow

SERVES 6 TO 8

A specialty of Lyon. Delicious to savor and delightful to look at. The recipe was invented by Brillat-Savarin and named for his mother Aurore.

DOUGH

butter for pan

1 batch of Classic Puff Pastry (p. 11) or Quick Puff Pastry (p. 12)

FILLING

2 pheasants, boned
½ pound veal, cubed
¾ pound pork, cubed
¼ pound pork fat
salt and pepper
1 tablespoon ground dried mushrooms

1 jigger (1½ ounces) Cognac
1 egg
2 to 3 ounces foie gras, cut into strips
1 truffle, diced (optional)

Fillet the breast of the pheasants. Cut it into strips and reserve together with the liver of the bird. Grind the dark pheasant meat, all the scraps, the gizzard, and skin together with the veal, pork, and pork fat. Place in a mixing bowl and add salt and pepper to taste, the mushrooms, Cognac, and egg. Mix well.

Preheat oven to 375°F. Butter a baking sheet (10 x 15 inches). On a lightly floured board, roll out half of the dough to a rectangle 14 x 8 inches. Place on the prepared baking sheet. Spread half of the meat mixture over the dough, leaving a 1-inch border all around. On top of the meat arrange the strips of pheasant breast and strips of foie gras. Scatter the diced truffle over all. Spread remaining meat mixture on top.

Roll out remaining dough to a rectangle of the same size, and place it over the filling. Trim excess dough with a knife. Seal the edges all around to give the pie the form of a pillow. Pierce top with a fork to make holes, and insert an aluminum foil funnel to allow steam to escape. Bake for 35 minutes. Reduce heat to 350°F. and bake for 40 to 45 minutes longer.

Serve with Madeira Sauce (p. 18).

WINE: Hermitage

TOURTE DE BASTOGNE   (B E L G I U M)
Bastogne Pot Pie

SERVES 4 TO 6

I do not have a great passion for fruits, jams, and sweet stuff when put together with meats and poultry. However, this pie, if taken in small doses, is delicious. I have friends who adore it. Well, we all know that old adage, *"de gustibus . . .",* etc.

This specialty comes from Bastogne, a town famous for its hams. Americans will remember the name since it was around Bastogne that the Battle of the Bulge took place during World War II.

DOUGH

butter for pan   ½ batch of Brioche Dough I (p. 13)

FILLING

1½ ounces (3 tablespoons) butter	2 bananas, sliced thin
1 onion, chopped	2 tart apples, sliced thin
1 pound fresh sausage meat	2 tablespoons vinegar
½ cup raisins, soaked in warm water	4 thick slices of ham, about ¼ pound, cut into strips
½ cup dried prunes, chopped	1 ounce (2 tablespoons) Calvados

Melt butter in a skillet. Add onion and cook until soft and translucent. Add sausage meat and cook for 5 minutes. Add both dried and fresh fruits; cook for 20 minutes. Drain off some of the fat. Add vinegar and let it evaporate. Butter a 9-inch soufflé dish or a meat-loaf pan (9 x 5 x 3 inches). Spoon half of the sausage mixture into the prepared dish and top with ham strips. Add remaining sausage mixture. Smooth top.

On a floured board, roll out dough into a circle for the soufflé dish, or a rectangle if you are using a loaf pan. Dough should be large enough to cover the top of the *tourte*. Cut excess dough with scissors but leave 1 inch extra overhanging the rim. Fold over and crimp the dough to enclose filling. Make a hole in the center. Insert a funnel made of aluminum foil to permit steam to escape. Decorate top of the dough with cutouts if desired. Let *tourte* rest for 20 minutes before baking.

Preheat oven to 375°F. Bake for 25 minutes, then add Calvados through the funnel. Reduce heat to 300°F. and bake for 10 minutes longer.

Cool a little before slicing.

WINE: Bâtard-Montrachet

CROSTATA TICINESE   *(S W I T Z E R L A N D)*
Sausage Pie from Ticino

SERVES 8

Canton Ticino is in the Italian-speaking part of Switzerland.

DOUGH

butter for pan

1 batch of Wheaten Egg Dough
(p. 7)

FILLING

3 or 4 mild fresh Italian sausages,
about 1 pound

1 leek

1 tablespoon butter

1 teaspoon oil

1 package (9 ounces) frozen
artichokes, defrosted

4 eggs

1 pound ricotta cheese, drained

3 tablespoons cream

2 triangles of Petit-Suisse cheese,
sliced

3 tablespoons grated Parmesan
cheese

4 ounces Swiss Gruyère cheese,
grated

4 slices of ham, cut into julienne

½ cup chopped parsley

salt and pepper

Place sausages in a skillet, pierce them with a pointed knife, cover with water, and cook until all water is absorbed. Cool, and cut into round slices. Wash the leek well; cut the white part into round slices and chop the green part. Butter a 10-inch quiche pan.

While sausages cook, roll the dough out on a floured surface into a circle large enough to line bottom and sides of prepared pan. Fit dough into pan, and trim excess dough. Chill the dough.

Heat butter and oil in a skillet. Add leek pieces and sauté lightly. Add artichokes, stir, reduce heat, cover, and cook for 5 to 8 minutes, until tender. Set aside. Beat the eggs in a mixing bowl. Add ricotta and cream, and beat until creamy and smooth. Stir in remaining filling ingredients, with salt and pepper to taste, and stir in leek and artichoke mixture.

Preheat oven to 425°F. Arrange the sausage slices on the bottom of the dough, reserving a few for decoration. Spoon ricotta mixture on sausages and smooth the top. Decorate with reserved sliced sausages. Bake for 10 minutes. Reduce temperature to 375°F., and bake for 20 minutes longer, or until top is set and lightly browned.

Serve warm or at room temperature.

WINE: Nostrano (from Ticino)

Around the North Sea and the Channel

Great Britain · Ireland · Holland

The British are masters in the art of pie making, and so are the Irish. Other dough-covered preparations are called puddings. Both pies and puddings are usually made with meats. The crusts are sometimes elaborately baked in molds resembling animals and the entire production is beautiful to look at as well as pleasing to the palate. Very often a pie will look like *pâté en croûte*, with truffles, ham, and hard-cooked eggs distributed in the forcemeat. Lamb and mutton pies are favorites in Scotland and Ireland.

Cornwall offers seafood pies like the Star-Gazy Pie, also the famous Cornish pasties filled with a mixture of lamb, potatoes, and onions, as well as pasties with many other fillings.

Game pies, in great variety, abound throughout the British Isles. They are favorite treats for buffet meals, and most welcome in picnic baskets. Irish cooks use pheasants, partridges, and other game, often wrapping them in puff pastry.

Steak and kidney pie has become an international favorite, and appears on menus of famous eating places all over the world. Kidneys without the steak, and brains, are made into pastry dishes in Ireland.

Holland shares with Britain the cold waters of the North Sea, rich in fish and shellfish. The English Channel (which the French call *la Manche*), which washes the southern coasts of England, carries this bounty to all fishermen there and on to ports of Ireland as well. One of the world's great fish, Dover sole, is used by all three countries for hundreds of dishes. The Dutch pie here is only one example. The Irish use all sorts of tiny shellfish—cockles, winkles, and closheens, a variety of scallop—in pastry wrappings. These countries can fish scallops in their own waters, to be purchased whole, in the shell, so they still have the roe or coral, like an orange red tongue, attached to the white muscle. In addition to its delicate and delicious flavor, it adds color to any dish.

Salmon, a favorite in Britain, especially Scotland, and Ireland, and still fished there in cold river waters, is made into a variety of pies, as are trout and other freshwater fish.

Holland, with its longtime Indonesian connection (now ended, of course), has exotic fare available. They also make the huge pancakes, baked in the oven, that are so popular all along the Rhine Valley.

YORKSHIRE PUDDING
(YORKSHIRE, ENGLAND)
SERVES 8

This may not be the traditional way of making Yorkshire Pudding, but it is a good way. I have even used duck or chicken dripping instead of beef with excellent results. Easy to make, this pudding is undoubtedly a more elegant accompaniment to an American "roast beef" than baked potatoes.

1 cup all-purpose flour	3 eggs
pinch of salt	2 tablespoons beef dripping or lard
pinch of nutmeg (optional)	
1 cup milk, or ½ cup milk and ½ cup water	

Preheat oven to 400°F. In a mixing bowl combine flour, salt, and nutmeg if used. Make a well in the middle and add the milk, no water at this point, and eggs. Beat with an electric beater. Refrigerate until ready to use.

If using half milk and half water, just before cooking stir in the water. Use a baking dish from which you can serve. Put the dripping or lard in the dish and place dish in the oven until fat is very hot. Beat batter energetically, pour into the hot dish, and bake the pudding for 30 to 35 minutes, or until puffed and nicely browned.

Serve hot.

SPINACH YORKSHIRE PUDDING. Add 1½ cups very finely chopped cooked spinach, very well drained, to the batter. Use only milk.

KAASPANNEKOEKEN *(HOLLAND)*
Dutch Oven Pancake

SERVES 6

These pancakes have a long history in the cuisine of northern Europe. They take the place of the pizzas and tarts of the South. This one makes a delicious breakfast dish.

2 tablespoons oil	1 cup all-purpose flour
8 ounces mushrooms, sliced thin	1 cup milk
salt and pepper	1 cup shredded Gouda cheese
4 eggs	1½ ounces (3 tablespoons) butter

Pour the oil into a 10- to 11-inch iron skillet. Heat, and add mushrooms; cook over high heat, stirring constantly, until mushrooms start to give out moisture. Cook until moisture has evaporated. Season with salt and pepper to taste and set aside. In a mixing bowl, beat the eggs with an electric beater for 1 minute. Add the flour and, gradually, the milk. Continue beating and add the cheese.

Preheat oven to 475°F. Add the butter to the skillet of mushrooms and place skillet in the oven. As soon as the butter starts to bubble, pour in the pancake batter. Bake for 20 to 25 minutes, or until puffy and nicely colored.

Serve hot directly from skillet.

VARIATION: Substitute sausages, cut into rounds, for mushrooms. This way the pancake becomes a nutritious luncheon dish.

FISHERMAN'S PIE (COUNTY CORK, IRELAND)

SERVES 6 TO 8

A specialty from County Cork. In Ireland as well as in Britain scallops are sold whole, still retaining the coral (roe). Unfortunately, in the United States this delicious morsel is discarded in commercial fishing. Unless you collect the scallops yourself, you will have a pie without coral. This is one of the many pies from this part of the world with a crust made from potatoes.

5 ounces (1¼ sticks) butter, approximately
bread crumbs
2 cups milk
salt and pepper
12 ounces raw shrimps (about 16), shelled and deveined
1 pound large scallops or bay scallops, with coral if possible
2 tablespoons flour

1 ounce (2 tablespoons) sherry
¼ pound mushrooms, coarsely chopped
2 tablespoons minced parsley
2 hard-cooked eggs, coarsely chopped
2 cups mashed cooked potatoes
3 tablespoons grated Parmesan cheese
¼ cup heavy cream

Preheat oven to 350°F. Butter an ovenproof dish from which you can serve. Sprinkle with bread crumbs. Set aside.

In a saucepan, heat the milk with salt and pepper to taste, and bring to a boil. Add the shrimps; as soon as they start to turn pink, add the scallops; simmer for 5 minutes. Set aside. In another saucepan melt 1 ounce butter, add the flour, and cook until well blended. Remove from heat. Strain the milk from shrimps and scallops. Measure 2 cups; if you are short, add a little more milk. Remove shrimps from saucepan and set aside. Cut each large scallop into 4 pieces and set aside in a mixing bowl. If you are using bay scallops, leave them whole, or cut into halves.

Pour the milk, a little at a time, into the butter and flour, and stir until sauce liquefies. Heat again and cook, stirring, until sauce starts to boil. Let it puff once or twice. Add the sherry and pour the sauce into the mixing bowl with the scallops. Melt another 1 ounce butter in a skillet and sauté mushrooms until tender. Add mushrooms and parsley to the scallops. Mix; taste for seasoning. Add the chopped eggs and mix gently again. Spoon the mixture into the prepared dish, and smooth top with a spatula.

Combine potatoes, 2 ounces butter, 1 tablespoon of the cheese, and the cream. Beat with a wooden spoon to make a fluffy, light mixture. Spoon this into a pastry bag and pipe decoratively all around the top of the scallop mixture, leaving a well in the middle. Arrange shrimps in this well like a bouquet of flowers. Dot with remaining butter and sprinkle with remaining cheese. Bake for 15 to 20 minutes, until top is nicely colored. If necessary, place under broiler for a few minutes.

DRINK: Cider

STAR-GAZY PIE *(CORNWALL, ENGLAND)*

SERVES 6

A specialty from Cornwall where fresh herrings or pilchards are often used instead of mackerels. This is a good pie with which to learn to look "your fish in the eye," the way we Italians do.

DOUGH
1 batch of Short Pastry (p. 9)

FILLING

2 ounces (¼ stick) butter, plus butter for pan
bread crumbs
1 tablespoon oil
6 small mackerels, about 12 ounces each, cleaned, boned, but with heads left on

4 eggs
salt and pepper
pinch of marjoram
pinch of tarragon
2 tablespoons vinegar
1 tablespoon cream

Preheat oven to 400°F. Butter a 12-inch round casserole or deep pie dish. Sprinkle with a thick layer of bread crumbs. Set aside. Heat 2 ounces butter and the oil in a skillet. Gently sauté fish on both sides, turning once. You may need to do this in 2 batches. If necessary, use a little more butter and oil. Arrange the fish in the prepared casserole, spoke fashion, with tails converging in the middle, and heads propped up at the outer rim and pointed upward. Beat the eggs, add salt and pepper to taste, herbs, vinegar, and cream. Pour into the casserole.

On a floured board roll out dough to a sheet ¼ inch thick, and cover the casserole. Seal dough all around, but make slits to let the fish heads gaze out. Bake for 10 minutes. Reduce heat to 350°F. and cook until top is golden brown, about 20 minutes longer. Insert a toothpick in the center; if it comes out clean, custard is set.

DRINK: Pale ale

SALMON PIE   (*ENGLAND*)

SERVES 6

Although typically English, this pie is not usually found in restaurants. It is a very homey dish made to use up leftover fish. The preferred fish is salmon, but cod, scrod, and similar kinds can be used too.

In my younger days I lived in England for three years and shared a flat with my dear friend Giuliana Trevisan. We could not afford salmon all the time, but our kind fisherman knowing of what we jokingly called the Britannic Campaign, during which we were learning the language and never had enough money, would present us with big heads of fresh salmon to which big chunks of neck meat would be attached. Those pieces, plus the cheeks of the fish, would result in a delicious pie. We learned this basic recipe from our substitute family, the Babbingtons.

butter	pinch of ground sage
4 tablespoons bread crumbs	2 eggs, lightly beaten
1 pound fresh salmon	salt and pepper
1 small potato, boiled	milk
4 ounces bacon, chopped	

Butter a 9-inch pie pan from which you can serve. Sprinkle with some of the bread crumbs.

Poach or pan fry the fish. Skin, bone, and flake it. Mash the potato.

In a mixing bowl place the potato, fish, bacon, remaining bread crumbs, sage, eggs, and salt and pepper to taste. Add just enough milk to moisten the mixture and blend all the ingredients well. Pour mixture into prepared pan. Smooth top and dot generously with butter. Bake at 350°F. for about 45 minutes.

GOUDSE ASPERGUS VIS TAART (*HOLLAND*)
Gouda, Asparagus, and Fish Pie

SERVES 6

DOUGH

1 batch of Pâte Brisée I (p. 6)

FILLING

4 or 5 ripe medium-size tomatoes, peeled, seeded, coarsely chopped	1 cup cooked rice
2 tablespoons oil	4 tablespoons bread crumbs, approximately
1 ounce (2 tablespoons) butter, plus butter for pan	8 ounces Gouda cheese, shredded
1 sprig of fresh dill, chopped, or pinch of dried dill	3 fillets of sole, cut into halves
	salt and pepper
	12 cooked asparagus, tender parts only

Place tomatoes, oil, and 1 tablespoon butter in a skillet. Cook uncovered over medium heat until liquid has evaporated. Add the dill toward the end. Remove from heat and stir in the rice and 1 or 2 tablespoons bread crumbs. Do not make the mixture too dry. Preheat oven to 375°F. Butter a 9-inch pie pan.

On a lightly floured surface, roll out the dough into a circle large enough to line bottom and sides of prepared pan. Fit dough into pan, and trim excess dough with scissors. Pierce the bottom of the dough with a fork; flute edges. Sprinkle dough with bread crumbs and half of the shredded cheese.

Sprinkle fillets of sole with salt and pepper and wrap each piece around 2 asparagus spears. Arrange rolls, spoke fashion, in the pastry-lined pan. Spoon tomato and rice mixture over the rolls and scatter remaining cheese on top. Dot with remaining butter and sprinkle lightly with bread crumbs. Bake for 35 to 40 minutes, or until fish starts to flake when touched with a fork.

Cool slightly before serving.

BACON PIE DOROTHY DOLGLISH   *(E N G L A N D)*

Dorothy is a dear and long-standing friend of mine, and an excellent cook.

DOUGH

butter for pan and for rubbing on
    dough

1 batch of Short Pastry (p. 9)

FILLING

1 pound bacon, cut into strips
4 eggs
2 cups cream
pinch of grated nutmeg
pinch of sugar
¾ teaspoon salt

pinch of cayenne pepper
pinch of black pepper
½ cup grated Cheddar cheese
½ cup grated Swiss Emmenthaler
    cheese

Preheat oven to 450°F. Butter a 10-inch quiche pan. On a floured board, roll out the dough into a circle large enough to line bottom and sides of prepared pan. Fit the dough into the pan, pierce the bottom of the dough with a fork, and chill.

Fry bacon until crisp. Break into small pieces. Beat the eggs in a mixing bowl. Add cream and remaining ingredients except cheeses. Mix well. Rub a little butter over the pastry, and sprinkle bacon pieces over it. Add the cheeses. Pour egg mixture over all. Bake for 10 minutes, then reduce heat to 300°F. Bake until a toothpick inserted in the middle of pie comes out clean, usually about 25 minutes.

NOTE: You can add all kinds of extras if you like, such as fried onions. You can also make the custard richer and more solid by adding another egg or two.

DRINK: Beer

NASI GORENG   *(H O L L A N D)*
Curried Rice, Pork, and Vegetable Pie

SERVES 4 TO 6

Holland is famous for the Indonesian touches in its cuisine. This is an exotic recipe that has become traditional. A flavorful one-dish meal, just right for lunch or a light supper, which can very nicely be made with leftovers. The lattice top, cut from a very thin omelet, makes the dish elegant to present at the table.

1½ ounces (3 tablespoons) butter	3 eggs
1 teaspoon oil	1½ cups cooked mixed peas and
2 large onions, sliced	carrots
½ pound lean pork, diced	pinch of curry powder
2 cups cooked rice	1 tablespoon soy sauce
salt and pepper	1 tablespoon minced fresh parsley

Heat 1 ounce of the butter and the oil in a 10- to 11-inch iron frying pan. Sauté the onions and pork, stirring often; cook for 15 to 20 minutes. Stir in half of the rice, with salt and pepper to taste. Remove from heat.

Preheat oven to 350°F. Make a thin omelet with 1 egg and set aside. Flatten the rice mixture in the skillet, and scatter half of the cooked vegetables over it. Add remaining rice and remaining vegetables in the same fashion. Beat remaining 2 eggs in a mixing bowl. Add salt and pepper to taste, the curry powder, and soy sauce. Pour over the rice mixture. Bake in the preheated oven for about 20 minutes.

Cut the omelet into strips. Remove pie from oven and arrange the strips of omelet on top of the rice, lattice style. Return pan to oven and bake for 5 to 8 minutes longer.

KINGDOM OF FIFE PIE

DOUGH

1 batch of Quick Puff Pastry (p. 12)
1 egg beaten with 2 tablespoons
    milk or water

FILLING

1 rabbit, 4 pounds approximately
¼ cup oil
1 tablespoon butter
3 tablespoons vinegar
salt and pepper
¾ pound pickled pork

2 hard-cooked eggs, sliced
2 slices of bacon, chopped
1 tablespoon minced parsley
pinch each of thyme and marjoram
½ cup bread crumbs
1 egg, lightly beaten

STOCK

bones of the rabbit
6 peppercorns
1 onion, with 2 cloves stuck in it
1 bay leaf

1 celery rib
1 carrot
1 parsley sprig
salt and pepper

Bone rabbit; reserve bones. Cut meat into serving pieces. Place all the ingredients for stock in a heavy pot, cover with water, bring to a boil, and simmer for about 2 hours. Strain and cool.

Spoon the oil and butter into a skillet. (In Scotland, drippings from roasts are used for frying.) Add the rabbit pieces and sauté until brown. Add the vinegar and let it evaporate. Add salt and pepper to taste. Add the pickled pork, cook just to heat through, and turn mixture into an ovenproof casserole from which you can serve. Arrange the sliced eggs all over rabbit and pork.

Preheat oven to 425°F. Put all remaining ingredients in a mixing bowl and mix well. Spread on rabbit mixture. Pour in enough stock to come two-thirds to the top of the pie dish.

On a floured board roll out the pastry into a sheet ¼ inch thick and large enough to cover the top of the casserole and overhang a little. Place pastry over the casserole, and trim excess with scissors; reserve scraps. Press the overhanging pastry all around to enclose pie well. Decorate pie with the scraps of pastry. Cut a few slits on the top of the pie. Bake for 15 minutes. Reduce heat to 325°F. and continue baking for 1½ hours longer. Cover pie loosely with aluminum foil when pastry starts to brown. Paint the pie with the egg wash 15 minutes before removing it from oven.

WINE: Brouilly

LAMB CISTE   (IRELAND)
SERVES 6

A traditional Irish dish, nowadays found only in private homes. It is excellent to serve as a complete meal; just add a salad and a nice dessert. The word *ciste* comes from the Latin *cista*, meaning basket or box. This dish, then, is lamb in a basket!

DOUGH

2 cups all-purpose flour

1 cup grated suet, or ½ cup vegetable shortening

1 teaspoon baking powder

½ teaspoon salt

½ cup milk, approximately

FILLING

6 small lamb chops, trimmed of fat, bone on

3 lamb kidneys, cut into pieces

1 large carrot, sliced

2 medium-sized onions, sliced

1 tablespoon minced parsley

½ teaspoon thyme

1 bay leaf

salt and pepper

2 cups stock or bouillon, approximately

Place the chops around the sides of a medium-size flameproof casserole with the bone ends sticking up. Add the kidneys, carrot, onions, and herbs, and season with salt and pepper. Add enough stock or bouillon barely to cover the kidneys and vegetables. Cover as tightly as possible with aluminum foil, bring to a boil, and simmer gently for 30 minutes. Taste for seasoning.

Preheat oven to 400°F. Place flour and suet in a mixing bowl. Combine quickly with fingers, without overworking. Add baking powder and salt, and enough milk to gather the mixture into a consistent dough. Turn out on a floured board and gently roll into a ¼-inch sheet. Cut out a lid and top the casserole with it. Press this lid down, but let the bones of the lamb chops protrude. Secure the edges of the dough all around casserole. Make decorations with scraps of dough, if you wish. Bake for 15 minutes. Cover loosely with foil and continue baking for 1½ hours longer.

Remove the top by loosening the crust around the edges with a knife. Then cut pie into 6 wedges. The *ciste* is served by placing 1 wedge, 1 lamb chop, and some of the kidney-vegetable stew on each dish.

MUTTON PIE   (SCOTLAND)

SERVES 6

A specialty from Scotland, where mutton is greatly appreciated. Lamb can be used if you prefer.

DOUGH

butter for pan   1 batch of Short Pastry (p. 9)

FILLING

4 tablespoons oil   1 teaspoon tomato paste
½ pound lean mutton, diced   2 tablespoons vinegar
2 shallots, finely chopped   12 mushrooms, chopped
½ teaspoon crumbled dried thyme   salt and pepper
1 tablespoon minced fresh parsley

Preheat oven to 375°F. Butter a 9-inch deep pie dish. Heat the oil in a skillet and sauté the mutton over high heat until brown. Add shallots, thyme, and parsley, and cook briefly over moderate heat for a few minutes. Combine tomato paste and vinegar and add to mutton. Add mushrooms and cook until water released by mushrooms has evaporated. Season with salt and pepper to taste, and set aside.

On a floured board, roll out the pastry into a ¼-inch-thick circle, large enough to line bottom and sides of prepared dish. Fit pastry into pan and trim excess pastry with scissors. Reserve leftover dough for topping. Pour mutton mixture into pastry-lined pan. Roll out remaining pastry into a lid to top pie. Press edges together to enclose pie well. Make a hole in the center. Bake pie for about 30 minutes. Cover pie if top starts to color too much. Cook for 15 minutes longer.

CHICKEN, VEAL, AND HAM PIE
(GREAT BRITAIN)
SERVES 8

DOUGH

1 batch of Hot-Water Raised Pastry (p. 15) or Short Pastry (p. 9), ready to use

oil or butter for pan
1 egg
1 tablespoon milk or cream

FILLING

1 frying chicken, 3 pounds
1 pound boneless veal from the leg, cubed
¾ pound country-cured ham, in 1 slice, cubed
1 teaspoon ground sage
1 pinch of ground allspice
2 shallots, peeled and halved

1 jigger (3 tablespoons) Cognac or other brandy
salt and pepper
1 bay leaf, crumbled
1 tablespoon butter
1½ cups chicken stock, approximately

Bone and skin chicken. With the bones and skin make a stock (see p. 19), or use already prepared stock. Place the meat from the chicken legs in a food processor fitted with the steel blade. Add one-third of the veal and one-quarter of the ham. Sprinkle in half of the sage, the allspice, and the shallots. Process until the mixture is very finely chopped, with the consistency of a forcemeat. Add the brandy and mix. Cut the rest of the cubed veal and ham into smaller cubes and cube the rest of the chicken meat.

Preheat oven to 400°F. Grease a hinged or collapsible mold or a springform pan 8 x 8 x 4 inches thoroughly. Roll out two-thirds of the dough into a circle large enough to line bottom and sides of prepared pan. Fit dough into pan, and trim excess dough with scissors. Leave about ½ inch of dough hanging over the edge of the pan all around. Place 1 thin layer of the forcemeat at the bottom of the dough. Scatter a layer of the cubed meat over. Season with a pinch of sage, and salt and pepper to taste. Repeat until all meats are used. Finish with a layer of forcemeat, add the bay leaf, and dot with 1 tablespoon of butter. Roll out remaining dough for the lid and top pie with it. Beat the egg lightly with the milk or cream to make egg wash. Brush a little of this on the overhanging dough. Fold it up over the edge of the lid and seal the pie all around. Make decorations with scraps of dough. Paint top with remaining egg wash. Cut a hole in the center of pie and insert a funnel of aluminum foil to allow steam to escape.

Place the pie on a baking sheet and bake for 25 minutes. Reduce heat to 325°F. and continue baking for about 2 hours longer. Cover pie loosely with foil as soon as it starts to brown, to prevent burning. Remove pie from oven and cool at room temperature. Remove the foil funnel, and chill the pie for 15 minutes.

Using a small funnel, pour cooled stock into the steam hole. Tilt the mold from side to side to distribute liquid well. Refrigerate overnight, or for a minimum of 6 hours.

Unmold pie and serve at room temperature.

STEAK AND KIDNEY PUDDING
AND STEAK AND KIDNEY PIE   (ENGLAND)

The glory of England, steak and kidney pudding, and pie, is still made much in the same manner as in the days of Charles Dickens, although the pie is a more modern version. The filling in both is similar. The addition of oysters is a luxurious touch, but not a necessary one; oysters can be omitted without taking away any of the authentic taste of this sturdy classic.

The real difference between the two preparations consists in the method of cooking, and of course the enclosing pastry. While the pudding is steamed in a basin, the pie bakes in the oven.

PUDDING   *SERVES 6 TO 8*

DOUGH

2 cups all-purpose flour
salt
1 teaspoon baking powder

1 cup very finely grated beef suet
1 cup cold water, approximately

FILLING

1½ pounds lean beef from the rump, cut into thin strips 4 x 2 inches

1 veal kidney, about 1 pound, cubed, fat removed

8 ounces mushrooms, quartered (optional)

⅓ cup flour

pinch of marjoram

pinch of thyme

1 small onion, minced

¾ cup beef stock

Place the flour, salt, baking powder, and suet in a bowl and mix well. Add enough water while stirring to make a fairly soft dough. Roll out two-thirds of the dough and line a greased 1-quart basin or mixing bowl so that there are not too many folds.

Combine the beef, kidney, and mushrooms in a mixing bowl. In a jar with a tight-fitting top combine the flour, herbs, and onion. Shake to mix well and sprinkle the meat mixture with it. Toss the pieces so that each one is well coated. Roll a piece of kidney and a piece of mushroom into each slice of meat. Pack these into the prepared pudding basin. Add any remaining piece of meat or kidney or mushroom. Pour in the stock. Roll out the remaining pastry, moisten edge, and fit over the meat. Cover tightly with aluminum foil and a piece of cloth. Place in a steamer over rapidly boiling water, or on a rack in a pan with boiling water extending two-thirds of the way up the bowl. Cook for 3½ to 4 hours, replenishing the water as necessary.

Unmold onto a warm dish and serve hot.

WINE: Beaujolais

PIE

SERVES 6 TO 8

DOUGH

2 cups all-purpose flour

salt

6 ounces (1½ sticks) butter

1 cup ice water

½ teaspoon lemon juice

1 small egg, lightly beaten

FILLING

2½ pounds beef chuck, cubed, fat removed

⅓ cup flour

pinch each of marjoram and thyme

3 tablespoons rendered beef fat (from the cubed chuck)

2 bay leaves

1 veal kidney, cubed, and fat removed

1 small onion, minced

¾ cup beef gravy, homemade or canned

½ cup beef stock

In a mixing bowl combine the flour and salt. Chop in the butter. Mix the water and lemon juice, and add enough of it to the butter and flour mixture to make a soft dough. Do not work too much; the butter will remain lumpy. Chill for 15 minutes.

Toss the beef cubes in the flour seasoned with the herbs. Heat the rendered fat and brown the meat, a few pieces at a time. Place the browned meat in a 1½-quart casserole. Add the bay leaves. Coat the kidney cubes with remaining flour and add to the casserole. Add onion, gravy, and enough stock to extend two-thirds of the way up the dish. Set aside.

On a lightly floured board roll out the chilled pastry into a rectangle about 6 x 18 inches. Fold into three, press the dough lightly, and roll out again. Repeat the rolling and folding 4 times in all, chilling in between if necessary. Chill for 10 minutes.

Preheat oven to 450°F. Roll out pastry about 1 inch larger than the dish. Cut off a ½-inch strip all around, moisten it; and line the edge of the dish with the strip. Moisten the newly made rim and top with the pastry round. The pastry should not be stretched at any point. Trim and decorate the edge. Make a hole in the center to allow steam to escape. Decorate with pastry leaves made from trimmings. Brush with the beaten egg. Bake for about 20 minutes. Reduce oven temperature to 325°F., cover the pastry loosely with aluminum foil, and continue cooking for about 1½ hours longer.

Serve hot.

CORNISH PASTIES

(CORNWALL,
ENGLAND)
4 PASTIES

These pasties were originally made by the mothers and wives of workmen for their lunch. The workman's pasty had his initial marked in the dough. Pasties are now found all over the British Isles, a nice luncheon with a glass of beer or a cup of tea. In Cornwall and Devonshire a similar pasty is called squab pie, not because it is filled with squab, but because it was stuffed like a plump cushion, from a dialect word meaning "to fill with stuffing." The pasty is still practical to tote to work.

DOUGH

2 batches of Short Pastry (p. 9)
1 egg, beaten with 2 tablespoons
    milk or water

FILLING

¾ cup diced cooked pork
¾ cup diced cooked veal
1½ cups diced boiled potatoes
½ cup finely chopped onion

¼ cup finely minced parsley
1 tablespoon whisky
good pinch of pepper

Preheat oven to 400°F. In a mixing bowl place all the filling ingredients and toss everything together. Set aside. On a floured board roll out the dough to a sheet ¼ inch thick. Cut into four 10-inch rounds. Divide the meat mixture among the rounds, placing it on one side. Moisten the edges of the dough with water and fold half of each round over to enclose the filling. Press the edges together and seal them well.

Place the pasties on an oiled baking sheet and cut 2 small slits on the top of each one. Brush with egg wash. Bake for 15 minutes, reduce heat to 350°F., and bake for 30 minutes longer, or until tops of pasties are nicely browned.

VARIATION: For snacks, make small pasties. Cut out the rounds 4 to 5 inches across. Fill each one with 2 tablespoons of the filling, press dough edges together, and bake. Makes about 16 small pasties.

DRINK: Beer

ENGLISH RAISED PIES

The "raised pies" of England are famous. One can find them in every pub, together with the delicious Scotch eggs, or buy them freshly made in food shops. Recipes for those pies are usually frightening: They tell you how difficult it is to "raise" the dough and detail all the disasters that can happen if one doesn't do it right. What I find difficult these days is to use all that lard for the crust without which, the recipe says, the pie will collapse. Some ethnic foods don't taste the same outside their native locale. I believe that "raised pies," made in the orthodox way, are better left in the pub where one can wash down all that lard with a good pint of Guinness. For this reason, I am offering an alternative choice using "short pastry," which also calls for lard, but in a more sensible quantity. Vegetable shortening can be substituted for lard, if one wishes.

For those who would like to try the classic "raised pastry" crust, there is a recipe for the original "Hot-Water Raised Pastry" as they make it in England. I assure you, it is not all that difficult. Just try to "raise" the dough as thin as possible, but make sure there are no cracks in the casing. Otherwise, when stock is poured in, it will ooze out.

For the mold, I suggest using a springform pan (8 x 4 x 4 inches), which is easier to line with dough. The classic molds have hinged or collapsible sides and are always round. I have also used empty tuna fish cans to make individual pies with excellent results; the pastry in that case is slightly different.

MELTON MOWBRAY PIE   (LEICESTERSHIRE, ENGLAND)

SERVES 6

This pie was invented in the town so famous for its Stilton cheese, but this particular recipe is freely adapted from one given to me by John Golden, the editor of the New York section of *Cuisine*. John shares with me the belief that there is a lot of good food to be eaten in England and some quite extraordinary.

Have all ingredients ready before preparing the dough, especially if you decide to make the hot-water raised pastry. Short pastry can be prepared in advance and chilled.

DOUGH

1 batch of Hot-Water Raised Pastry (p. 15), or Short Pastry (p. 9)

1 egg beaten with 1 tablespoon milk or cream

FILLING

4 pounds pork shoulder with bones
¼ cup dry white wine
½ teaspoon crumbled sage
¼ teaspoon grated nutmeg

¼ teaspoon ground allspice
2 to 3 teaspoons anchovy paste
salt and pepper

PORK STOCK

bones from pork shoulder
1 or 2 veal knuckles
1 carrot
1 medium-size onion, studded with 3 cloves

1 celery rib, halved
1 parsley sprig
1 bay leaf
2½ quarts water
Kosher salt

Bone the shoulder, or have butcher do it for you. Reserve the bones for stock.

Make the stock: Place all stock ingredients in a heavy pot, cover, and bring to a boil. Simmer for 3 hours, skimming scum as it surfaces. Strain the stock, and discard the solids. Return stock to a clean pot and reduce to about 3 cups. Line a strainer with a triple layer of cheesecloth, rinsed in cold water and squeezed hard. Let stock drip through the damp cheesecloth. You should have 2 cups or more of stock. Test the stock for jelling. If it does not make a firm jelly, add 1 teaspoon unflavored gelatin to the stock and dissolve it, stirring, over low heat. Let the stock cool, then refrigerate if you are not planning to use it promptly, but it should be liquid when used. You will need about 1½ cups. Refrigerate the balance for another recipe.

Make the filling: Cube the pork meat, and place it, the wine, flavorings, and seasoning to taste in a mixing bowl. Toss to combine well. Let the meat absorb the flavor of the wine mixture for at least 1 hour.

Preheat oven to 400°F. Grease a hinged or collapsible mold, or a spring-form pan 8 x 4 x 4 inches. Prepare the pastry according to directions. Reserve enough dough for the lid, and line the prepared mold. Fill dough with the pork mixture, including any remaining wine. Roll out the dough for the lid and top the pie with it. Trim excess dough but let ½ inch of dough hang over the edge. Use a little egg wash, or water, to moisten the underside of the overhanging edge and seal the pie all around. Make decorations with dough scraps. Paint top with egg wash. Cut a hole in the center and insert a funnel made with aluminum foil to allow steam to escape.

Place pie on a baking sheet and bake for 25 minutes. Reduce heat to 325°F. and continue baking for about 2 hours longer. Cover pie loosely with aluminum foil as soon as it starts to brown, to prevent burning. Remove pie from oven and cool at room temperature. Remove the funnel and chill the pie for 15 minutes.

Using a small funnel, pour 1½ cups cool jellied stock, or as much as the pie will hold, into the steam hole of the pie. Tilt the mold from side to side to distribute liquid well. Refrigerate pie overnight, or for a minimum of 6 hours, to give the stock time to set.

Carefully unmold the pie and serve at room temperature.

NOTE: In Melton Mowbray, the dough is raised *outside* of a mold. The filling is made of pork and seasonings only, and the traditional pie is round, about 5 inches across. The small pies, popular as snacks and picnic food, are a recent development.

WINE: Beaujolais Blanc

GAME PIE   (E N G L A N D)

SERVES 6

This is a most unusual but not uncommon English pie. The preferred meat for this recipe is venison, but hare, wild rabbit, pheasant, or grouse can be used as well. It is difficult to give the proportions for this pie because it depends on what the hunter brings in. I have calculated this recipe for approximately 4 pounds of meat.

DOUGH
butter for pan
1 batch of Short Pastry (p. 9)

FILLING

4 pounds game (approximately), cut
    into small pieces
6 slices of bacon
¾ pound tongue, diced
1 bouquet garni made with 1 bay
    leaf, sprig of thyme, a few
    peppercorns

2 cups stock (beef or chicken)
    (p. 19)
1 jigger (1½ ounces) of sherry

Preheat oven to 375°F. Butter an ovenproof deep casserole large enough to contain all the meats and condiments. Place in it layers of game, bacon, and tongue. Bury the *bouquet garni* in the middle of the casserole. Add the stock and sherry. On a lightly floured board, roll out the dough into a circle large enough to top the casserole. Fit over the casserole and trim excess dough with scissors; seal all around edges. Cut a vent on top of the pie and insert a funnel to allow steam to escape. Bake pie for about 3 hours. Cover top with foil when crust starts to brown.

    Serve hot. Discard *bouquet garni* before serving.

WINE: Bordeaux Rouge

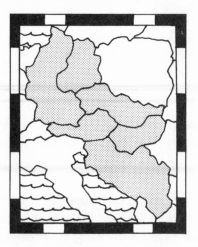

Middle Europe
Germany · Czechoslovakia · Austria
Hungary · Yugoslavia

This chapter contains recipes from a large part of Europe—the continental part of the former German Empire and most of the departed Austro-Hungarian Empire. These recipes range from the rustic preparations of peasants and gypsies to the sophisticated creations of Viennese chefs. In Austria, Hungary, and Yugoslavia one still sees the influence of the East, brought in by the Turks who dominated large parts of Hungary for 150 years and parts of Yugoslavia even longer. One of the specialties in the cuisine of all three countries is the strudel, based on the same paper-thin dough sheets so familiar in Greek and Middle Eastern pastry dishes. The Yugoslavs call their strudel *pita!*

An enormous variety of dumplings can be found in Germany and especially in Czechoslovakia, with the dough wrapped around everything from bread cubes to meat or cheese to plums or cherries. *Kuchen* (German for cake), made with a dough that is not oversweet, is used for savory as well as sweet dishes, and similar preparations are made in Hungary.

KÁPOSZTÁS POGÁCSA   (HUNGARY)
Cabbage Biscuit

ABOUT 2 DOZEN

George Lang in his erudite book *The Cuisine of Hungary* relates how the ancient Magyars ate *lángos,* in George's own words, "ancestor of the pizza." I accept this since I feel that basic foods, like bread, porridge, pizza, noodles, were eaten at the same time by many people early in human history. Take the eternal dispute over spaghetti: although it is true that Marco Polo didn't bring noodles from China, the Chinese were undoubtedly eating noodles at that time. The Etruscans, who had a highly developed civilization before the Romans, adorned their tombs with the equipment used to make pasta, and this was in the fourth century B.C. Horace, the Roman poet, who missed by a few days the turn of the first century, was singing praises to a bowl of noodles and chick-peas in the Rome of the Caesars.

The following recipe is therefore another version of the universal pizza, and I could have called it *pizzette Ungheresi* since these biscuits are just like small pizzas. It is freely adapted by me from Mr. Lang's recipe, with the kind permission of the author.

1 small head of cabbage	1½ cups all-purpose flour
salt	1 teaspoon baking powder
8 tablespoons lard or vegetable	1 egg yolk
shortening, lard or oil for pan	1 tablespoon sour cream
½ tablespoon sugar	1 tablespoon fresh dill
½ teaspoon pepper	1 whole egg

Shred cabbage, mix with 1 tablespoon salt, and let it stand for 1 hour. Drain and squeeze dry. Melt 2 tablespoons lard or vegetable shortening in a skillet. Add the sugar and carefully brown it, but do not let it burn. Add the cabbage and cook over low heat for 30 minutes, until thoroughly done. Add the pepper, stir, and remove from heat. Cool.

In a mixing bowl blend remaining lard or vegetable shortening with the flour and baking powder until mixture resembles coarse meal. Add the egg yolk, a pinch of salt, the sour cream, and the dill. Mix and gather into a ball. Turn dough out on a floured board and knead quickly for a few minutes. Form into a ball, wrap, and chill for about 30 minutes.

Remove dough from refrigerator and knead the cabbage in. Form again into a ball, wrap, and chill for 30 minutes longer.

Preheat oven to 375°F. Lightly grease 2 or 3 baking sheets. Remove dough from refrigerator and roll it between sheets of wax paper to ½-inch thickness. Work as quickly as possible. Cut into 3-inch circles. Place circles on the prepared baking sheets, and score with a knife. Beat the whole egg with 2 tablespoons water and brush circles with the mixture. Bake for 30 minutes, or until tops are nicely colored.

NOTE: George Lang makes these biscuits very small, 1 inch around, and serves them with cocktails. He prefers the large version to accompany roasts instead of Yorkshire pudding.

HOUSKOVÉ KNEDLÍKY (CZECHOSLOVAKIA)
Giant Bread Dumpling

SERVES 6

It is not surprising to find recipes in Czechoslovakia reminiscent of dishes from other places. This land in the heart of Europe was crossed by many travelers who stayed for a while and invariably left some of their customs. However, the reverse is true—many recipes from Moravia and Bohemia were adopted by Viennese cooks and others and became world famous in a new context.

Many *knedlíky* (the Czech name for dumplings) are made without eggs. Others are made with eggs, potatoes, finely chopped greens, yeast, and cheese, and dessert *knedlíky* contain fruits. Some are steamed, others boiled. One of my favorites is called "giant dumpling" and here it is.

3 to 4 tablespoons oil
1 cup bread croutons
2 ounces (½ stick) butter
salt
4 eggs, separated

1 pound all-wheat flour, or 8 ounces
    all-purpose flour combined
    with 8 ounces semolina
2 cups milk
butter or oil for napkin

Heat 3 to 4 tablespoons oil in a skillet and quickly fry the croutons. Drain on paper towels. In a mixing bowl cream 2 ounces butter; add the salt and 1 egg yolk at a time, beating after each addition. Gradually stir in the flour, or flour and semolina mixture, and the milk. Beat the mixture until smooth and creamy. Add the fried croutons. Beat the egg whites until stiff and fold into the egg-yolk mixture.

Dampen a large linen napkin. Grease the center with oil or butter. Place the batter on the greased part and enclose in the napkin, giving a round pizzalike form to the dumpling. The best way to do this is by setting the napkin on a round pan before pouring in the batter. Transfer dumpling in the napkin to a pan of boiling water. The pan should be large enough to let the dumpling float and expand. Cook at a steady simmer for 1 hour.

Turn onto a board or a serving dish. Remove napkin. Cool for 10 minutes before cutting, preferably with a string. Serve with butter and grated cheese, alone or as an accompaniment to meat or fish.

ASPARAGUS STRUDEL

(A U S T R I A)
12 SLICES OR MORE

DOUGH

12 phyllo sheets

4 ounces (1 stick) butter, melted

FILLING

1½ pounds asparagus, washed and
    trimmed

1 cup Béchamel Sauce (p. 17)

2 tablespoons cream or milk

¼ cup grated Parmesan cheese

1 cup shredded mozzarella cheese

2 eggs, lightly beaten

salt and pepper

Unroll the sheets of phyllo on your working counter. Cover them with a sheet of wax paper, then with a damp towel to prevent drying. Cover the pile of sheets again while working with one at a time.

Preheat oven to 375°F. Plunge asparagus into boiling water and cook for 5 to 6 minutes. Drain and rinse under cold water. Keep wrapped in paper towels. Spoon the béchamel sauce into a mixing bowl. Add the cream or milk, and stir in the Parmesan, the mozzarella, and eggs. Taste for seasoning and add salt if needed and a good pinch of pepper. Cut the tender parts of the asparagus into 1-inch pieces. Discard the tough parts. Fold asparagus into the béchamel mixture.

Brush 4 sheets of phyllo, one at a time, with melted butter and place one on top of the other. Spread one-third of the asparagus mixture over the sheets. Top with 4 more buttered sheets of phyllo and repeat until all ingredients are used. Roll the layered sheets like a strudel. Place on a baking sheet with nonstick lining, and tuck pastry ends underneath. Brush the top with butter and bake for about 30 minutes. Strudel is done when top is crisp and golden.

Cool before slicing.

NOTE: These can also be shaped like individual turnovers.

WINE: Grinzinger Spätlese

GERÄUCHERTE FISH-PASTETE   *(AUSTRIA)*
Smoked Fish Tart

SERVES 6

DOUGH

9-inch baked tart crust, made with
    Pâte Brisée I (p. 6)

FILLING

4 ounces (1 stick) butter, at room
    temperature
5 eggs, separated
8 ounces smoked fish without bones
    (whitefish, salmon, trout, eel),
    chopped

2 tablespoons grated cheese
2 teaspoons snipped fresh chives
1 tablespoon very fine toasted bread
    crumbs

Preheat oven to 375°F. Cream the butter in a mixing bowl. Add 1 egg yolk at a time, beating after each addition. Stir in remaining ingredients except egg whites. Beat egg whites until stiff but not dry. Fold half of them into the mixture. Pour into prepared tart crust. Top with remaining egg whites, shaping the foam like a turban. Bake for 20 to 25 minutes, until top is golden brown.

NOTE: For the smoked fish you can substitute 6 ounces sardines.

JADRANSKA STRUŠA

Adriatic Roll

(YUGOSLAVIA)

SERVES 6 TO 8

I had this dish in Dubrovnik at the delightful Hotel Argentina, whose chefs are often schooled in Italy. In fact, one can detect a foreign touch in the dough, which is rather unusual in Yugoslavia.

DOUGH

2 ounces (½ stick) butter

5 tablespoons flour

salt and pepper

2 cups milk

5 eggs, separated

FILLING

1 tablespoon butter

1 onion, chopped fine

8 ounces fresh mushrooms, sliced
    thin

2 pounds cooked shrimps or crab
    meat or lobster, coarsely
    chopped

1 tablespoon minced parsley

8 ounces cream cheese, at room
    temperature

salt and pepper

Prepare filling first. Heat 1 tablespoon butter in a skillet. Add onion and cook over low heat until soft and translucent. Add mushrooms and cook until all water released by mushrooms has evaporated. Add seafood and parsley. Cook for 5 minutes, stirring to combine ingredients well. Stir in the cream cheese, mix well, and remove from heat. Set aside.

Preheat oven to 400°F. Butter a baking sheet, 15 x 10 inches, with sides, with half of the butter. Cover with wax paper, butter again, and sprinkle with flour. Toss out excess flour. Set baking sheet aside.

Melt remaining 1 ounce butter in a saucepan. Add the flour and salt and pepper to taste. Cook, stirring, for a few minutes and remove from heat. Gradually add the milk, stirring constantly, until sauce is liquid and smooth. Place pan over low heat again and cook, stirring constantly, until sauce thickens and starts to bubble. Remove from heat. Cool. Beat egg yolks and add, a little at a time, to the cooled sauce. Warm up the sauce, stirring constantly, but do not let it boil. Cool by stirring once in a while.

Beat the egg whites until stiff. Fold into the sauce and pour the batter into the prepared baking sheet. Spread evenly with a spatula. Bake for 15 to 20 minutes, until puffed and lightly colored.

Turn sponge out on a clean towel and peel off wax paper. Quickly spread the filling on the sponge and roll with the help of the towel. Place roll, seam side down, on a serving platter. Cool slightly before slicing.

NOTE: The white sauce can be prepared in advance up to the addition of the egg yolks. Refrigerate. Warm up before adding the egg whites.

WINE: Pošip (Dalmatian White)

LAUCHTORTE   *(A U S T R I A)*
Leek Tart

SERVES 12

DOUGH

butter for pan	3 cups all-purpose flour
2 packages active dry yeast	2 eggs
1 cup lukewarm water (105° to 115°F.)	1 teaspoon salt

FILLING

20 leeks	4 eggs
1½ ounces (3 tablespoons) butter	3 ounces Westphalian ham, chopped
1 tablespoon oil	
salt and pepper	3 ounces salt pork, chopped

Dissolve yeast in the water and set in a warm place for 10 minutes. Place flour on a board, make a well in the center, and pour in the yeast mixture, eggs, and salt. Mix with a wooden spoon and stir in the flour, gathering the whole into a dough. Knead until smooth and elastic, about 20 minutes. Form into a ball and set in a floured bowl in a warm place, covered, for about 1½ hours, or until doubled in bulk.

Trim and wash the leeks, cut into rings, and wash again to be sure all sand has been removed. Drain well. Heat butter and oil in a large skillet. Add the leeks, cover, and cook over low heat until leeks are tender but not brown, about 40 minutes. Stir often. Add salt and pepper while cooking. Remove from heat and cool completely.

Beat the eggs in a mixing bowl. With a slotted spoon, lift the cooked leeks from the skillet (to prevent dilution of the eggs with cooking liquid). Add leeks to eggs. Butter a 10-inch springform pan. Set aside. Preheat oven to 400°F.

Roll the dough out to a circle ½ inch thick and large enough to line bottom and sides of prepared pan. Fit dough into pan, letting the excess dough hang over the edge. Scatter the ham and salt pork on the dough. Pour in the leek and egg mixture. Trim excess dough with scissors and fold the edge inward, making a decorative border. Grind a little pepper on top of filling. Bake the tart for 40 to 45 minutes, until top is set and golden brown.

Remove tart from oven and cool for 10 to 15 minutes before removing the rim of the springform pan. This torte is also good at room temperature.

PILEĆA PITA
Chicken Pie

(YUGOSLAVIA)

SERVES 8

DOUGH

butter for pan

1 batch of Very Short Pastry (p. 10)

FILLING

4 eggs

2 tablespoons flour

2 cups buttermilk

2 tablespoons olive oil, warmed

1 cup chicken stock

2 garlic cloves, mashed

1 teaspoon sweet paprika

pinch of tarragon

3 cups chopped cooked chicken

Preheat oven to 375°F. Butter a 10-inch pie pan. On a floured board roll the dough out into a circle large enough to line bottom and sides of the pan. Fit dough into the pan, and trim excess dough with scissors; reserve scraps. Chill the lined pan and remaining dough.

Combine eggs and flour in a saucepan. Pour in the buttermilk and stir until smooth. Add 1 tablespoon warm oil and the chicken stock. Cook the sauce over medium heat, stirring, until it thickens. Remove from heat. Stir garlic and paprika into remaining oil, and add to the sauce together with the tarragon. Mix well. Combine sauce with cooked chicken, and spoon into the pastry-lined pan.

Roll out remaining dough and make a lattice top for the pie. Bake for 35 to 40 minutes, until top is nicely browned.

Cool before slicing.

WINE: Pitovske Plaže (Dalmatian Red)

KALBSBRIES UND HUHN IN BRIOCHE
Sweetbread and Chicken Pie   *(A U S T R I A)*

SERVES 8

Sweetbreads and brains are a favorite combination in Austria, and Viennese chefs love to include them in many delicate preparations.

DOUGH

butter for pan   1 batch of Brioche Dough II (p. 14)

FILLING

1½ ounces (3 tablespoons) butter   3 tablespoons Madeira or sherry
½ pound sausage meat   wine
2 or 3 lamb or veal sweetbreads,   1 cup fresh peas, blanched
    prepared according to   1½ cups chopped cooked chicken
    directions (p. 59)   salt and pepper
1 goose liver, or 2 or 3 chicken   1 egg
    livers   ¼ cup heavy cream

Melt 1 tablespoon butter in a skillet. Add sausage meat and sauté until brown. Remove to a bowl. Pour off most of the fat from the skillet and add 1 more tablespoon of butter. Sauté prepared sweetbreads on both sides, turning often, for 10 to 15 minutes. Remove, cool, and dice. Add to sausage meat in the bowl. Add remaining butter to the skillet and cook the goose or chicken livers, turning often, for 5 to 6 minutes. Livers should remain pink inside. Remove livers, cool, dice, and add to mixing bowl.

Pour Madeira or sherry into skillet and deglaze the pan over heat, scraping the brown particles clinging at the bottom of pan. Boil the liquid for a few minutes and add to the mixing bowl. Stir in the peas and chicken, season the filling to taste, and toss to combine mixture well.

Preheat oven to 400°F. Butter a 10-inch springform pan. On a floured board roll the dough out to a circle large enough to line bottom and sides of prepared pan. Fit dough into pan. Trim excess dough with scissors and reserve scraps. Spoon sweetbread mixture into dough-lined pan. Beat egg and cream together, reserve 2 tablespoons of it, and pour remainder into the pie. Roll out scraps of dough and make a lattice top on the pie. Paint with reserved egg and cream mixture. Bake for 30 minutes. Reduce temperature to 375°F., and continue baking for 10 minutes longer. If top tends to get too brown, cover loosely with aluminum foil.

Cool before cutting.

WINE: Grinzinger Spätlese

SCHINKENBEIN STRUDEL   *(G E R M A N Y)*
Ham Bone Strudel

10 TO 12 SLICES

The special taste of this strudel comes from the ham or prosciutto bone adding its distinctive flavor to the steaming cabbage and onions. Ask your butcher to reserve a bone when he finishes a ham or prosciutto. Have him cut it into pieces and store them in the freezer until you are ready to use them.

DOUGH

10 phyllo sheets

4 ounces butter (1 stick), melted

FILLING

1 tablespoon butter

1 tablespoon oil

1 onion, sliced

3 cups shredded cabbage

1 ham or prosciutto bone, 3 inches long

⅓ cup broth or bouillon

1 teaspoon tomato paste

2 cups chopped cooked lamb

2 cups cooked rice

2 tablespoons bread crumbs

2 eggs

1 tablespoon flour

allspice

pepper

2 tablespoons grated Parmesan cheese

¼ pound Brudder Bazil or smoked mozzarella cheese, shredded

Unroll the phyllo sheets on a flat surface. Cover with wax paper, then with a damp cloth towel to prevent drying. Cover the pile of sheets again after removing each one.

Heat butter and oil in a heavy saucepan. Add onion, cover, reduce heat, and cook until onion is soft. Add cabbage, bury the bone in it, cover, and cook at a simmer for 20 to 25 minutes. Add a little of the broth and continue cooking. Combine remaining broth and tomato paste; add to cabbage and cook for 10 minutes longer. Add lamb and rice, and heat through. Add bread crumbs, stir to combine ingredients well, remove from heat, and cool. Remove ham bone.

Beat eggs in a mixing bowl. Add flour, allspice, and pepper to taste, and Parmesan cheese. Add the lamb and cabbage mixture and stir until well blended.

Preheat oven to 400°F. Butter a baking sheet 15 x 10 inches. Place 1 phyllo sheet on the baking sheet and brush with melted butter. Top with remaining sheets, brushing each one with butter. Spoon the meat mixture in an even log shape down the full length of the pastry. Scatter the Brudder Bazil or smoked mozzarella over the log, pushing some of the shreds into the meat mixture. Carefully fold over the dough and roll into a strudel. Tuck in the ends. Place strudel on the prepared baking sheet. Brush top with more of the melted butter. Bake for 40 minutes, brushing the strudel with melted butter every 10 minutes.

Cool slightly before cutting.

DRINK: Beer

Eastern Europe
Poland · Russia
Rumania · Bulgaria

Russia, or rather the Soviet Union, has an enormous territory which has been subject to many outside influences, mainly German, Italian, and French in the western part. The Mongolian invasions in the Middle Ages brought many culinary changes, introducing not only new ingredients but new ways to cook. In the southern areas one sees the influence of the Orient, and finds the luscious fruits indigenous to Russia. The recipes here range from the flat bread of the Armenians (not unlike Greek *pita*) to the elaborate *kulebiaka*, served as a main dish at fancy banquets.

Poland has also been subject to many outside influences, but through it all has preserved its interesting cuisine. Well-made *pierogi* have delicate pastry (not at all like the rather tough and doughy versions to be found in the supermarket freezer case). The delicious sausage, kielbasa, often found in filled Polish pastries, has become an American favorite, and is now made extensively in the United States.

123

Rumania and Bulgaria, part of the mysterious Balkans, were once part of the Eastern Roman Empire, but were later swallowed up by the Ottomans; their "captivity" continued for almost five hundred years. Both show this influence, especially in the use of soured milk products, rice, lemon juice instead of vinegar, and here too the paper-thin sheets of phyllo pastry.

PEDA   *(A R M E N I A)*
                                                        2 LOAVES

2 packages active dry yeast
2 cups lukewarm water (105° to
   115°F.)
2 tablespoons sugar
1 tablespoon salt
3 tablespoons melted butter or oil

5½ cups all-purpose flour,
   approximately
oil and flour for baking sheets
½ cup cold water
2 teaspoons sesame seeds or poppy
   seeds, optional

Empty yeast into the large bowl of an electric mixer. Add lukewarm water and let stand for about 5 minutes. Stir in sugar, salt, and melted butter or oil. Add 4 cups of the flour, 1 cup at a time, beating at medium speed. Continue beating for 5 minutes, or until dough is smooth and pulls away from the sides of the bowl. Gradually add 1¼ cups more flour, mixing with a heavy-duty mixer or a wooden spoon. Turn dough out on a floured board and knead until smooth and elastic, using a little more flour as needed. Place dough in a greased bowl, turn over to grease top, and cover. Let rise in a warm place until doubled in bulk, about 1 hour.

Lightly grease 2 large baking sheets and dust with flour. Punch down dough, divide into 2 equal parts, and shape each into a smooth ball. Set each ball on a baking sheet, cover lightly with clear plastic wrap, and set aside at room temperature for 30 minutes. Then press, pull, and shape each loaf into a flat oval about 11 x 14 inches; if dough is too elastic to hold its shape, let it rest for a few minutes longer. Cover again with clear plastic wrap and let rise in a warm place for 45 to 60 minutes, or until doubled in bulk.

Using a soft brush dipped into cool water, brush top and sides of each raised loaf. With a toothed wheel, score a border all around, 1½ inches wide. Mark crosswise and lengthwise into squares about 2 inches apart. Do not cut through. Allow loaves to rise uncovered, until almost doubled, about 45 minutes. Preheat oven to 450°F.

Bake 1 loaf at a time in the center of the oven until golden brown, about 15 minutes. Mix 2 teaspoons flour and ½ cup cold water in a small pan until smooth. Place over medium heat and cook, stirring, until mixture boils and thickens into a glaze. Remove from heat and let stand, covered, until ready to use. With a soft brush, apply glaze lightly over sides and top of the loaves. To sprinkle with seeds, repaint each loaf lightly with glaze and immediately add seeds.

Serve warm or cool. This bread freezes well. Reheat uncovered in a 350°F. oven for 5 to 8 minutes.

WHOLE-WHEAT PEDA. Use 2½ cups whole-wheat flour and about 2½ cups all-purpose flour. Add all of the whole-wheat and 1 cup all-purpose flour in the first mixing stage. Mix in remaining all-purpose flour and finish as directed in the recipe.

SMALL PEDA. Divide dough into 8 equal pieces, shape each into a smooth ball, and place on 2 large greased and floured baking sheets. Let dough rest for 30 minutes, then flatten each to about 6½ inches in diameter. Let rise for 45 minutes. Mark and glaze the same way as the large loaves.

MAMALIGA   (R U M A N I A)
Cornmeal Pie

SERVES 4 TO 6

Rumanians are said to look and act very much like Italians. Their language is similar and some of the food goes back to the Romans, the conquerors and name givers of Rumania.

Mamaliga and *polenta*, the refined daughters of *pulmentum*, the Roman mush, are even made the same. Today, the ancestral ceremony of slowly stirring the cornmeal into the boiling water is similarly reenacted in the valleys of Transylvania and the grassy edges of the Po River. The *mamaliga* or *polenta* is then poured onto a wooden board where it slowly spreads itself into a soft, shiny disc, the color of an autumn sun. In its pristine state the disc is cut with a string and served like bread.

An imaginative cook can give a different dimension to this simple, nourishing food, by adding sauces, condiments, and filling, which transform a simple *mamaliga* into an appealing and elegant dish.

3 cups water

salt

1 cup yellow cornmeal

½ pound brynza or feta cheese,
    crumbled

¼ cup grated Parmesan cheese

bread crumbs

butter

Preheat oven to 350°F. Butter a 9-inch ovenproof dish from which you can serve. Bring water and salt to a boil. Very slowly add the cornmeal, stirring. Cook the mixture, still stirring, until thick and smooth.

Spoon a layer of the *mamaliga* into the prepared dish. Cover with a layer of brynza or feta cheese and half of the Parmesan cheese. Cover with remaining *mamaliga*. Sprinkle with remaining Parmesan and bread crumbs. Dot generously with butter and bake until top is golden brown, 20 to 25 minutes.

KHACHAPURI   *(R U S S I A)*

Khachapuri is a delicious Georgian specialty. I fell in love with it when I saw it demonstrated at a food festival by John Clancy, the food expert and author. I remember discussing with him the similarity of this bread to the Italian *Fiadone* (p. 33), the traditional Easter *pizza rustica* of my native region Abruzzo. I freely adapted this recipe to suit my taste. In America it makes an ideal dish for a Sunday brunch. It can also be made in smaller sizes and shapes for cocktails and snacks. In the Caucasus, small *khachapuri* are sold by street vendors just like pretzels in New York.

DOUGH

2 packages active dry yeast

1 tablespoon sugar

1 cup lukewarm milk (105° to
    115°F.)

3 cups flour, plus flour for kneading

pinch of salt

4 ounces (1 stick) butter, at room
    temperature, plus butter for
    bowl and baking pan

1 egg

FILLING

2 pounds Munster cheese, finely
    minced

2 eggs, beaten

1 ounce (2 tablespoons) butter, at
    room temperature

Combine yeast, a pinch of sugar, and ½ cup lukewarm milk; stir. Set aside for 5 minutes or so, until mixture starts to bubble. Place the flour on a pastry board, make a well in the center, and add remaining sugar, remaining milk, the yeast mixture, salt, 4 ounces butter, and egg. Mix in the flour and start kneading. Add flour every once in a while to keep the dough from sticking. Knead for 10 to 15 minutes. Place dough in a lightly buttered bowl. Cover and set in a warm spot until doubled in bulk, 1 hour or more.

Punch the dough down and let it rise again for 30 to 40 minutes.

Preheat oven to 375°F. Prepare filling by mixing cheese, eggs, and butter together. Set aside. Butter a 9-inch round springform cake pan. Punch dough down again and roll out on the floured board into a circle 22 inches in diameter. Line the pan with the dough, and let remaining dough hang over the edges of the pan. Pour the filling into the dough and start folding dough over, pleating it all around the pan so that the pleated ends are gathered together in the center. Twist this meeting point into a knob. Let the bread rest for 10 to 15 minutes.

Bake for 1 hour, or until bread is golden brown.

KHLIAB RAISKA PTITSA *(BULGARIA)*
Bird-of-Paradise Bread

TO MAKE 1 ROUND LOAF

Bulgaria shares with Rumania the heritage of Turkish influence. They were both part of the Ottoman Empire, but unlike Rumania, which was able to retain a local government run by its own people, Bulgaria was completely dominated by the Turks. Although both countries vehemently tried to reject the legacy of the Muslims by using pork and wine with relish, touches of the exotic Ottoman cuisine appear over and over again.

Most Bulgarian pies are made with eggs, cheese, and vegetables, with meat just an occasional addition, chiefly because the quality is rather poor. Bulgaria stands on its own with the use of game; the St. Nicholas Feast Pie (p. 140) is one of the best examples of a game dish. Even this *ptitsa*, one of the most famous Bulgarian specialties, traditionally made for Easter, suggests game. But it is a suggestion only, since it has nothing to do with birds and there is no game in it. This recipe was originally printed in *A Quintet of Cuisines*, published by Time-Life Books.

1 package active dry yeast
½ teaspoon sugar
¼ cup lukewarm water (110° to 115°F.)
3 to 3½ cups all-purpose flour
2 teaspoons salt
½ cup unflavored yogurt
4 eggs
2 ounces (½ cup) brynza or feta cheese, rubbed through a sieve or food mill
1 tablespoon salted butter, softened

1 egg lightly beaten with 1 tablespoon milk
¼ pound Kashkaval, or substitute sweet Munster cheese, sliced ¼ inch thick and trimmed into 4 triangles about 4 inches long
¼-inch-thick slice boiled ham, cut into four 1-inch squares
4 ripe black olives, preferably Mediterranean type
1-inch square of sweet red pepper or pimiento, cut into a star

Dissolve the yeast and sugar in the lukewarm water. Let the mixture stand for 2 to 3 minutes, then stir well. Set the bowl in a warm place for about 5 minutes, or until the mixture almost doubles in volume.

Combine 3 cups of flour and the salt in a mixing bowl, make a well in the center, and pour in the yeast mixture, yogurt, eggs, and brynza or feta cheese. With a large spoon, gradually stir the flour into the other ingredients, continuing to stir until the mixture is smooth and the flour is completely absorbed. The dough should be just firm enough to be gathered into a ball. If it is too soft, add the remaining ½ cup of flour a tablespoon at a time, beating vigorously after each addition and using only enough of the flour to give the dough its proper consistency. It should not be too firm.

On a lightly floured board, knead the dough for about 15 minutes, or until the dough is smooth and elastic. Sprinkle it from time to time with a little flour to prevent it from sticking to the board.

Shape the dough into a ball and place it in a lightly greased bowl. Cover with a kitchen towel and set aside in a warm, draft-free place for about 1 hour, or until the dough doubles in bulk.

Butter a large baking sheet with the tablespoon of softened butter. Punch the dough down, shape it into a round loaf about 8 inches in diameter, and set the round on the buttered sheet. Brush the entire surface of the dough evenly with the egg-and-milk mixture, then arrange the cheese triangles, the ham cubes, olives, and red pepper or pimiento attractively on top. Set the dough aside in a warm place for about 30 minutes until double in bulk.

Preheat oven to 400°F. Bake *ptitsa* in the middle of the oven for 15 minutes, reduce the heat to 350°F., and bake for 30 to 40 minutes longer, or until the loaf is golden brown. Transfer to a cake rack to cool. Serve at room temperature.

NOTE: I have also baked this in a 12-inch pizza pan and it works beautifully.

KAVKASKIE
Caucasian Pirozhki

(RUSSIA)

30 PIROZHKI

DOUGH

½ cup cold water
2 ounces (½ stick) butter, plus
    butter for pan

salt
1 cup flour
3 large eggs

FILLING

2 cups Béchamel Sauce (p. 17)
¾ cup finely grated cheese
½ cup Duxelles (p. 19)
1 egg, separated

¼ cup milk
flour
bread crumbs
oil for deep-frying

Place water, 2 ounces butter, and salt to taste in a saucepan, and bring to a boil. Remove from heat, add 1 cup flour, and beat vigorously with a wooden spoon until paste is perfectly smooth. Place back over heat and stir until the paste begins to leave the bottom and sides of the pan. Remove from heat and add 3 eggs, one at a time, stirring after each addition. At this point the paste can be refrigerated.

Preheat oven to 350°F. Butter a baking sheet 10 x 15 inches. Spread the dough as thin as possible on the baking sheet. Bake for 25 to 30 minutes, or until top is slightly browned. Remove from oven and cool on a rack.

Mix 1 cup béchamel, the grated cheese, and the duxelles. Divide the baked pastry into 2 equal parts. Spread one part with the béchamel and cheese mixture, top with other part, and cut into 3-inch squares. Dilute remaining béchamel with the egg white and 2 tablespoons of the milk. Beat the egg yolk with remaining milk. Coat each square with some of the béchamel, dip into flour, then into the egg-yolk and milk mixture, finally into bread crumbs. Chill for at least 20 minutes. Deep-fry in oil heated to 375°F.

VEGETARIANSKI PASTI   *(BULGARIA)*

Vegetarian Pasty

SERVES 6

An interesting variety of pie goes under the name of *pasti*. The pie is baked and later finished with an egg batter poured over to form the crust.

2 medium-size eggplants, sliced into circles	salt and pepper
Kosher salt	1 tablespoon minced parsley
½ cup oil, approximately	4 to 5 firm medium-size tomatoes, sliced crosswise
2 large onions, sliced thin	1 tablespoon butter
2 ripe pear-shaped tomatoes, peeled and chopped	1 tablespoon flour
1 cup uncooked rice	1 cup milk
2½ cups boiling water	3 eggs

Place eggplant slices in a colander, sprinkle with kosher salt, and let drain for 15 minutes. Spoon 2 tablespoons oil into a skillet. Add onions and sauté until soft and translucent. Add the chopped tomatoes and rice. Cook, stirring, until rice is well coated with sauce, then pour in boiling water, cover, reduce heat, and cook until rice is done. Season with salt and pepper to taste, stir in the parsley, and set aside. Press liquid out of the eggplants and pat dry. Fry in hot oil until golden on both sides. Drain on paper towels.

Preheat oven to 375°F. Lightly oil an ovenproof dish from which you can serve. Make 1 layer of eggplant slices at the bottom of prepared dish. Add some of rice mixture and smooth top. Continue layering with eggplant and rice until both are finished. Eggplant slices should be last. Top with a layer of tomato slices. Bake for 20 minutes.

Melt the butter in a saucepan. Add the flour and cook over low heat, stirring, until mixture is quite brown. Remove from heat and gradually add the milk, stirring until sauce is liquefied and smooth. Return to heat and cook, still stirring, until sauce thickens and starts to boil. Remove from heat immediately. Stir to cool a little and add the eggs, one at a time, stirring vigorously after each addition. Pour this sauce on the *pasti* and continue baking for 10 to 15 minutes longer, or until top is puffed and a nice golden color.

Serve hot.

VARIATION: Top *pasti* with a batter made with 4 eggs beaten with 1 tablespoon flour and mixed with 1½ cups plain yogurt, instead of the basic sauce.

KULEBIAKA
Cabbage Loaf

(R U S S I A)

SERVES 4

A recipe from Mrs. Victoria Martin, a Russian-born and French-raised amateur cook. It was given to Lynn Visson for her book in progress on the heritage of Russian cuisine. It is with Lynn's and Mrs. Martin's kind permission that I repeat the recipe here.

DOUGH

2 cups all-purpose flour

2 teaspoons sugar

1 teaspoon salt

6 ounces (1½ sticks) sweet butter

4 ounces cream cheese, at room
     temperature

½ to ⅔ cup dairy sour cream

1 egg, beaten

FILLING

1 medium-size cabbage

1 onion, chopped fine

6 to 8 tablespoons chicken fat

1 bay leaf

pinch of thyme

1 tablespoon snipped dill

1½ teaspoons salt

¼ teaspoon pepper

Sift flour, sugar, and salt into a mixing bowl. Cream butter and cream cheese. Add sour cream. Stir until mixture is smooth. Combine with dry ingredients. Gather into a ball, wrap, and chill for 1 hour, or overnight. Bring dough to room temperature, and divide into 2 parts.

Core and shred cabbage. Place in a heavy saucepan with the onion. Add chicken fat, bay leaf, thyme, dill, salt, and pepper, and cook over low heat, until vegetables are soft. Taste for seasoning. Cool.

Preheat oven to 425°F. Roll out dough, 1 part at a time, to make 2 equal rectangles, each about 8 x 5 inches. Spread 1 rectangle with the filling and smooth the top, leaving at least a ¾-inch border free of filling. Cover with the other rectangle and pinch edges firmly all around to seal *kulebiaka*. Brush top lightly with beaten egg. Pierce top of pastry to allow steam to escape. Bake on a lightly greased baking sheet for 45 minutes, or until golden brown.

NOTE: Leftover cabbage mixture can be used in an omelet or combined with rice.

DRINK: Vodka

KUGELIS   *(L I T H U A N I A)*
Potato Kugel

Potatoes, "devil's apples," were viewed with suspicion for a long time in Eastern Europe. Nowadays they are the expected accompaniment to almost any dish.

butter for pan	1 tablespoon chopped fresh parsley
4 slices of bacon, chopped	1 garlic clove, minced
1 medium-size onion, chopped	4 medium-size potatoes, peeled and
1 tablespoon cornstarch or flour	grated
½ cup milk	4 eggs, lightly beaten
3 heaping tablespoons plain yogurt	salt and pepper

Preheat oven to 375°F. Butter a shallow 9-inch baking dish. Cook bacon in a skillet for 3 minutes. Add onion and cook over low heat until onion is soft and translucent. Spoon cornstarch or flour into a mixing bowl. Gradually pour in the milk and the yogurt. Mix well until smooth. Add all remaining ingredients including onion and bacon mixture. Season with salt and pepper to taste. Pour into prepared dish. Bake for about 1 hour, or until top is nicely browned.

GRZYBY PASZTECIKI   *(P O L A N D)*
Mushroom Pasties

Mushrooms abound in every forest in Poland and appear in almost every recipe. No wonder! If you have ever tried those imported Polish mushrooms, you will know the difference.

DOUGH

1 cup sifted all-purpose flour	salt
2 ounces (½ stick) butter	cornstarch
4 to 5 tablespoons dairy sour cream, approximately	

FILLING

½ pound fresh mushrooms

1 dried Polish mushroom, soaked

2 ounces (½ stick) butter

1 tablespoon oil

1 cup finely chopped onion

salt and pepper

¼ teaspoon grated nutmeg

Prepare the filling first. Rinse the mushrooms to remove all traces of soil. Pat dry and chop fine. Chop the dried mushroom too. Heat the butter and oil in a large skillet. Add the onion and cook over low heat, stirring frequently, until the onion is golden brown. Add all the mushrooms and cook, stirring frequently, until liquid released by mushrooms evaporates. Season to taste with salt, pepper, and nutmeg. Cool and refrigerate.

Place the flour in a mixing bowl. Add the butter and chop it in until the mixture resembles coarse meal. Add the sour cream and salt to taste; mix and gather into a ball. Wrap dough in wax paper and chill for a few hours.

Preheat oven to 400°F. Pull off 1 piece of dough the size of a golf ball, and shape it into a ball. Roll it lightly in cornstarch and place between 2 sheets of wax paper. Roll lightly with a rolling pin. Remove the dough from the wax paper and add about 1 teaspoon of filling. Moisten the edge of the dough with water and fold over. Press with the tines of a fork and place on an ungreased cookie sheet. Continue making *paszteciki* until all the dough is used. Bake for 15 to 20 minutes.

Serve hot, as an appetizer.

VARIATION: These pasties also can be filled with cooked meats combined with 1 chopped hard-cooked egg and 2 to 3 tablespoons of cream.

DRINK: Krupnik Honey Liqueur

KULEBIAKA
Salmon Loaf

(RUSSIA)

SERVES 16

In 1892 Mikhail Pyliaev wrote in *Staroezhit'e (Life of the Past)* that up to the seventeenth century Russians used only cabbage, garlic, onions, cucumbers, and beets. Salad was unheard of. From this state of affairs to the creation of the most prestigious pastry dish in the world, a lot of water has flowed down the Volga. Imitated and varied, *kulebiaka* runs the gamut from peasant rusticity to extreme sophistication. In my somewhat simplified version, I use my own brioche dough, with which I feel very secure.

This is a dish demanding patience and a little time. Fortunately, it can be done in stages and all the components can be prepared a day before serving. The brioche dough can be prepared a few weeks in advance and kept frozen. The end result is a guaranteed delight.

In his version of this dish, Craig Claiborne calls it "a celestial creation."

DOUGH

2 batches of Brioche Dough II
    (p. 14)
2 egg yolks beaten with 2
    tablespoons water

½ pound (2 sticks) butter, melted,
    plus 1 ounce butter at room
    temperature

SALMON AND MUSHROOM FILLING

2 skinless and boneless salmon
    fillets, each about 1½ pounds
1 ounce (2 tablespoons) butter
2 tablespoons finely chopped onion
2 tablespoons finely chopped
    shallot

salt and freshly ground pepper
¾ pound fresh mushrooms, thinly
    sliced
¼ cup snipped fresh dill
2 cups dry white wine

VELOUTÉ SAUCE

1 ounce (2 tablespoons) butter
3 tablespoons flour
dash of white pepper

3 tablespoons lemon juice
5 egg yolks
salt and pepper

RICE AND EGG FILLING

3 hard-cooked eggs
1¾ cups firmly cooked rice
¼ cup minced fresh parsley

1 tablespoon snipped dill
salt and freshly ground pepper

Preheat oven to 400°F. Cut each salmon fillet into slices about ⅓ inch thick. Each fillet should produce 12 slices. Butter a rectangular baking dish, 13½ x 8½ inches and 2 inches deep, with 1 ounce butter. Sprinkle with chopped onion and shallot, and salt and pepper to taste. Arrange 2 parallel rows of salmon slices slightly overlapping. Sprinkle salmon with salt and black pepper to taste. Scatter the mushrooms over the salmon. Sprinkle with fresh dill, and pour the wine over all. Cover with aluminum foil and bring the liquid to a boil on top of the stove. Place the dish in the preheated oven and bake for 15 minutes.

Remove the baking dish, uncover, and pour the accumulated liquid into a saucepan. Carefully spoon off most of the mushrooms and transfer them to another dish. Bring the cooking liquid to a boil over high heat. Tilt the dish containing the salmon. More liquid will accumulate as it stands. Spoon or pour this liquid into the saucepan containing the rest of the cooking liquid.

Make the sauce: Melt 1 ounce butter in a saucepan and stir in the flour, using a wire whisk. When blended, add the cooking liquid, stirring rapidly with the whisk. Cook for about 5 minutes, stirring often. Add the reserved mushrooms and continue cooking for about 20 minutes, adding any liquid that accumulates around the salmon. Add the white pepper and lemon juice. Beat the egg yolks with a whisk and scrape them into the sauce, stirring vigorously. Cook for about 30 seconds, stirring, and remove from the heat. Add salt and a generous amount of pepper to taste. Spoon and scrape this sauce, it should be quite thick, over the salmon to cover the fish all over with an even layer, but try to avoid having the sauce spill over the sides of the salmon. Let salmon and sauce cool.

Butter a neat rectangle of wax paper. Arrange this, buttered side down, on the sauce-covered salmon and refrigerate until thoroughly cold. This can be done a day in advance.

Make the rice and egg filling: Chop the eggs and put them in a mixing bowl. Add remaining ingredients, with seasoning to taste, and blend well.

Remove salmon from the refrigerator. Using a knife, cut it lengthwise down the center into halves.

Place brioche dough on a lightly floured board. Pat the dough flat and roll it into a rectangle 21 x 18 inches. Sprinkle about one-third of the rice mixture down the center of the rectangle. Pick up half the chilled salmon and carefully arrange it, mushroom side down, over the rice mixture. Sprinkle with another third of the rice mixture. Top this, sandwich fashion, with another layer of the chilled salmon filling, mushroom side up. Sprinkle with remaining rice. Bring up one side of the brioche. Brush liberally with a mixture of beaten egg yolks and water. Bring up the opposite side of the brioche dough to enclose the filling, overlapping the 2 sides of the dough. Brush all over with more of the egg-yolk wash. Trim off the ends of the dough. Brush with egg-yolk wash and bring up the ends, pinching to enclose the filling.

Butter a baking sheet with 1 ounce butter at room temperature. Carefully place the *kulebiaka* on the baking sheet. Cut a hole in the center of the *kulebiaka* to allow steam to escape. Brush around the hole with egg-yolk wash. Roll out the scraps of dough to make cutouts to decorate the top of the pastry, including a little decorative collar of dough around the center hole. Brush with the rest of the egg wash before affixing decorations so they will not fall off.

Roll out a 6-foot length of aluminum foil. Fold it over into thirds to make one long band about 4½ inches wide. Brush the band with melted butter. With the buttered side next to the dough, arrange the band neatly and snugly around the brioche, to keep the sides of the loaf from collapsing before the dough has a chance to become firm while baking. Fasten a paper clip where the two ends of the foil band overlap. Tie a cord around the center of the foil band to secure it. Run the cord around three times and tie the ends. Make certain the bottom of the band fits snugly around the dough. Set the pan in a warm place for about 30 minutes.

Preheat oven to 400°F. Bake the loaf for 15 minutes. Reduce temperature to 375°F. and bake for 10 minutes longer. Cover dough with a sheet of aluminum foil to prevent excess browning. Continue baking for 20 minutes, a total baking time at this point of 45 minutes. Remove foil and continue baking for 15 minutes more. Remove *kulebiaka* from the oven. Pour remaining melted butter through the steam hole into the filling.

Cut into 1-inch slices, and serve with melted butter on the side.

PIEROG NADZIEWANY RYBAZE Z ŚMIETANIE
Fish Pie with Sour Cream (*P O L A N D*)

SERVES 6

Although there is a conflict in Poland between the Communist policy and the traditional observance of religion, certain Catholic holidays, such as Easter, are still celebrated. Lent is very much observed, to the point that when fish becomes difficult to obtain, beavers' tails are permitted, since the animal lives in the water. This pie is made with pike, which abounds in the Baltic area, or carp which is found in the many lakes in Poland. The origin of the pie is Jewish, and dates back to a time when Poland was made an open country for the persecuted Jews of Europe by Casimir III, called the Great, who had fallen in love with a beautiful Jewish woman. It was at this time that the Polish people got accustomed to the cosmopolitan dishes brought in by this new influx of people. Now part of the national heritage is *karp po zydowsku,* a cold jellied carp *alla Giudea,* or Jewish style, traditionally eaten at Christmas.

DOUGH
1 batch of Pâte Brisée I or II (pp. 6 or 7)

FILLING

1½ ounces (3 tablespoons) butter	1 tablespoon chopped parsley
8 ounces fillet of pike or carp, cut into small pieces	2 eggs
	½ cup dairy sour cream
4 ounces rice, cooked	1 tablespoon snipped fresh dill
salt and pepper	

Melt 2 tablespoons of the butter in a skillet. Add the fish and cook until it starts to flake. Add rice, and salt and pepper to taste. Stir until rice is heated through. Add parsley and remove from heat.

Preheat oven to 375°F. Butter a 9-inch pie pan. On a floured board roll out dough to a circle large enough to line bottom and sides of prepared pan. Fit the dough into the pan. Pour fish mixture into it. Beat eggs with 2 tablespoons sour cream and pour on the pie. Bake for 30 minutes, until top is set and nicely colored.

Serve with remaining sour cream mixed with dill.

DRINK: Vodka

PIROG S KASHEI   *(R U S S I A)*
Kasha and Meat Pie

SERVES 6

This is a good pie to make when you have leftover potted or stewed meat cooked with onion, carrot, and celery. However, if your leftover meat is simply roasted, just chop vegetables, sauté them in a little oil and butter, and add them to the meat.

DOUGH

1 package active dry yeast
½ cup lukewarm milk (105° to 115°F.)
pinch of sugar
2 cups all-purpose flour

1 egg, lightly beaten
1½ ounces (3 tablespoons) butter, melted and cooled
1½ teaspoons salt
butter for pan

FILLING

1 cup chopped cooked veal
1 cup chopped cooked beef or pork
½ cup sauce from the meat, or tomato sauce
1 cup cooked kasha
2 eggs, lightly beaten
1 tablespoon chopped parsley
½ cup chopped cooked spinach, escarole, endive, or cabbage, or a mixture

1 teaspoon flour
3 tablespoons dairy sour cream or plain yogurt
1 tablespoon lemon juice
1 teaspoon tomato paste
1 garlic clove, mashed
2 tablespoons pine nuts (pignoli)

Combine yeast, milk, and sugar and let stand for 10 minutes. Place 1 cup flour in a mixing bowl. Make a well in the center and add the yeast mixture. Blend in the flour. Gather dough into a ball and place it in a buttered bowl. Cover, and set in a warm place to rise for about 40 minutes.

Turn dough out on a floured board. Punch dough down. While kneading, blend in remaining ingredients. Work dough for about 15 minutes, until smooth. Gather into a ball and place in a buttered bowl. Cover and let rise again for about 1 hour, or until doubled in bulk. Punch down before using.

Preheat oven to 375°F. Butter a 9- to 10-inch pie pan. On a floured board roll out three-quarters of the dough into a circle large enough to line bottom and sides of prepared pan. Fit dough into pan. Trim excess dough with scissors but let 1 inch overhang the sides. Pierce the bottom of the dough with a fork, and chill.

In a mixing bowl combine all the ingredients for the filling. Mix well and pour into pastry-lined pan. Roll out remaining dough into a lid and cover the pie. Pinch all around to seal pie well. Make several slits on top of the pie to let steam escape. Bake for 45 minutes. If top tends to brown too quickly, cover loosely with foil.

SCHUMATA PASTI

Pork Pie with Leeks

(BULGARIA)

SERVES 6

This *pasti* is a specialty from the hamlet of Schumata.

DOUGH

½ batch of Crusty-Wrap Dough
   ready to use (p. 5)

FILLING

1 ounce (2 tablespoons) butter	salt and pepper
1 tablespoon oil	paprika
1½ pounds boneless lean pork, cut into small cubes	1 jar (9 ounces) pickled sweet green peppers, drained and cut into pieces
¼ cup wine	
1 pound leeks, 5 or 6, trimmed, well washed, and chopped	1 egg
1 garlic clove, chopped	1 tablespoon flour
	2 tablespoons milk

Heat the butter and oil in an iron skillet or earthenware casserole. Sauté the pork cubes until brown. Add the wine, cover, and cook until wine has almost evaporated. Add the leeks and garlic, and continue cooking until vegetables are soft. Add salt and pepper to taste and a pinch of paprika. Add the peppers and cook for a few minutes longer, just to heat through.

Preheat oven to 400°F. Beat egg well. Combine flour and milk and add to egg. Stir this batter into the pork mixture and sprinkle with paprika. Remove from heat and let cool.

Roll out the dough, or stretch with hands, into a circle large enough to cover the top of the cooking vessel. Let dough hang over the edge a little. Pinch dough all around rim to seal the pie. Cut a vent in the middle of the pie and insert a funnel to allow steam to escape.

Bake for 30 to 40 minutes, or until top is crusty and nicely browned.

VARIATION: Substitute veal for pork and pickled eggplants for peppers.

ST. NICHOLAS FEAST PIE   (BULGARIA)
Game or Duck Pie

SERVES 8

In the town of Bansko, in southwestern Bulgaria, this pie is baked in a huge earthenware vessel sealed with a rough pastry. It is baked all night at a very low heat. The dish usually contains several kinds of meats, including pork, game birds of various kinds, chicken, and rabbit. Leaves of fresh and fermented cabbage are layered among the meats. It is a traditional dish made in this village for the festival of St. Nicholas.

DOUGH

1 batch of Wheaten Egg Dough
   (p. 7)

FILLING

¼ pound bacon, in 1 slice, diced
1½ ounces (3 tablespoons) butter
1 tablespoon oil
8 oven-ready quails, about 5 ounces
   each, or 1 duck, 4 pounds, cut
   into serving pieces
1 onion, finely chopped
1½ cups uncooked rice
3 cups water
¼ cup dried currants
¼ cup white raisins

salt and pepper
1 head of white or Savoy cabbage,
   washed and trimmed
¼ cup chopped fresh Italian fennel,
   or ½ teaspoon fennel seeds
1 garlic clove, minced
thyme
marjoram
½ cup each of water and vinegar
   combined with pinch of sugar

Cook half of the bacon dice in a large skillet over moderate heat until brown and crisp. Remove bacon to a paper towel; pour off the fat. Put 1 ounce of the butter and the oil in the same skillet. Gently brown and cook the quails, turning often. However, if using duck, the heat should be high, and when duck is done, it must be drained on paper towels. Remove quails to a plate.

Pour off most of the fat from the skillet, leaving 2 to 3 tablespoons. Heat fat again and add onion. Cook until onion is translucent. Add rice, and stir to coat the rice well with the fat. Reduce heat and pour in the water, currants, raisins, and salt and pepper to taste. Stir, cover, and simmer over low heat until rice is tender but not overdone and liquid is absorbed. Set aside.

Remove 3 or 4 large leaves from the cabbage head. Blanch leaves in boiling water, drain flat on a paper towel, and set aside. Shred remaining cabbage.

Place remaining bacon dice in a skillet and cook until bits start to fry. Add the shredded cabbage, fennel, garlic, herbs to taste, and the mixture of water, vinegar, and sugar. Add a pinch of salt and a good grinding of pepper. Cover and cook over low to medium heat until cabbage is tender, about 45 minutes.

Preheat oven to 375°F. Cut the blanched cabbage leaves into 4 pieces each. Fill each piece with a teaspoon of the cooked rice mixture, roll into a small ball, and set aside. Use remaining butter to coat an ovenproof earthenware casserole large enough to contain the quails cut into halves or the pieces of duck, in one layer. Place a layer of rice at the bottom of casserole. Arrange the birds and their juices, or the duck pieces, on top of the rice. Tuck the cabbage balls between pieces of meat. Spread cabbage mixture over this.

Roll out the dough into a circle large enough to cover the top of the casserole. Let dough hang over the edge a little and pinch all around rim to seal pie. Cut a vent in the center and pierce top in several places with a fork. Reduce oven temperature to 350°F. and bake casserole for 30 to 35 minutes. If top tends to brown too much, cover loosely with foil.

DRINK: Slivovitz

PIROG IZ ZAICHEVO MIASA   (*R U S S I A*)
Hare Pie

SERVES 6 TO 8

DOUGH

butter for pan   1 batch of Short Pastry (p. 9)

FILLING

4 pounds skinned and dressed hare or rabbit	4 hard-cooked eggs, chopped
	4 ounces cream cheese
2 cups bouillon	2 raw eggs, lightly beaten
3 ounces (6 tablespoons) Madeira wine	4 ounces pork fat, diced
	1 tablespoon butter
salt and pepper	1 tablespoon flour
1 tablespoon lemon juice	nutmeg

Bone the hare or rabbit, dice the best pieces of meat, grind the rest, and reserve. Place all the bones in a heavy saucepan. Add bouillon and 2 ounces of the Madeira, with salt and pepper to taste. Add the lemon juice and water, if necessary, to cover the bones by 1 inch. Bring to a boil and simmer for 1 hour. Strain the broth. Measure 1 cup of the broth for the sauce, and reserve the rest.

In a mixing bowl combine the chopped eggs, cream cheese, and raw eggs; mix well. Add the ground hare or rabbit meat, and salt and pepper to taste. Butter a 9-inch springform pan.

On a floured board roll out three-quarters of the pastry into a circle large enough to line bottom and sides of prepared pan. Let dough hang over the edges, but trim excess with scissors. Spread a layer of the ground meat mixture on the bottom of the pastry. Scatter the diced meat and the pork fat all over, and top with remaining ground meat mixture. Sprinkle with a few spoons of reserved hare broth.

Preheat oven to 375°F. Roll out remaining pastry to make a lid, and cover the pie. Fold over the overhanging dough edge and pinch together all around in a decorative fashion. Decorate pie with scraps of dough. Invert a funnel in the middle of the pie to allow steam to escape. Bake the pie for 20 minutes. Reduce temperature to 350°F. and continue baking for 45 minutes longer. Pour a little of the hare broth into the funnel every 15 minutes while the pie is baking.

Melt 1 tablespoon butter in a small saucepan over low heat. Add the flour and cook briefly, stirring constantly. Remove from heat and gradually add the reserved 1 cup of hare broth, stirring until sauce is smooth and liquid. Return to heat and cook, stirring, until sauce thickens and starts to boil. Add nutmeg to taste and remaining Madeira, and season with salt and pepper.

Let pie cool a little before slicing. Serve Madeira-flavored sauce with the pie.

WINE: Red Burgundy

WLOSZCZYZNA PIEROG   *(P O L A N D)*
Vegetable and Sausage Pie

SERVES 6

Wloszczyzna means "Italian manners" and also green vegetables because green vegetables were introduced to Polish cuisine by Italian cooks, as were tomatoes. *Pomidor,* the Polish name for tomato, is similar to the Italian *pomidoro* or *pomodore.* Some of the touches of Italian influence in Polish cuisine can be traced back to Queen Bona Sforza of the Milanese family, who introduced Italian cooking to Poland when she married King Sigismund I in 1518.

DOUGH

butter for pan	1 egg
1 batch of Pâte Brisée II (p. 7)	½ teaspoon salt

FILLING

1 pound sausage meat	1 green pepper
2 tablespoons oil	1 teaspoon paprika
2 onions, chopped	½ teaspoon cayenne pepper
4 or 5 fresh tomatoes, about 1½ pounds, or 3 cups canned tomatoes	salt

Preheat oven to 400°F. Lightly butter a 9-inch pie pan. Roll the sausage meat into walnut-size balls. Heat 1 tablespoon oil in a skillet and cook sausage balls until browned on all sides. Arrange them in the prepared pan. While sausage cooks, chop the onions, and peel, seed, and chop the fresh tomatoes; if using canned tomatoes, crush them. Remove stem, ribs, and seeds from green pepper, and chop the pepper. Heat remaining oil in the skillet. Add onion and sauté until lightly browned. Add tomatoes, green pepper, paprika, cayenne, and a little salt. Simmer, stirring occasionally, for 5 to 8 minutes, or until liquid has evaporated. Spoon the sauce over the sausage balls and let the mixture cool.

Roll the dough out on a floured board to a circle large enough to cover the pie, with ¾ inch extra all around. Cover the pie, and turn the extra dough underneath edge of pie pan to seal all around. Pierce a hole in the center for steam to escape. Mix the egg with ½ teaspoon salt, and brush this all over the dough. Bake for 15 minutes, or until dough is beginning to brown. Reduce temperature to 350°F. and continue baking for 15 to 20 minutes longer, or until top is well browned.

DRINK: Vodka

PIEROŻKI Z MIĘSEM
Meat-Filled Dumplings

(POLAND)

45 DUMPLINGS

DOUGH

1½ cups milk

2 ounces (½ stick) butter

1 package active dry yeast

2 tablespoons sugar

⅓ cup lukewarm water (105° to 115°F.)

4 to 5 cups unbleached flour

1 teaspoon salt

3 eggs, lightly beaten

FILLING

½ cup oil

1 tablespoon butter

¾ cups finely chopped onions

12 ounces fresh mushrooms, chopped

salt and pepper

2½ cups cooked meat, chopped

Pour the milk into a saucepan and bring just to the boil. Remove from the heat and add the 2 ounces of butter. Let stand until the butter melts and the mixture is just warm. Meanwhile dissolve the yeast and a pinch of sugar in the lukewarm water. Stir to mix well.

In a large bowl combine 4 cups of flour, the remaining sugar, and the salt; stir. Make a well in the center and add 2 eggs, the warmed milk and butter, and the yeast mixture. Mix the flour into the liquid ingredients, working rapidly and beating with a wooden spoon until well blended. Gather mixture into a dough. Turn onto a floured board and knead, adding more flour as needed, until the dough is smooth and no longer sticky. Gather the dough into a ball and place in a buttered bowl. Cover and let rise in a warm place until doubled in bulk, about 1½ hours. Punch down and let rise again for about 1 hour.

Make the filling: Heat the oil and 1 tablespoon butter in a skillet. Add the onions and cook until golden in color. Add the mushrooms and cook until liquid released by the mushrooms has evaporated. Add salt and pepper to taste. The mixture should not be very dry. Add the meat and cook just to heat through.

Preheat oven to 350°F. Turn dough out on a lightly floured board. Knead it briefly, and divide it into 4 parts. Work with one part at a time, and keep the remainder covered. Roll out 1 piece into a long snakelike rope. Cut this into 1½-inch lengths. Roll each piece into a ball and flatten with the hands into a 3-inch circle. Add 1 level teaspoon of filling to each circle. Fold the dough over to enclose the meat. Press around the edges to seal. Place the dumpling on a baking sheet. Continue making *pieroźki* until all the dough and filling are used. Brush them with the remaining beaten egg. Bake for 25 minutes.

Serve hot. These are also good cold, and they can be reheated.

DRINK: Vodka

PIEROG KIELBASA NADZIEWANY Z KAPUSTA

Kielbasa Pie with Cabbage (P O L A N D)
SERVES 6

Polish pork is excellent. Raised without chemicals and fed as nature commands, the pig makes the juiciest hams and most flavorful sausages. Kielbasa is the Polish sausage best known in the United States, but those you buy here are locally made and equally good.

DOUGH

1 batch of Quick Puff Pastry (p. 12)

FILLING

3 slices of bacon, diced
1½ pounds kielbasa sausage, cut
    into ½-inch slices
1 onion, sliced
1 head of Savoy or green cabbage,
    shredded

1 teaspoon caraway seeds
1 teaspoon sugar
juice of ½ lemon
salt and pepper
2 tablespoons water
1 potato

In a flameproof casserole fry the bacon until browned. Drain bacon and reserve it. Add the sliced sausage and fry until browned. Add the onion and cook until soft. Stir occasionally. Add the shredded cabbage, caraway seeds, sugar, lemon juice, and seasoning to taste. Mix well. Add water, cover the pan, and simmer gently for 5 to 8 minutes. Peel and grate the potato and stir into the cabbage. Cover and continue cooking for 15 minutes, or until the cabbage is tender and potato has disintegrated. Cool.

Preheat oven to 400°F. Roll out the pastry on a floured board to a round large enough to cover the casserole. Fit it over the dish, turning pastry underneath the edge of the casserole to seal all around. Cut a few decorative vents on top. Bake for 30 to 40 minutes, or until top is golden.

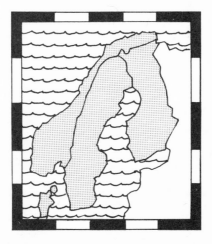

Scandinavia

Denmark · Norway
Sweden · Finland

Scandinavian countries are famous for their breads; baking is a true art among their people. No wonder we find some of the most original and tasty flat breads in these countries. Some are crispy wafers, others are pliant and warm or braided and artistically decorated. Some are shaped like oversize crackers with seeds on top. Many are like the savory pizzas of Italy or the delicate koulorias of Greece. Mainly whole-grain flour is used in the making of breads and pies; potatoes and cornmeal are also prominent.

Because of the extended coastline of Scandinavia and the many lakes in its territory, fish is predominant in the cuisine, and savory pies are very often filled with it. Cheese and meats are also used, combined with mushrooms and herbs.

Pancakes and waffles are eaten in great quantity all over Scandinavia. In fact, it is not uncommon for a dinner to begin and finish with some sort of delicate *plättar*, or pancakes. We include some here, since I agree with James Beard who says that they belong to the world of bread, just like pizzas.

PINAATTIOHUKAISET   *(FINLAND)*
Spinach Pancakes

SERVES 6 TO 8

1½ cups milk
1 teaspoon salt
⅛ teaspoon grated nutmeg
1 cup flour
2 ounces (½ stick) butter, melted

4 eggs
½ teaspoon sugar
1 pound fresh spinach, or 10 ounces
    frozen spinach, cooked,
    squeezed, and chopped

In a mixing bowl combine milk, salt, nutmeg, and flour. Using an electric mixer beat in half of the melted butter. In a separate bowl beat the eggs and sugar; add to the batter. Gradually beat in the spinach. Brush a little of the remaining butter in a heavy skillet and make about 24 pancakes. Brush more butter on the skillet as needed for each batch of cakes. Keep them warm.

Serve them for lunch with sour cream or Finnish style, as an accompaniment to meat and fish, instead of bread or vegetables.

SUOMALAISLEIPA   *(FINLAND)*
Flat Rye Bread

1 LARGE LOAF

2 packages active dry yeast
3 teaspoons dark brown sugar
1¼ cups lukewarm water (105° to
    115°F.)
1 tablespoon butter, melted, plus
    butter for pan

1½ teaspoons salt
2 cups all-purpose flour
1½ cups rye flour

Dissolve yeast and 1 teaspoon sugar in ¼ cup of the lukewarm water. Let stand for a few minutes, then mix. Set the mixture in a warm spot until it bubbles. Pour the mixture into a mixing bowl. Add remaining water and sugar, and mix. Add melted butter, salt, all-purpose flour, and 1 cup of the rye flour. Gather into a smooth ball and let rest at room temperature for 10 minutes. Knead the dough for 10 to 15 minutes, until smooth and elastic, adding the rest of the rye flour if necessary. Place the dough in a buttered bowl, cover, set in a warm spot, and let rise until doubled in bulk, about 1 hour.

Butter a baking sheet and sprinkle with flour. Preheat oven to 375°F. Punch dough down and knead again for 10 minutes. Shape into a round flat loaf 9 to 10 inches in diameter. Set on the prepared baking sheet. Mark parallel lines 2 inches apart on the dough by pressing down with a wooden spoon handle. This will permit you to break the bread into large strips after it is baked. Bake until crusty brown, about 30 minutes.

Serve still warm.

LEFSER   *(NORWAY)*
Potato Griddle Cakes

24 CAKES

Good either crisp or soft, *lefser* can be served with butter, cheeses, or preserves. Soft ones are wrapped around Gjetost (goat cheese) or a thin wedge of sharp Cheddar.

2½ pounds baking potatoes	1 teaspoon salt
1 ounce (2 tablespoons) butter or margarine	3 cups all-purpose flour
¼ cup milk	salad oil

Peel potatoes and cut into pieces. Cook in boiling water just to cover until tender; drain. Mash potatoes or beat with an electric mixer until very smooth. Measure 4 cups of mashed potatoes. Add butter or margarine, milk, and salt; mix well. Let cool to room temperature.

Stir in enough of the flour, about 2 cups, to form a smooth dough. Add flour gradually, the less the better. On a floured board, shape dough into a log and divide into 24 pieces. Roll each piece of dough out on a floured board to form a very thin round about 10 inches in diameter. Turn each *lefse* over frequently while sprinkling board with flour when necessary to prevent sticking. Lay out the rolled *lefser*, side by side, on lightly floured wax paper until all are shaped, or roll out 1 *lefse* as you cook another.

Heat the griddle over medium heat, and lightly oil it. To cook each *lefse*, place it on the griddle. *Lefse* will start to bubble immediately; cook, turning often, until bubbles are lightly browned on both sides, about 2 minutes. Stack *lefser* as they cook, cover with foil, and place in a 200°F. oven to keep warm.

Lefser can be refrigerated for a week or frozen, well wrapped in foil.

For crisp *lefser*, place cooked ones in single layers on baking sheets. Bake in a 425°F. oven for about 3 minutes.

KARJALANPIIRAAT   (*F I N L A N D*)
Karelian Pasties

12 PIECES

Whole rye flour is used extensively in Finland and the most characteristic pies are made with this flour. The oval-shaped *piiraat* comes from the eastern province of Karelia, now belonging to Russia. The shape of the *piiraat* varies from village to village. It can be eaten hot or cold, usually accompanied by a mixture of butter and hard-cooked eggs flavored with a touch of ginger and a few drops of aquavit. Aquavit is usually served as the drink which best complements the delicate flavor of these pasties.

DOUGH

1½ ounces (3 tablespoons) butter
1 teaspoon salt
1½ cups all-purpose flour

1½ cups rye flour
1 cup water
butter for baking sheets

RICE

1 cup water
¾ cup uncooked rice
2 cups milk
1½ cups half and half

salt
½ teaspoon pepper
1½ ounces (3 tablespoons) butter
2 tablespoons melted butter

EGG BUTTER

4 ounces (1 stick) butter, at room
    temperature
3 hard-cooked eggs

½ teaspoon of ground ginger
salt and pepper
aquavit (optional)

To make the dough: In the bowl of a food processor place the butter and the salt. Combine both kinds of flour and add to the food processor. Turn the machine on and off until mixture resembles coarse meal. Gradually add the water and stop machine as soon as a ball forms on the blades. If dough still appears moist, sprinkle on a little more all-purpose flour and process a few seconds longer. Turn dough onto a floured pastry board and knead for 5 minutes, adding more flour if necessary. Refrigerate until ready to use.

To cook the rice: Bring 1 cup of water to a boil, add rice, and cook until water is absorbed, 10 to 15 minutes. Add the milk and the half and half while stirring. Add salt to taste and the pepper. Bring to a boil again and cook the mixture uncovered over low heat, stirring often, for 45 minutes to 1 hour. Mixture must be thick but not dry. Add the 3 tablespoons of butter and stir again.

Preheat oven to 450°F. Lightly butter 2 baking sheets, 11 x 14 inches, and set aside.

Divide dough into 12 pieces. Keep pieces covered with a towel while making pasties. Roll 1 piece of dough at a time into a thin oval. Place 2 tablespoons of filling on the oval. Crimp the edges of dough along the sides of the filling like a ruffle, leaving the center exposed. Set on prepared baking sheet. Roll and fill the other pieces of dough. Brush pasties with the melted butter. Repeat brushing once while baking and once as pasties are removed from oven. Bake for 20 to 25 minutes.

Serve warm or at room temperature.

EGG BUTTER. Mix ingredients together and spread on hot pasties.

NOTE: 1 shredded carrot, braised together with a chopped onion, can be mixed with the rice before filling the pasties.

JANSSON'S FRESTELSE   (S W E D E N)
Jansson's Temptation

SERVES 6

This potato pie is as popular as a pizza. It is eaten late at night after a party or the theater, accompanied by a strong drink with which to brave the cold winter night. It is named after Erik Jansson, a religious fanatic who disdained the pleasures of the flesh, but fell prey to this temptation.

8 medium-size potatoes, boiled
1 ounce (2 tablespoons) butter, plus
    butter for casserole and dotting
2 tablespoons oil
2 to 3 medium-size onions, thinly
    sliced

fine bread crumbs
16 anchovy fillets, drained
salt and pepper
1 cup heavy cream
¼ cup milk

Preheat oven to 400°F. Cut 3 boiled potatoes into strips; mash remaining potatoes. Set aside. Heat the butter and oil in a skillet. Add onions and cook, stirring, until soft and translucent. Butter an ovenproof casserole or deep dish from which you can serve. Coat with bread crumbs. Place a layer of mashed potato in the prepared dish. Alternate layers of onions, anchovies, and potato strips, ending with more mashed potato. Season each layer with salt and pepper. Combine cream and milk and pour into the casserole. Sprinkle with bread crumbs and dot with butter. Bake for 1 hour, until top is crusty and brown.

FISKEFARCE PIE
Creamed Fish Pie

(NORWAY)

SERVES 8

DOUGH
butter for pan
1 batch of Wheaten Egg Dough (p. 7)

FILLING
3 pounds fresh haddock or cod
    fillets
1 tablespoon potato flour
1 tablespoon wheat flour
2 eggs

salt and pepper
3 ounces (¾ stick) butter, cut into
    pieces
1 tablespoon Dijon-style mustard
1½ cups milk

Preheat oven to 375°F. Butter a 10-inch pie pan. On a floured board roll out the dough into a circle large enough to cover bottom and sides of prepared pan. Fit dough into pan and trim excess dough with scissors. Flute edges and pierce the bottom of the dough with a fork. Reserve scraps of dough.

Skin fish, if necessary, and cut into small pieces. Place fish and all remaining ingredients but milk in the bowl of a food processor. Add 2 tablespoons milk and turn the machine on and off 2 or 3 times. With the machine on, start to add the rest of the milk slowly and process until mixture becomes creamy. Pour mixture into the dough-lined pan. Roll out scraps of dough and cut strips to make a lattice on top of pie. Bake for 45 minutes, or until filling is set and top is golden in color.

MAKRIL KAKA   *(S W E D E N)*
Mackerel Pie

SERVES 6

DOUGH

butter for pan   1 batch of Pâte Brisée I (p. 6)

FILLING

1 ounce (2 tablespoons) butter   pinch of paprika
1 tablespoon oil   salt and pepper
2 leeks, thinly sliced   6 mackerel fillets, about 12 ounces
4 medium-size tomatoes, peeled   each
   and chopped   2 tablespoons bread crumbs
2 sprigs of fresh dill, snipped   ½ cup dairy sour cream

Preheat oven to 375°F. Butter a 10-inch pie pan. On a floured board roll the dough out into a circle large enough to cover bottom and sides of prepared pan. Fit dough into pan and trim excess dough with scissors. Flute edges, and pierce the bottom of the dough with a fork. Chill.

Heat butter and oil in a large skillet. Add leeks and cook over medium heat, stirring often, until vegetables are wilted. Add tomatoes and cook uncovered for 15 minutes. Add dill and seasoning to taste. Place fillets in the skillet, spoon the sauce over them, and cook, covered, for 5 to 8 minutes.

Sprinkle the dough with the bread crumbs. Carefully remove fish fillets from the sauce and place in the dough-lined pan. Increase heat under the skillet and cook the sauce for a few more minutes to let most of the moisture evaporate. Remove from heat and stir in the sour cream. Pour over the fish. Bake for 25 to 30 minutes, until rim of pie is golden brown.

BURBOT PASTY PIE   (*F I N L A N D*)
Cod Pie

This is a specialty from Helsinki. The recipe calls for cod liver, but since it is not easy to find here, I have used fish roe. If you can find burbot, which is a freshwater cod, use it in preference to other species. It has fewer small bones than other cods and very good liver and roe.

DOUGH

1 batch of Quick Puff Pastry (p. 12) or Classic Puff Pastry (p. 11)	1 egg yolk, lightly beaten

FILLING

1¼ cups cubed fish roe	½ cup snipped fresh dill
1 cup rice, cooked	salt and freshly ground pepper
6 hard-cooked eggs, sliced	Wine and Butter Sauce (recipe
1½ pounds boneless cod, chopped	follows)

Preheat oven to 400°F. Roll out puff pastry to ¼-inch thickness and cut out 2 fish-shaped pieces. Place 1 pastry piece in an ovenproof dish from which you can serve. In alternating layers, place fish roe, rice, sliced eggs, and chopped cod. Sprinkle the dill on and season with salt and pepper to taste. Fit the other pastry piece on top and press edges together. Decorate top by "scaling" fish with the nozzle of a pastry bag. Brush the pastry with the egg yolk. Bake for 45 minutes. Serve with the sauce.

WINE AND BUTTER SAUCE

¾ cup dry white wine	10 ounces (2½ sticks) butter, melted
¼ cup finely chopped onion	¾ cup heavy cream, boiling
6 egg yolks	salt and pepper

Bring wine to boil in a saucepan and add onion. Boil for about 5 minutes. Remove from heat, and beat in the egg yolks, one at a time, until sauce is creamy and thick enough to coat a spoon. Return to heat and gradually add the melted butter, stirring all the while. Pour in the cream, still stirring constantly. Season to taste with salt and pepper. Do not let the sauce boil after adding egg yolks. Serve in a sauceboat.

KALAKUKKO   *(F I N L A N D)*
Fish Turnover

This recipe originated in the lake district of Finland. As soon as the fish is caught, it is wrapped in the rye dough. The turnover has become internationally known. Fish is a staple in this part of the country and is cooked in many ways. Although the Finns use their small and bony varieties of fish for this specialty, I have chosen freshwater fillets easily available in this country.

DOUGH

2 packages active dry yeast
¼ teaspoon sugar
1 cup lukewarm water (105° to 115°F.)
1½ cups rye meal

1½ cups all-purpose flour
1 teaspoon salt
2 ounces (½ stick) butter, cut into pieces

FILLING

6 slices of bacon
1 pound fillets of whitefish, trout, or carp

salt and pepper

Dissolve yeast and sugar in the water, and set in a warm place. In a mixing bowl combine the rye meal, 1 cup of the all-purpose flour, and the salt. Chop in the butter until mixture resembles coarse meal. Add the yeast mixture and gather into a ball. Place in a buttered bowl, set in a warm place, and let rise for 1 hour, or until doubled in bulk.

Cook the bacon in a skillet until crisp. Drain on paper towels, reserving the fat. Cut the fish fillets into 3 strips, more or less the length of the bacon slices. Sprinkle with salt and pepper.

Punch the dough down and pat into a 10- to 12-inch oval. Place 3 slices of bacon lengthwise in the center of the oval. Top with fish strips, and then with remaining bacon. Dribble some of the bacon fat over. Moisten edges of oval all around and bring up the sides of the dough to enclose the fish. Tuck in ends. Butter a baking sheet. Place the turnover, seam side down, on the sheet and pat it to a nice oblong shape. Brush with remaining bacon fat. Cover loosely with foil, and set in a warm place for about 45 minutes.

Preheat oven to 375°F. Reduce temperature to 350°F. and bake the turnover for about 1¼ hours, or until top looks nice and crusty.

Cool for 15 minutes before slicing.

NOTE: Pike, white or yellow perch, and black bass are also suitable for this turnover.

REJE POSTEJ
Shrimp Pie

(DENMARK)

SERVES 6

DOUGH
½ batch of Short Pastry (p. 9)

FILLING

1 ounce (2 tablespoons) butter
1 teaspoon oil
1 onion, sliced
1 pound raw shrimps, shelled and
deveined
¼ pound fresh mushrooms
1 tablespoon dried mushrooms,
soaked
4 eggs

1 cup milk
1 cup heavy cream
salt and pepper
nutmeg
2 bacon slices, cooked and
crumbled
1 cup grated Gruyère cheese
¼ cup plain yogurt
1 tablespoon flour

Preheat oven to 400°F. Heat butter and oil in a skillet. Add onion and cook until tender and translucent; remove onion with a slotted spoon. Add shrimps to skillet and sauté until they turn pink; remove shrimps. Chop both kinds of mushrooms, add them to the skillet, and cook until moisture evaporates.

Roll dough out into a circle large enough to line a 9-inch pie pan. Fit dough into the pan, and chill it.

Chop the shrimps and combine them with onion and mushrooms. Spoon into the pastry-lined pan. Beat the eggs with milk, cream, and salt, pepper, and nutmeg to taste. Pour over the shrimp filling. Sprinkle top with crumbled bacon and grated cheese. Bake for 10 minutes, then reduce temperature to 325°F. and continue baking for 30 minutes longer.

Combine yogurt and flour, and spread over the pie. Slide the pie under the broiler for a few minutes, until browned.

TUNGA OCH POTATIS PASTEJ   *(S W E D E N)*
Tongue and Potato Pie

SERVES 6 TO 8

Potatoes are venerated in Sweden; many eat them twice a day. This is an odd passion, when one remembers that potatoes were forced on the Swedes during the famine of 1771–1772. This recipe provides a good way to use cooked tongue.

2 eggs
2 tablespoons water
6 to 8 slices of boiled fresh beef
    tongue, or more
bread crumbs
3 ounces (¾ stick) butter or
    margarine
2 tablespoons oil

1 pound asparagus
1 medium-size onion, finely
    chopped
1 tablespoon flour
1 cup broth from cooking tongue,
    or bouillon
2 cups mashed boiled potatoes
salt and pepper

Preheat oven to 375°F. Beat the eggs with 2 tablespoons water. Dip tongue slices into the beaten eggs, then coat with bread crumbs. Heat 2½ ounces of the butter or margarine and the oil in a skillet. Reduce heat to medium and brown tongue slices on both sides. You may need more butter. Arrange the browned slices, slightly overlapping, in a baking dish from which you can serve.

Wash and trim asparagus. Bend each stalk; it will break where the tough fibers begin. Remove all tough ends. Blanch the tender stalks, drain, rinse with cold water, and drain again. Set aside.

Melt remaining 1 tablespoon butter in a small saucepan. Add onion and cook, stirring, until soft. Add flour and continue to cook for a few minutes longer. Remove saucepan from heat and gradually add the broth, stirring with a wire whisk until sauce liquefies. Return pan to low heat and cook until sauce thickens and comes to a boil. Place mashed potatoes in a mixing bowl, pour hot sauce over potatoes, and beat to blend mixture well. Add salt and pepper to taste. Spoon potato mixture over prepared tongue slices. Place blanched asparagus stalks on potato mixture in a decorative fashion. Bake for 25 to 30 minutes.

Serve hot.

FLÄSKPANNKAKA   *(S W E D E N)*
Bacon Pancake

SERVES 6

A basket of *fläskpannkaka*, an earthy soup, and a succulent roast goose make a favorite dinner for a cold winter night in Sweden.

2 eggs	6 tablespoons chopped cooked pork
2½ cups all-purpose flour	or bacon
¼ cup milk	salt and pepper
2 ounces (½ stick) butter, melted	
and cooled	

Beat eggs in a mixing bowl. Gradually add flour, milk, butter, pork or bacon, and salt and pepper to taste. Stir well. Let batter stand in a cool place for 1 hour.

Preheat oven to 375°F. Beat batter again before using it. Pour into a greased iron skillet and bake for 45 minutes.

Serve warm, cut into wedges.

HOKAREPANNA   *(S W E D E N)*
Coachman's Pie

SERVES 8

1 ounce (2 tablespoons) butter, plus	1 veal kidney, sliced thin
butter for casserole	2 lamb kidneys, sliced thin
2 pounds potatoes	salt and pepper
4 medium-size onions	½ cup flat beer
2 tablespoons oil	½ cup beef broth
¾ pound lean pork, diced	pinch of sugar

Preheat oven to 375°F. Butter a deep ovenproof earthenware casserole 9½ inches in diameter. Set aside. Peel potatoes and cut into thin slices. Place in a bowl and cover with cold water. Peel onions and cut into thin slices. Heat 1 ounce butter and the oil in a skillet. Add onions and cook over low heat until wilted. Remove onions and reserve. Add pork to skillet and cook for 10 minutes. Add both kidney slices and sauté on both sides, adding more oil or butter if necessary. Season with salt and pepper. Remove meats and reserve.

Pour beer and broth into skillet, add sugar, and boil liquid for about 5 minutes. Scrape up any brown particles clinging to the bottom of the skillet. Remove skillet from heat. Arrange a layer of potato slices, in an overlapping fashion, on the bottom and sides of prepared casserole. Season with salt and pepper. Continue layering in this order: Spread half of the meats on the potatoes, cover with a thin layer of potatoes, season with salt and pepper. Spread half of the onion, remaining meats, and end with all remaining potato slices arranged in an overlapping circular design on the top. Season with salt and pepper. Pour the liquid in the skillet over potato mixture. Bake for 1½ hours, basting once or twice with a bulb baster. Pie is done when top is nicely brown and crisp, and liquid has been absorbed. It is advisable to pull 1 slice of potato from the sides of casserole to make sure it is done. If top tends to brown too much, cover loosely with foil.

SKINKE POSTEI MED SURFLÖTESAUS
Ham Pie with Sour Cream and Dill Sauce   (N O R W A Y)
SERVES 6

DOUGH

butter for pan
1 batch of Wheaten Egg Dough
   (p. 7)

FILLING

1½ pounds cooked ham
1 tablespoon butter
1 garlic clove, minced
1 cup finely chopped onions
¼ pound mushrooms, chopped fine
½ cup finely chopped celery
freshly ground pepper
1 cup chicken broth

2 cups fine bread crumbs
2 whole eggs, lightly beaten
¾ cup heavy cream
¼ teaspoon grated nutmeg
2 tablespoons chopped fresh
   parsley
Sour Cream and Dill Sauce (recipe
   follows)

Butter a 9-inch pie pan. On a floured board roll out three-quarters of the dough into a circle large enough to cover bottom and sides of prepared pan.

Fit dough into pan, and trim excess dough with scissors. Pierce the bottom of the dough with a fork, and chill.

Preheat oven to 400°F. Cube ham and grind or chop very fine. (This can be done in a food processor.) Turn ham into a mixing bowl and set aside. Heat the butter in a skillet, and add garlic, onions, mushrooms, and celery. Cook until vegetables are tender. Sprinkle with pepper and cook for 5 minutes longer. Add the chicken broth and cook for 5 to 8 minutes. Pour the mixture into the bowl with the ham. Add the bread crumbs, eggs, cream, nutmeg, and parsley. Blend well. Spoon mixture into the pastry-lined pan. Smooth the top.

Roll out remaining dough and cover pie. Seal edges all around in a decorative fashion. Decorate pie with scraps of dough if desired. Pierce top in several places to allow steam to escape. Bake for 45 minutes.

Cool pie for at least 15 minutes before slicing. Serve with Sour Cream and Dill Sauce.

SOUR CREAM AND DILL SAUCE

2 CUPS SAUCE

1 tablespoon butter
¼ cup finely chopped onion
pinch of tarragon
1 tablespoon flour
¾ cup chicken broth

½ cup tomato purée
1 cup dairy sour cream
salt
2 tablespoons snipped fresh dill

Heat the butter in a saucepan. Add the onion and cook until onion is tender and translucent. Add tarragon and flour, stirring with a whisk. Add chicken broth and tomato purée and stir rapidly until sauce is thickened and smooth. Stir in sour cream and salt to taste. Heat thoroughly, stirring. Stir in the dill just before serving.

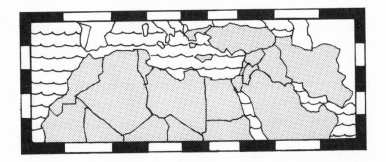

Around the Mediterranean and Middle East
Greece · Cyprus · Turkey
Iran · Arab States
Israel · Egypt · North Africa

It was in these countries that the humble circle of dough reached its apotheosis. According to historians, man first learned to cultivate the soil in this area, and to cook his food to make it more palatable. The simple mixture of grain and water, probably baked on hot stones, developed into the flat bread, *pita* or *khoubz*. This bread, which goes back to biblical times and much further, has never been replaced by the leavened bread Westerners use. Flat breads appear everywhere, at modest meals and Pantagruelian banquets. Torn into pieces, opened like a pouch, wrapped around food, used like a spoon to catch drippings and scoop out solids, such breads accompany every sort of comestible.

The Greeks introduced *phyllo* (or *fillo*) pastry into the American market. This pastry, though, derives from a flaky dough of Persian origin, and it is used throughout the Middle East, wrapped around Turkish *börek*, Tunisian *brik*, Moroccan *b'stilla*, Lebanese veal and eggplant pie, and countless other pastry dishes in the entire area.

161

Lebanon, Syria, Jordan, and Iraq had developed sophisticated civilizations long before the Ottoman Empire swallowed them up. These thousands of years of civilization in this arc of the Mediterranean Sea have not been wasted when it comes to food. Although each country has its own cooking style, touches of the exotic imported from Rome as well as the Far East and the influences of the Arabs, the Turks, and the French, all invaders at some time, have left their mark on the culinary art. Perhaps because of the similarities in culture and tradition, the food varies little from country to country in spite of the political differences, even enmity, that divide them. As the expansion of Islam carried its culture to a large part of Africa, along with it went the same pastry and bread. The savory pies in Africa are made in an array of shapes, often in individual portions, ideal for carrying and eating outside. These make unusual and practical food for picnics.

ELIOPSOMO   (CYPRUS)
Onion and Mint Olive Bread

ONE 10-INCH LOAF

1 package active dry yeast
1 teaspoon sugar
1½ cups lukewarm water (105° to
    115°F.), approximately
5 cups all-purpose flour
3 tablespoons olive oil
2 teaspoons salt, or less if olives are
    very salty

1 medium-size onion, chopped
1½ tablespoons chopped fresh mint,
    or 2 teaspoons dried mint
10 Greek olives, pitted and coarsely
    chopped
melted butter or oil (optional)

Dissolve the yeast and a pinch of the sugar in ½ cup of the water, and let it set in a warm place for 10 minutes. In a large mixing bowl, combine the flour, oil, remaining sugar, and the salt. Stir in the onion and mint, make a well in the center, and add the yeast mixture and enough more warm water to gather the mixture into a dough, which should be soft and elastic. Add more water if necessary. Add the olives to the dough. Turn out on a floured board and knead for 10 minutes. Place in a large floured bowl, cover, and set in a warm place until doubled in bulk, 1 to 1½ hours.

Punch dough down and knead thoroughly. Form into a round loaf and set in an oiled pan. Cover and allow to rise again in a warm place until doubled in bulk. Preheat oven to 450°F.

Bake bread for 10 minutes, then reduce heat to 350°F. and continue baking for 30 to 35 minutes longer, or until loaf is nicely browned and crisp. Brush with butter or oil. Cool on racks.

PITA BREAD   *(G R E E C E)*
4 PITAS

Pita is an ancient food, indigenous to the Middle East. It reached our shores with a wave of relatively new immigrants, some of whom opened unpretentious little eateries offering a succulent new sandwich plumped up with meats and exotic spreads made with vegetables, legumes, and seeds. Presented this way, pita became popular in the United States, and indeed it is a nutritious repast that lends itself to many variations.

2 packages active dry yeast
¼ teaspoon sugar
2 cups lukewarm water (105° to 115°F.)

¼ cup olive or vegetable oil
1½ tablespoons salt
6 cups all-purpose flour
cornmeal

Dissolve yeast and sugar in ½ cup lukewarm water; let stand in a warm place for about 10 minutes. Stir in remaining water, the oil, salt, and 5 cups of the flour. Gather into a ball and turn dough out onto a floured board. Knead for about 10 minutes, adding enough of the remaining flour until dough is smooth and elastic. Place dough in a greased bowl and turn to grease other side; cover. Let rise in a warm place until doubled in bulk, 1½ to 2 hours.

Punch down dough; let it rest on a floured surface for 10 minutes. Divide dough into 4 parts; shape each part into a ball. Roll each ball on a lightly floured surface into a 9-inch circle. Cover; let rise for 30 minutes.

Preheat oven to 500°F. Sprinkle baking sheet with cornmeal; place 1 pita on the baking sheet. Bake until brown and puffy, about 8 minutes. Remove from oven; while warm wrap in aluminum foil to cool. Repeat baking process with 3 remaining pitas. To serve, split the pita, and spoon in desired filling.

NOTE: Stone-ground whole-wheat flour can be substituted for the all-purpose flour; increase yeast to 3 packages.

IFLAGUN
Spicy Flat Bread

(E G Y P T)

Claudia Rodin in *A Book of Middle Eastern Food*, which is full of much valuable information, dates the origin of this spicy and flavorful bread to medieval times. In the book *Wusla il al Habib*, it is described "as the bread of the Franks and Armenians." Whatever the origin, to eat a piece of this bread is quite an experience; it combines the flavors of the many lands touched by that sea the Romans called *mare nostrum*, the Mediterranean.

DOUGH

¾ cup milk

¾ cup lukewarm water (105° to 115°F.)

1 tablespoon vegetable shortening

1 tablespoon butter

½ teaspoon salt

1½ tablespoons sugar

1½ packages active dry yeast

3½ cups all-purpose flour

oil

FILLING

1 egg

pinch of ground ginger

2 tablespoons roasted sesame seeds

1 teaspoon rosemary, crumbled

1 teaspoon poppy seeds

2 tablespoons grated cheese (Parmesan, or Cheddar)

pinch of salt

1½ tablespoons pistachio nuts, chopped

1 teaspoon freshly ground black pepper, or more

Combine milk and water, place on the heat and warm up, but do not boil. Add the shortening, the butter, salt, and sugar. Stir over very low heat until fat melts. Allow to cool. Dissolve yeast in remaining lukewarm water. Set aside in a warm place for about 10 minutes, then combine with the first mixture.

Sift the flour into a mixing bowl. Make a well in the center and add the liquid mixture. Beat the flour into the liquids and gather into a dough. Turn dough out on a lightly floured board and knead it, slapping it on the board for 20 minutes. Oil a large bowl and place the dough in it. Turn dough upside down to coat with oil. Cover and place in warm spot to rise until doubled in bulk, about 1 hour.

Punch the dough down and knead again for a few minutes. Pat into a flat round and place on an oiled baking sheet or pizza pan. Beat the egg in a mixing bowl. Add all remaining ingredients and stir to a thick paste. Spread on prepared dough. Once more allow the bread to rise in a warm place for about 1 hour. It will not be quite doubled.

Preheat oven to 450°F. Bake *iflagun* for 10 minutes. Reduce temperature to 375°F. and continue baking until the bread is crusty and sounds hollow when tapped at the bottom.

FLAOUNES   *(G R E E C E)*
Cheese-Mint Pies
                                                      20 PASTRIES

These delicious pastries are traditionally made for Easter.

DOUGH

½ cup oil

1 large egg

4 teaspoons granulated sugar

3 pieces of mastic (see Note 2) (optional)

¼ cup milk, warmed

3½ cups all-purpose flour

1 teaspoon baking powder

¼ teaspoon salt

FILLING

2 cups fresh ricotta cheese

1 cup grated mixed kefalotiri (or Romano) and kasseri (or provolone) cheeses

3 small eggs

3 tablespoons fine semolina

2 tablespoons finely crushed fresh mint

sesame seeds

With an electric mixer, beat the oil with 1 egg until thick. Add 3 teaspoons of the sugar. Pound the mastic with the remaining teaspoon of sugar and add to the batter; then add the warm milk. Sift the flour with the baking powder and salt into a mixing bowl. Gradually add dry ingredients to the oil mixture. Mix by hand when the dough becomes thick. Knead for 5 to 10 minutes, until smooth and elastic. Cover and set aside to rest for about 2 hours.

Preheat oven to 350°F. Combine the ricotta and the grated cheeses in a mixing bowl. Lightly beat the 2 eggs. Remove 3 tablespoons of the beaten egg to a cup for egg wash. Add the rest of the eggs to the cheeses. Stir in the semolina and mint; the filling should be rather thick. Divide the dough into 2 parts and divide each part into 10 balls. Keep covered while working. Roll out each ball into a 6-inch circle as thin as possible. Place 2 tablespoons of the filling in the center of each circle and raise edges to form an oval or boatlike shape, leaving the cheese filling exposed in the center. Add 2 tablespoons water to the reserved beaten egg in the cup and brush the top of the dough with this egg wash. Sprinkle the *flaounes* with sesame seeds. Bake for 20 to 25 minutes, or until the dough is crisp and nicely golden.

Serve hot or cold.

NOTE 1: A more delicate version made in Cyprus has cinnamon instead of mint. Add ½ cup raisins with the cheese; use only cottage or ricotta cheese.

NOTE 2: Mastic is an aromatic resin extracted from the mastic tree, mainly in the island of Chios. It can be found in Greek and Middle Eastern shops.

WINE: Aphrodite (from Cyprus)

LEEK AND CHEESE PIE   (ISRAEL)

SERVES 6

In the past, leeks were considered brain food and were favored by Talmudic scholars.

DOUGH
butter for pan
1 batch of Short Pastry made with
   vegetable shortening (p. 9)

FILLING
12 leeks   pepper
¾ teaspoon salt   ½ cup grated Swiss cheese
2 ounces (½ stick) butter   4 eggs, separated
3 tablespoons flour   bread crumbs

Preheat oven to 350°F. Butter a 10-inch ovenproof dish from which you can serve. Set aside.

On a lightly floured board roll out the dough into a circle large enough to line the bottom and sides of prepared dish. Fit dough into the dish, trim excess dough with scissors, flute edges, pierce bottom in several places with a fork, and refrigerate.

Trim leeks, wash them well, and cut into 1-inch lengths, including tender green parts. Place in a saucepan, add water to cover and the salt, and cook until leeks are almost tender. Drain, but reserve the cooking liquid.

Melt the butter in a small saucepan. Add the flour and stir, while cooking over low heat. Remove from heat and gradually add 1 cup of the reserved cooking liquid. Return to heat and cook the sauce, stirring, until it thickens and starts to boil. Add salt and pepper to taste. Stir in the cheese. Add the egg yolks, one at a time. Place well-drained leeks in the prepared pastry-lined dish. Beat egg whites until stiff and fold into the cheese sauce. Pour or spoon sauce over leeks. Delicately sprinkle with bread crumbs. Bake for 15 to 20 minutes, or until top is golden brown.

Serve immediately.

TIROPITAKIA
Cheese Triangles

(GREECE)

24 TRIANGLES

DOUGH
18 phyllo sheets, 12 x 8 inches
8 ounces (2 sticks) sweet butter,
    melted

FILLING

3 ounces (¾ stick) sweet butter
6 tablespoons flour
2 cups milk
4 egg yolks
pinch of grated nutmeg
2 cups crumbled feta cheese

1½ cups grated kefalotiri or
    pecorino Romano cheese
1½ cups grated Gruyère cheese
¼ cup snipped fresh dill
2 tablespoons minced fresh parsley
freshly ground pepper

Unroll the phyllo sheets on a flat surface. Cover with wax paper, then with a damp towel to prevent drying. Cover the pile of sheets again after removing each one.

Melt 3 ounces butter in a large saucepan over medium-low heat. Add flour, and cook and stir for 3 minutes. Remove pan from heat and gradually pour in the milk, stirring until sauce is smooth and liquid. Return to the heat and cook, stirring constantly, until sauce starts to boil; reduce heat. Cook, stirring, for a few minutes. Beat egg yolks just until blended; pour in 1 cup of the sauce, stirring. Stir egg-yolk mixture into remaining sauce. Return to heat; again stirring constantly, heat to the boiling point. Cook for 2 or 3 minutes; flavor with nutmeg. Remove sauce from heat and pour into a large bowl. Cool.

Stir cheeses, dill, and parsley into cooled sauce; season to taste with pepper. Set aside.

Preheat oven to 325°F. Place 1 phyllo sheet on a clean surface; cut lengthwise into thirds. Brush top surfaces with melted butter. Place 1 teaspoon of the filling in top corner of 1 strip, fold corner over to opposite edge, making a triangle. Continue folding, as you would a flag, keeping the triangular shape with each fold. Place on a buttered baking sheet. Repeat with remaining sheets of phyllo and the filling. Brush finished triangles with melted butter. Bake for 30 to 35 minutes, until golden.

Serve hot. These triangles can be frozen. Thaw, and bake for 35 to 40 minutes.

NOTE: Leftover filling can be reserved for another use. It is excellent mixed with vegetable, rice, and pasta casseroles; bake for about 30 minutes.

DRINK: Ouzo

SPANAKOPITTA DIANA
Spinach Pie

(GREECE)

SERVES 8 TO 10

DOUGH

1 pound phyllo sheets
8 ounces (2 sticks) sweet butter,
    melted

FILLING

8 scallions, chopped
1 ounce (2 tablespoons) butter
4 packages (10 ounces each) frozen
    spinach, or 4 pounds fresh
    spinach
5 eggs, lightly beaten
½ pound feta cheese, crumbled

8 ounces cottage cheese
2 tablespoons semolina
½ cup chopped parsley
½ cup snipped fresh dill
salt and pepper
2 tablespoons olive oil

Unroll the phyllo sheets on a flat surface. Cover with wax paper, then with a damp towel to prevent drying. Cover the pile of sheets again after removing each one.

Sauté the scallions in 1 ounce of butter until tender. Cook the spinach according to package directions if frozen; if fresh, wash thoroughly and cook in the water that clings to the leaves until wilted. Drain, pressing out as much moisture as possible, chop.

Preheat oven to 375°F. Place a baking sheet on the oven shelf. Mix together the scallions, eggs, feta cheese, cottage cheese, semolina, parsley, dill, and chopped drained spinach. Season with salt and pepper to taste. Stir in the oil. Butter a 2-quart decorated ring mold.

Brush 1 phyllo sheet with melted butter, and cut the sheet lengthwise into 2 pieces. Use the pieces to line the ring mold. Allow pastry to extend about ½ inch over the sides of the pan. Fit the sheet down into the pan and over the center opening. Press against the sides of the mold. Repeat with other sheets of pastry, working around the mold in even layers, using half to three-quarters of the pastry sheets. Fill pastry with the spinach mixture. Cut out and discard the disk of pastry covering the center hole. Brush another sheet of pastry with butter and cut into half-moons to fit over the filling. Repeat with several layers, brushing each layer with butter. Draw up the overhanging pieces of dough over the covered filling. Place ring mold on the baking sheet and reduce oven temperature to 350°F. Bake for 1¼ hours, or until golden brown, puffed, and crisp. Let the *pitta* stand in the mold for 5 to 15 minutes before unmolding on a warm platter.

ATHENAEKA TIROPITAKIA (Spinach Triangles). You will need about 2 cups of the *spanakopitta's* filling. Just reduce ingredients of the filling to half. If you still have some leftover, use in an omelet or fill tomatoes which you can bake.

DOUGH

2 cups flour

1 egg

1 tablespoon olive oil

½ teaspoon salt

4 to 8 tablespoons cold water

oil for deep-frying

FILLING

2 cups filling for Spanakopitta
    Diana (see above recipe)

Place flour in a mixing bowl and make a well in the center. Add the egg, olive oil, and salt; mix. Add water gradually to make a workable dough. Knead the dough well on a lightly floured board and divide it into 12 pieces of equal size. Shape each piece into a ball and cover with a towel to prevent drying. Roll out each ball of dough into a thin circle 4 to 5 inches in diameter. Place a heaping tablespoon of filling in the center of each half and fold over, to enclose the filling. Deep-fry the pieces in hot oil until golden and puffy all over. Serve hot or at room temperature.

FILLED KHOUBZ OR PITA BREADS

A meal in Arab countries usually begins with a flat bread or *khoubz*, topped, stuffed, or dipped into some delectable concoction. Wedges of *pita* with a bowl of *baba ganouj, hummus,* etc., are fast becoming usual features at an American cocktail party too, and are, therefore, included here. I am practically addicted to these things. Another favorite of mine are the lamb "pouches" with which one can solve the problem of that leftover roast leg of lamb. They are excellent served as an appetizer or for lunch.

BABA GANOUJ
Eggplant Dip

(ARAB STATES)

SERVES 6 OR MORE

2 medium-size eggplants
2 or 3 garlic cloves, minced
1 tablespoon olive oil
½ teaspoon dry mustard (optional)
¼ teaspoon ground cuminseed
  (optional)

2 to 4 tablespoons tahini sauce
  (sesame paste)
juice of 1 lemon, or more
2 tablespoons minced fresh parsley
black olives
tomato slices

Roast eggplants over direct heat (preferably gas), turning them often until skin is charred. (Eggplants can be roasted in the oven but the flavor will not be authentic.) Slash the eggplants so that the somewhat bitter juice can run out while they are cooling. Peel eggplants; do not wash them. Cut into cubes and place in the bowl of a food processor, or blender. Add remaining ingredients except garnishes. Process until smooth but not liquid. Place in a serving bowl, garnish with olives and tomato slices, and serve at room temperature with heated pitas.

HUMMUS BI TAHINI
Chick-Peas with Tahini

(ARAB STATES)

SERVES 6 OR MORE

1 cup dried chick-peas, soaked
  overnight
2 or 3 garlic cloves, minced
½ cup tahini (sesame paste)
pinch of salt

2 tablespoons olive oil
juice of 2 lemons, or more
2 tablespoons chopped fresh
  parsley
paprika

Boil soaked chick-peas until soft. Cool and drain. Reserve a few chick-peas for garnish. Place the rest in the bowl of a food processor, or blender, together with the garlic, tahini, salt, and olive oil. Turn the machine on and pour in the lemon juice while processing. Stir in the parsley. Turn into a serving bowl and sprinkle with paprika. Serve with pita breads.

KOFTA PITA
Lamb Pouches

(ARAB STATES)

SERVES 6 OR MORE

DOUGH

6 Pita breads (p. 163)

FILLING

3 onions, finely chopped
1½ ounces (3 tablespoons) butter
1 tablespoon oil
2 cups finely chopped cooked lamb
½ cup white raisins

¼ cup dried currants
½ cup pine nuts (pignoli)
1 tablespoon tomato paste
2 garlic cloves, minced
½ cup minced fresh parsley

Sauté onions in butter until almost brown. Add all remaining filling ingredients and heat through. Cut the breads into halves and fill each pouch with some of the lamb mixture.

Before serving, heat pouches in a preheated 350°F. oven for 15 minutes.

AGET KARNABET
Cauliflower and Egg Pie

(LEBANON)

SERVES 6

1 medium-size cauliflower
2 medium-size potatoes
2 tablespoons oil
2 garlic cloves
2 ounces (½ stick) butter, plus
　　butter for casserole
½ cup plain yogurt, drained
3 eggs, separated

salt and pepper
pinch of grated nutmeg
pinch of ground cloves
1 tablespoon lemon juice
¼ teaspoon cream of tartar
1 tablespoon bread crumbs
1 tablespoon grated pecorino
　　Romano

Core the cauliflower and separate into flowerets. Blanch flowerets in boiling water for 5 to 6 minutes. Drain. Boil potatoes until tender, then cool and peel. Heat the oil in a skillet. Add garlic and cauliflowerets. Shake skillet while cooking, tossing cauliflower lightly. Sauté evenly. Set aside.

Preheat oven to 400°F. Butter a 6-cup oval casserole. In the bowl of a food processor, or a blender, purée cauliflowerets and potatoes together with the butter, yogurt, and egg yolks. Turn into a mixing bowl. Add salt and pepper to taste, the nutmeg and cloves. Beat egg whites with lemon juice and cream of tartar, until stiff. Fold into the purée. Spoon mixture into prepared casserole; smooth the top. Combine bread crumbs and cheese, and sprinkle on top of casserole. Bake for 30 to 35 minutes, until top is puffed and golden brown.

UÇLU YUMURTA
Peaked Pie

(TURKEY)

SERVES 4

1 tablespoon oil
1 tablespoon butter
1 large onion, chopped fine
4 medium-size potatoes, boiled and
    mashed

1 cup plain yogurt
¼ cup grated Parmesan cheese
pinch of grated nutmeg
salt and pepper
4 eggs

Preheat oven to 350°F. Heat oil and butter in a skillet. Add onion and sauté until soft and translucent. In a mixing bowl combine mashed potatoes, sautéed onion, yogurt, half of the Parmesan, the nutmeg, and salt and pepper to taste. Butter a shallow baking dish and spread the potato mixture in an even layer in the dish. Make 4 hollows in the potato mixture, using the round end of one of the eggs. Separate the eggs carefully. Drop a yolk into each of the hollows, reserving the whites. Beat the whites with a pinch of salt until stiff but not dry; add remaining Parmesan. Spread most of the whites gently over the potato mixture and egg yolks. Drop about 1 tablespoon of whites on top of each egg to make a peak. Bake for about 10 minutes, or until top is golden brown.

Divide into 4 wedges, each one including an egg yolk.

PITA IMAM   (TURKEY)
Priest's Pita

This is my adaptation of a famous Turkish dish. According to the legend, when the Imam (priest) came to dinner and tasted the eggplants, he swooned.

DOUGH

4 Pita breads (p. 163)

FILLING

4 medium-size eggplants
½ cup olive oil
2 medium-size onions, minced
2 green peppers, minced
2 red peppers, minced
3 garlic cloves, minced

4 medium-size tomatoes, quartered
2 tablespoons minced fresh parsley
3 tablespoons pine nuts (pignoli)
2 tablespoons unflavored bread
    crumbs

Place the pita breads under the broiler for a few minutes until slightly warm. Cover them with a napkin and cool.

Remove stems from eggplants and cut them into cubes without peeling. Heat the oil in a large frying pan and sauté eggplants over low heat for a few minutes. Add onions, peppers, and garlic. Cook for 10 minutes. Add tomatoes and cook for 5 minutes. Add remaining ingredients, mix, and remove from heat. Let the mixture cool.

Open a pocket in each pita and insert some of the eggplant mixture into it. Serve the breads cut into wedges.

PSAROPITTA
Striped Bass Pie

(G R E E C E)

SERVES 6

DOUGH

12 phyllo sheets

6 ounces (1½ sticks) butter, melted

6 teaspoons fine bread crumbs,
   approximately

FILLING

5 cups loosely packed spinach
   leaves, washed and trimmed

2 tablespoons finely chopped
   parsley

1 tablespoon olive oil

¼ cup finely chopped shallots

¾ cup drained shucked oysters,
   about 12

salt and freshly ground pepper

6 center-cut fillets of striped bass,
   skinned, about ½ pound each

Unroll the phyllo sheets on a flat surface. Cover with wax paper, then with a damp towel to prevent drying. Cover the pile of sheets again after removing each one.

Preheat oven to 450°F. Combine spinach with parsley. Heat the oil in a heavy skillet, and add the shallots. Cook briefly, stirring. Add the spinach mixture and cook, stirring, until spinach is wilted. Add the oysters and salt and pepper to taste. Cook briefly. Chop mixture finely with a heavy knife. Brush a baking dish with butter.

Brush 1 phyllo sheet with melted butter; sprinkle with crumbs. Top with another sheet, and brush with butter and sprinkle with crumbs as before. Arrange 1 fish fillet down the center of the pastry. Spoon a tablespoon or so of the oyster and spinach mixture over it. Sprinkle with salt and pepper. Lift up the 2 phyllo sheets and fold over and over to enclose the fillet. Tuck edges under. Repeat with remaining phyllo sheets, fillets, and spinach mixture.

Brush the top of each package with melted butter and arrange them on a buttered baking sheet. Bake for 20 minutes, or until packages are well puffed and browned.

WINE: White Retsina

SAYYADIAH   *(TUNISIA)*
Fish and Rice Pie

SERVES 6 TO 8

Tunisians believe that fish brings good luck. On the day of a wedding, a newly married couple will step on a large fish to ensure happiness for themselves and keep the evil eye at bay.

3 tablespoons olive oil	1 ounce (2 tablespoons) butter
3 onions, minced	1½ tablespoons flour
salt	2 tablespoons lemon juice
cuminseed	salt
allspice	nutmeg
2½ cups water	2 eggs
2 pounds sea bass, haddock, cod, or halibut, preferably whole, dressed	saffron
	1 tablespoon very fine bread crumbs
1 cup uncooked rice	

Heat the oil in a deep skillet large enough to contain the fish. Add the onions and cook, covered, over very low heat, stirring often and adding a little water if mixture gets dry. Onions should remain white and become creamy. This will take about 45 minutes. Add salt, cuminseed, and allspice to taste, and pour in 2½ cups water. Bring to a boil and simmer for 10 minutes. Add the fish, bring liquid again to a boil, and immediately reduce heat. Cook fish for 15 to 20 minutes, or until done. If you are using an entire fish it will take a little longer. In any case, remove fish, and let it cool. Skin and bone the fish, and flake it; reserve.

Pour the liquid in which the fish was cooked into a bowl. Return 1½ cups of it to the skillet. Reserve remaining liquid. Bring the liquid in the skillet to a boil, and pour in the rice in a steady stream so that liquid continues boiling. Cover the skillet and reduce heat to a simmer. Cook until the rice is done and water has been absorbed.

Melt 1 tablespoon butter in a saucepan, add the flour, stir, and cook for a few minutes. Remove from heat. Measure 1 cup of the remaining liquid; if you do not have enough, add milk to make up the difference. Slowly pour liquid into the butter and flour mixture, stirring constantly, until sauce is smooth and liquefied. Add lemon juice and cook over low heat until sauce thickens and starts to boil. Add a pinch of salt and a pinch of nutmeg. Remove sauce from heat.

Beat the eggs, add the cooked rice and saffron to taste, and stir well. Preheat oven to 400°F. Butter a springform pan. Sprinkle with bread crumbs. Pour in half of the rice mixture and spread it on bottom and sides to form a shell. Combine the sauce with the flaked fish and fill the shell with it. Cover with remaining rice. Dot with remaining butter. Bake for 15 minutes. Reduce temperature to 375°F. and cook for 25 minutes longer, until top is golden brown.

KAVOUROPITTA
Crab-Meat Pies

(GREECE)

4 TO 5 DOZEN TRIANGLES

DOUGH

1 pound phyllo sheets (about 20
    leaves)
6 ounces (1½ sticks) butter, melted

FILLING

2½ ounces (5 tablespoons) butter
1 small onion, chopped
2 tablespoons all-purpose flour
2 cups milk
1 tablespoon chopped parsley
1 tablespoon snipped dill
½ cup chopped cooked mushrooms
1 tablespoon chopped shallots,
    cooked in butter

2 hard-cooked eggs, chopped
dash of Tabasco
1 tablespoon Worcestershire sauce
1 teaspoon sherry
pinch of basil
salt
1½ pounds lump crab meat
½ cup or more fine bread crumbs

Unroll the phyllo sheets on a flat surface. Cover with wax paper, then with a damp towel to prevent drying. Cover the pile of sheets again after removing each one.

Melt 2½ ounces butter in a skillet, and sauté onion until golden. Stir in the flour; cook briefly. Remove from heat and add the milk slowly; mix until smooth. Add all remaining filling ingredients. If the consistency is too loose, add more bread crumbs; if too thick, add more milk.

Preheat oven to 350°F. Working with 1 sheet at a time, cut the phyllo sheets into strips 3 inches wide. Brush a strip with melted butter. Place 1 full teaspoon of the crab-meat mixture in the top corner of the strip. Fold corner over to opposite edge, making a triangle. Continue folding as you would a flag, keeping the triangular shape with each fold. Place on an ungreased baking sheet. Repeat with remaining sheets of phyllo and the filling. Brush top of each triangle with melted butter. Bake for 15 to 20 minutes, until pastry is crisp and lightly browned.

Leftover filling can be frozen or put into an omelet.

NOTE: These can also be shaped into squares or into elegant puffs. To make puffs, put the filling into a 6-inch-square pile of buttered phyllo dough. Bring up the edges to enclose filling. Turn the bundle over and place in a buttered muffin cup. Bake for 20 minutes.

WINE: White Samos

MIDYA BOREG
Mussel Pie

(IRAN)

SERVES 6 TO 8

SHELL

1 cup olive oil

3 cups minced onions

1½ cups uncooked rice

¼ cup dried currants

pinch of ground allspice

pinch of ground cuminseed

salt

2 cups water

½ cup pine nuts (pignoli)

butter for pan

FILLING

3 dozen mussels

1 tablespoon minced fresh parsley

1 tablespoon snipped fresh dill

2 tablespoons lemon juice

2 teaspoons cornstarch

1 cup plain yogurt

Heat the oil in a heavy saucepan. Add onions and sauté until wilted. Stir in the rice, currants, spices, and salt to taste. Pour in the 2 cups water, stir, and bring to a boil. Reduce heat, cover saucepan, and cook for 20 minutes, or until liquid is absorbed and rice is tender. Stir in pine nuts. Set aside.

Scrub mussels, remove beards, and discard any with broken shells. Place mussels in a large skillet and set over heat. As soon as they start to open, remove mussels and discard shells. Discard any mussels that do not open. Remove shells over a cup or bowl to keep the mussel liquid. Filter the liquid through a double layer of moistened cheesecloth.

Preheat oven to 350°F. Butter a 10-inch ovenproof dish from which you can serve. Spread half of the rice on the bottom of the dish. Push some up around the edge to make a "shell." Arrange mussels on the rice and sprinkle with parsley, dill, and lemon juice. Reserve 4 or 5 tablespoons of the rice, and spread the rest on top of the mussels. Dribble a few tablespoons of the reserved mussel liquid over the rice. In a small saucepan combine the corn-starch, 1 tablespoon of the mussel liquid, and the yogurt. Place over moderate heat, stirring constantly, and remove as soon as sauce starts to bubble. Add the reserved tablespoons of rice and spread this mixture evenly over pie. Bake for 25 to 30 minutes, until top is lightly browned.

Serve hot.

BAGHALA POLO ALLA VILMA GARABAGHE
Chicken, Rice, Lima Beans, and Dill (I R A N)
SERVES 8 TO 10

Polo, which is a rice dish usually cooked in a shallow rimmed casserole and unmolded to show its crusty bottom, embodies the subtle tradition of Iranian cooking. This is my adaptation of a dish made for me by my friend, Vilma Garabaghe. She prepared this for me upon her return from Iran where she had lived for a while. I prefer to bake this in a springform pan, which works well for the unmolding operation.

1½ ounces (3 tablespoons) butter
1 tablespoon oil
1 large onion, sliced
4 chicken legs and thighs, cut into 4
    pieces
3 whole chicken breasts, skinned,
    each half cut into 2 pieces
3 cups water
1 teaspoon salt

3 cups uncooked rice
good pinch of ground saffron
2 eggs
1 cup snipped fresh dill
1½ packages (10-ounce packages)
    frozen lima beans, defrosted, or
    1 pound shelled fresh fava
    beans
very fine bread crumbs

VELOUTÉ SAUCE

1 tablespoon butter	salt and pepper
1 tablespoon flour	nutmeg
1 cup chicken stock	

In a heavy top-of-the-stove casserole heat 1 ounce of the butter and the oil. Sauté onion in it until lightly colored. Remove onion to a bowl. Add the chicken pieces and cook until nicely browned. You may have to do this in batches. Remove cooked chicken to the bowl with the onion.

Pour 3 cups of water into the casserole in which the chicken was cooked, add 1 teaspoon salt, and bring to a boil. Add rice in a slow stream so that water continues to boil. Stir rice, boil for 5 minutes, and drain. Place half of the rice in a mixing bowl. Add saffron and stir until rice is nicely colored; stir in 1 egg and set aside. Return the second half of the rice to the casserole, add the dill, the lima beans or fava beans, and the remaining egg. Mix well. Set aside.

Make the velouté sauce: Melt the butter in a small saucepan. Add flour and cook, stirring, for 5 minutes. Remove from heat and gradually add chicken stock, stirring constantly until sauce liquefies. Cook sauce over low heat until it starts to bubble. Add salt, pepper, and nutmeg to taste. Remove sauce from heat.

Butter an 11- to 12-inch springform pan with remaining 1 tablespoon butter. Coat pan lightly with bread crumbs. Spoon the yellow rice in and with a spatula spread it evenly on bottom and sides of pan. Spoon some of the sauce over. Arrange the chicken pieces and onion on the rice. Dribble some more of the sauce over. Stir the rest of the sauce into the rice, dill, and bean mixture. Spoon this mixture into pan and smooth the top. Cover the pan tightly with aluminum foil. Drape another piece of foil at the bottom of pan to catch drippings. Set pan in a cold oven, and set temperature to 350°F. Bake for 45 minutes to 1 hour, until rice is tender when tasted. Remove foil during the last 10 to 15 minutes to let the top brown lightly.

Carefully unmold on a serving plate and decorate with sprigs of dill and parsley, if desired.

B'STILLA   *(M O R O C C O)*
Chicken Pie

SERVES 12

"Food for the Gods" is the most frequently used expression to describe this unique pie from Morocco. The cuisine of this country is so interesting and has been so enthusiastically introduced to us by Paula Wolfert, in her book *Couscous and Other Good Food from Morocco* that no further introduction is necessary. The following recipe was given to me personally by Mrs. Wolfert and it is with her kind permission that it is included here. To eat it in the Moroccan style, dig three fingers into the hot pastry and pick out the chicken.

FILLING

4 pounds chicken legs and thighs

3 cups water

4 ounces (1 stick) unsalted butter

1 cup chopped fresh parsley

1 large onion, grated

1 cinnamon stick, 3 inches

1 scant teaspoon freshly ground
    pepper

¾ teaspoon ground ginger

¼ teaspoon ground turmeric

¼ teaspoon ground saffron

few sprigs of fresh coriander,
    chopped

pinch of salt

¼ cup vegetable oil

1 pound blanched whole almonds

½ cup powdered sugar

2 teaspoons ground cinnamon

4 ounces (1 stick) unsalted butter

¼ cup fresh lemon juice

10 eggs, well beaten

salt

DOUGH

4 ounces (1 stick) unsalted butter,
    clarified

½ to ¾ pound phyllo pastry sheets,
    preferably fresh

powdered sugar (garnish)

cinnamon (garnish)

Combine first 12 ingredients in Dutch oven, cover, and bring to a boil over high heat. Reduce heat and simmer for 1 hour, stirring occasionally.

Heat oil in a large skillet, add almonds, and brown lightly. Drain well. Transfer to the bowl of a food processor fitted with the steel blade and mix until coarsely broken. Add sugar and cinnamon and grind until almonds are coarsely chopped. Add 2 ounces butter and mix, using about 3 on and off turns. Set mixture aside.

Remove chicken and set aside to cool slightly. Discard cinnamon stick and any loose bones from Dutch oven. Reduce remaining liquid to about 1¾ cups by boiling rapidly. Reduce heat to simmer and add lemon juice. Pour eggs into simmering sauce and stir constantly until cooked and slightly congealed. They should become curdy but not too dry. Using a slotted spoon, transfer eggs to a baking sheet or jelly roll pan. Refrigerate until completely cool. Add salt to taste. Shred chicken into pieces about 1½ inches long; discard bones and skin.

Preheat oven to 425°F. Brush a deep, 12- to 14-inch pan with a little clarified butter. Cover pan with 1 sheet of phyllo, keeping unused sheets covered with damp towel. Drape several more sheets, one at a time, into the pan, allowing half of each of the sheets to extend beyond pan edges and remaining half to cover bottom of pan evenly, and drizzling only a little butter between layers.

Spread chicken pieces evenly on the bottom of the pan. Cover with well-drained eggs. Sprinkle with almond-sugar mixture. Working as quickly as possible, cover layers with all but 4 of the remaining pastry sheets, brushing each lightly with butter. Fold extended sheets over top of the pie to cover and enclose. Place remaining 4 sheets over the top, lightly buttering each. Tuck neatly around outer rim and lightly brush top with butter. Pour any remaining butter around edges. Bake for 10 minutes.

Remove pan from oven and shake pan to loosen pie. Run spatula around edges and carefully pour off excess butter. Invert onto the large buttered baking sheet, return to oven, and continue baking for 10 to 20 minutes, until crisp and golden brown.

Invert onto a serving plate and dust lightly or liberally with powdered sugar. Run crisscross lines of cinnamon over top and serve immediately.

Recipe can be halved.

ÖRDEK BÖREK   (T U R K E Y)
Sidqi Efendi Duck Pie

SERVES 6 TO 8

Sidqi Efendi was the author of a nineteenth-century Turkish cooking manual.

DOUGH

12 phyllo sheets	sugar
½ pound butter (2 sticks), melted	ground cinnamon or allspice
1 egg yolk	½ cup mixed chopped walnuts and
2 tablespoons duck cooking liquid	pine nuts (pignoli)

FILLING

1 duck, 4 pounds, including liver,	2 tablespoons oil
heart, and gizzard	2 onions, chopped
½ cup plain yogurt	2 cups uncooked rice
1 sprig of dill, snipped	1 teaspoon salt
1½ ounces (3 tablespoons) butter	½ cup raisins

Cut the duck into 8 pieces. Place them in a glass or pottery bowl. Combine yogurt and dill and pour it over duck. Refrigerate for 6 hours or overnight.

In a skillet large enough to hold the duck pieces in 1 layer, heat 2 tablespoons of butter and 1 tablespoon oil. Add onions and sauté until translucent. Drain duck pieces and add them to the skillet. Cook, turning pieces often, to sear them, for 15 to 20 minutes. Add enough water to barely cover the duck. Simmer covered for 40 minutes. Remove duck with a slotted spoon. Reserve the cooking liquid but do not strain it (there should be about 4½ cups liquid).

Cut liver, heart, and gizzard into small pieces. Heat remaining 1 tablespoon butter and 1 tablespoon oil, and sauté the cut-up giblets. Add the rice, stir to mix with oil and butter, and pour in 4 cups of the reserved duck cooking liquid. Scoop in the onions with a slotted spoon. Add salt. Bring liquid to a boil, then simmer until rice is tender and liquid is absorbed. Add raisins. Set aside.

Unroll the phyllo sheets on a flat surface. Cover them with a sheet of wax paper, then with a damp towel to prevent drying. Cover the pile of sheets again while working with one at a time.

Preheat oven to 350°F. Brush an 11-inch pie pan, 1½ to 2 inches deep, with some of the melted butter. Line with 1 phyllo sheet, or 2 sheets if one is not large enough to cover the pan. Brush pastry with melted butter and top with 5 more phyllo sheets, each one brushed with melted butter. Mix the egg yolk with 2 tablespoons duck cooking liquid to make an egg wash. Brush top layer of pastry with more than half of the egg wash. Sprinkle with a touch of sugar and some cinnamon or allspice. Dribble a few drops of duck broth over all, and scatter half of the chopped nuts on top. Cover with 4 more layers of phyllo, each sheet brushed with melted butter.

At this point you can bone the duck or leave it as it is (in the original dish the duck was not boned), and lay the pieces on the sheets of phyllo. Cover with the rice mixture and scatter the remaining nuts all over. Cover with remaining phyllo sheets, each one brushed with butter. Fold all the over-hanging pastry over pie. Do not worry if dough breaks. Brush top with butter and paint with remaining egg wash. Bake for 45 minutes, then in-crease the temperature to 425°F. and bake for 15 minutes longer, until top is crisp and deep gold in color. Sprinkle with a little more sugar and cinnamon or allspice.

Pass plenty of paper napkins if you do not bone the duck.

BOUREKAKIA ME KREAS   *(G R E E C E)*
Meat Pie

SERVES 8 TO 10

DOUGH

8 phyllo sheets   3 ounces (¾ stick) butter, melted

FILLING

1 medium-size onion, chopped   freshly ground pepper
1 ounce (2 tablespoons) butter   2 garlic cloves, minced
1½ pounds lean beef, ground   2 teaspoons bottled mint sauce
1 pound pork, ground   2 tablespoons chopped fresh
3 eggs   parsley
⅔ cup milk   plain yogurt (optional)
1½ cups soft white bread crumbs   chopped green onion (optional)
2 teaspoons salt

Unroll phyllo sheets on a working surface. Cover them with a sheet of wax paper, then with a damp cloth towel, to prevent drying. Cover the pile again while working with 1 sheet at a time.

Sauté onion in butter until golden. Add meats and cook until done. Set aside. Beat together eggs, milk, bread crumbs, salt, pepper to taste, garlic, mint sauce, and parsley until well blended. Add the onion and meat mixture and combine thoroughly.

Preheat oven to 375°F. Brush 1 phyllo sheet with melted butter and top with remaining sheets, each one brushed with butter. Spoon meat mixture along one edge of the sheets as you would for a strudel. Fold phyllo sheets over to enclose filling; tuck in ends. Place on a buttered baking sheet and brush top with more of the melted butter. Bake for 30 to 40 minutes, until phyllo is crispy and golden brown.

Transfer to a serving dish. Cut into 1-inch slices. If desired, accompany with yogurt mixed with chopped green onion.

WINE: Hymettus Red

KNISHES   *(ISRAEL)*
Filled Pastries

8 TO 10 PASTRIES

Whenever I ask Israeli friends for a "classic" recipe for knishes . . . *oi vei!* I get the most confused answers! The variations are incredible. But that is natural if one remembers the variety of nationalities flowing, at one time or another, into the land of milk and honey. So I am offering three of the best choices. The dough and first filling come from Felicia Berg, an accomplished cook. The second filling is a "secret recipe" my friend Janet Neipris will give to whoever asks. The third filling is my own adaptation of a "classic" recipe.

DOUGH

2 cups flour
1 tablespoon sugar
1 egg, beaten
1 tablespoon vinegar
½ to ¾ cup water

¾ cup or more vegetable shortening
1 egg yolk beaten with 2 to 3
     tablespoons water
oil for baking sheets

POTATO FILLING

3 pounds potatoes, boiled in salted
    water
1 cup chicken fat
1 large onion, minced

3 garlic cloves, minced
1 tablespoon Kosher salt
pepper

BEEF FILLING

¼ cup chicken fat
3 onions, chopped
2 pounds lean beef chuck, ground

2 eggs, lightly beaten
4 to 5 tablespoons bread crumbs
salt and pepper

KASHA AND CHICKEN FILLING

2 tablespoons chicken fat or
    shortening
1 large onion, chopped
2 eggs
1 cup kasha (buckwheat groats)

2 cups boiling chicken broth or
    water
¾ teaspoon salt
¾ cup chopped cooked chicken

For the dough: In the bowl of a food processor combine flour and sugar. Add the egg, vinegar, and enough water to gather the mixture into a ball. Wrap and chill for 15 minutes.

For the potato filling: Peel potatoes and purée through a food mill into a mixing bowl. Add 2 to 3 tablespoons chicken fat. Melt remaining fat in a skillet and sauté onion and garlic over medium heat until soft and translucent. Add to potatoes and stir in the salt and pepper to taste; mix well.

For the beef filling: Melt the chicken fat in a skillet. Add onions and cook until translucent. Add beef and brown. Pour off excess fat, and turn beef into a mixing bowl. Add eggs, bread crumbs, and salt and pepper to taste.

For the kasha and chicken filling: Melt 1 tablespoon of the fat or shortening in a skillet. Add onion and sauté until lightly browned. Remove onion with a slotted spoon and set aside; reserve the skillet. Beat the eggs in a mixing bowl. Add kasha. Heat the skillet in which the onion was cooked and add kasha; you may need a little more fat if skillet is dry. Cook over low heat, stirring, until grains separate. Add the boiling broth or water and the salt. Cover and cook over low heat for 15 minutes, or until liquid is absorbed. Do not overcook otherwise kasha becomes mushy. Add sautéed onion, the chopped chicken, and remaining fat. Heat through. Remove from heat and cool.

Preheat oven to 400°F. Brush the required baking sheets with a little oil. Roll dough into a ¼-inch-thick rectangle. Spread half of the shortening all over the dough. Fold dough over into thirds and then in half to form a square. Wrap and chill for 15 minutes. Roll dough out again into a rectangle and repeat spreading with shortening and folding. Refrigerate for 15 minutes. Repeat once more and roll the dough ¼ inch thick. Cut into pieces 6 x 9 inches.

With some of the filling form a patty 3 inches in diameter and 1½ inches thick. Place the patty at bottom edge of cut rectangle. Brush outer edge of dough with the egg and water mixture. Fold dough over filling and press edges to seal. If too much dough remains on the sides of filling, trim a little. Knishes should be well stuffed. Paint top with egg and water mixture. Repeat until all filling and dough are used. Place knishes on prepared baking sheets. Bake for about 35 minutes, or until knishes are lightly browned.

YOĞURTLU KEBAB (TURKEY)
Yogurt and Meat Pita

SERVES 4

I was introduced to this delicious dish by my Turkish friend, Gul Wines. She invited me to lunch at the Divan restaurant in New York, and Chef Ishmael kindly told me how the kebab was made. This is my own adaptation and I hope it will meet the approval of the chef. I serve these kebabs for lunch with great success. Wine is used here although in Moslem countries alcoholic beverages are forbidden.

DOUGH

4 Pita breads (p. 163)

FILLING

1½ pounds boneless lamb, cut into small cubes

¾ pound lean beef, cubed

1 leek

½ cup wine

4 tablespoons bottled mint sauce

1 garlic clove, sliced

1 sprig of fresh dill, snipped, plus additional dill for garnish

pepper

1½ cups plain yogurt, or more

3 tablespoons olive oil

salt

In a shallow glass or china dish, place the lamb cubes on one side and the beef cubes on the other. Trim the leek, wash well, and cut into thin slices. Wash again, and drain. Combine the wine, mint sauce, garlic, leek slices, dill, pepper to taste, and 2 to 3 tablespoons of yogurt. Pour over the meat, cover the dish, and refrigerate overnight.

Remove meats from the marinade. Reserve the marinade. Place all of the beef and half of the vegetables of the marinade in the bowl of a food processor. Chop coarsely; remove the mixture. Do the same with only half of the lamb cubes and half of the remaining vegetables. Make tiny patties with the lamb you have just chopped and set aside.

Pat the cubed lamb dry. Heat 2 tablespoons oil in a skillet. Quickly sauté the lamb cubes over high heat; add salt and pepper to taste. Remove cubes to a dish and keep warm. Add remaining oil to the skillet and carefully sauté the tiny lamb patties; do not overcook. Add salt and pepper to taste. Remove patties to a dish and keep warm. Sauté ground beef until meat loses its color; add salt and pepper and 3 to 4 spoonfuls of the liquid of the marinade.

Preheat oven to 400°F. Toast pita breads on both sides. Place on an ungreased cookie sheet. Spread as much yogurt as you wish on the pita breads, and top with equal amounts of ground beef, lamb patties, and lamb cubes. Bake for 10 to 15 minutes, until top starts to bubble.

Garnish with snippets of dill. Serve immediately.

NOTE: Sometimes I grind the meats, make patties, set the meat in a dish, flatten the ground beef, and pour the marinade over. It saves time when I am ready to assemble the kebab.

I also make this with roast lamb. I grind some meat and cube the rest. It is a good way to use leftovers.

MELITZANOPITTA

Eggplant Pie

DOUGH

6 phyllo sheets

4 ounces (1 stick) sweet butter, melted

6 tablespoons fine bread crumbs

FILLING

1 large eggplant, about 1 pound, cut into ½-inch cubes

salt

2 tablespoons olive oil

½ pound lean lamb, ground

1 medium-size onion, minced

3 garlic cloves, minced

2 large tomatoes, peeled, seeded, chopped

fine bread crumbs

¼ teaspoon orégano

pinch of mint

pinch of cinnamon

1 large egg

freshly ground pepper

2 tablespoons minced fresh parsley

1 tablespoon snipped fresh dill

8 tablespoons grated Parmesan cheese

salt

2 ounces (½ stick) sweet butter, at room temperature

2 tablespoons flour

1 cup milk, scalded

lemon wedges

1½ cups plain yogurt

Unroll the phyllo sheets on a flat surface. Cover with wax paper, then with a damp towel to prevent drying. Cover the pile of sheets again after removing each one.

Place eggplant cubes in a colander, sprinkle lightly with salt, and let stand for 20 minutes. Pat dry with paper towels. Heat olive oil in a skillet and add eggplant. Cook covered over high heat, shaking pan occasionally, for about 5 minutes; reduce heat and cook uncovered, stirring constantly, for 5 minutes longer. With a slotted spoon remove eggplant to a bowl and set aside.

Add lamb to skillet; sauté over high heat until light brown, about 5 minutes. Drain lamb on paper towels and reserve. Pour off all but 1 tablespoon pan juices from the skillet. Put onion and garlic in the skillet and sauté over high heat until soft, about 3 minutes; reduce heat to medium. Add tomatoes; cook until juices evaporate. Add 2 tablespoons bread crumbs and the drained lamb; cook, stirring constantly, for 3 minutes. Stir in orégano, mint, and cinnamon; mix, and cool to room temperature. Stir in the egg, a good grinding of fresh pepper, the parsley, dill, and 2 tablespoons Parmesan cheese. Taste and adjust seasonings. Reserve.

Melt 1 ounce butter in a small saucepan over medium heat until foam subsides. Add flour; cook and stir for 1 minute. Remove from heat and gradually pour in milk; stir until smooth. Cook over low heat, stirring constantly, until sauce thickens and starts to boil. Season to taste with pepper. Stir ⅓ cup of the sauce into the eggplant. Freeze remaining white sauce for another use.

Preheat oven to 400°F. Butter a baking sheet 12 x 16 inches. Place 1 phyllo sheet on a clean surface; brush top with melted butter. Top with 2 additional phyllo sheets, brushing each with melted butter. Sprinkle with 4 tablespoons of the bread crumbs. Top with 3 remaining phyllo leaves, brushing each with melted butter. Sprinkle with remaining 2 tablespoons bread crumbs and 2 tablespoons Parmesan cheese. Spread half of the eggplant mixture in the middle of the phyllo. Sprinkle with 2 tablespoons of the cheese. Spoon meat mixture over cheese; spread remaining eggplant over meat mixture. Sprinkle with remaining cheese. Fold phyllo leaves to enclose filling, strudel fashion; tuck ends underneath. Brush top phyllo sheet with butter. Carefully transfer to the buttered baking sheet. Bake for 20 minutes. Cover lightly with foil. Bake for 20 minutes longer, or until puffed and brown. Let stand for 5 minutes.

Transfer to a serving dish. Garnish with mint leaves, if used, and lemon wedges. With a serrated knife cut the pie into 1½-inch slices. Serve with chilled plain yogurt.

WINE: Red Retsina

ZAMPONPITTA   *(GREECE)*
Ham Pie

24 PIECES

This *pitta*, cut in the traditional diamond shape, is an ideal dish to serve for a party.

DOUGH

12 phyllo sheets

4 ounces (1 stick) butter, melted

FILLING

1 ounce (2 tablespoons) butter

2 onions, finely chopped

12 ounces fresh mushrooms, finely chopped

2½ pounds cooked lean ham, ground

1½ teaspoons grated lemon rind

3 eggs, lightly beaten

½ pound Samsoe or Gruyère cheese, shredded

2 tablespoons minced fresh parsley

2 slices of white bread, crumbled

¼ teaspoon grated nutmeg

salt and pepper

Unroll the phyllo sheets on a flat surface. Cover with wax paper, then with a damp towel to prevent drying. Cover the pile of sheets again after removing each one.

Melt 1 ounce butter in a large frying pan. Sauté onions until soft and translucent. Add mushrooms and cook until liquid released by mushrooms has evaporated. Cool. In a mixing bowl, combine remaining filling ingredients. Add the mushroom mixture and mix well.

Preheat oven to 350°F. Butter a baking pan 9 x 11 inches. Line prepared pan with 1 phyllo sheet. Brush with melted butter and top with 5 more sheets, each one brushed with melted butter. Let phyllo overhang edge of pan. Spoon in ham and cheese mixture; smooth top. Fold in overhanging dough. Cover with remaining phyllo dough, brushing each sheet with melted butter. With a razor blade or sharp knife, score top layers of the *pitta* in diamond shapes about 2 inches wide and 3 inches long. Bake for 45 minutes, or until the top is golden and crisp.

Cool slightly. Cut through completely following the scoring. Serve warm or at room temperature.

WINE: Lindos

SAMBOUSEK   (LEBANON)
Veal and Eggplant Pie

SERVES 8

Lebanon, once considered the Paris of the Middle East, is an unusual coun-try. Its capital, Beirut, was an international meeting place for a segment of affluent European society with a sprinkling of intellectuals from all over the world. Because Lebanon was a French mandate on and off until 1944, French influence is still very much apparent. It is not unusual to find a pie made not with the ever-present lamb, but with veal, which is rare in this part of the world. This pie is a fine example of Lebanese cuisine.

DOUGH

8 phyllo sheets   4 ounces butter (1 stick), melted

FILLING

1 large eggplant, peeled and cubed   salt and pepper
coarse or Kosher salt   1 medium-size onion, chopped
1 pound boned shoulder of veal,   ¼ cup dry white wine
    cubed   1 cup chopped peeled tomatoes
flour   pinch of basil
1½ ounces (3 tablespoons) butter   3 tablespoons minced fresh parsley
¼ cup olive oil   2 tablespoons plain yogurt
2 garlic cloves, mashed   2 eggs, lightly beaten

Unroll the sheets of phyllo on a flat surface. Cover them with a sheet of wax paper, then with a damp towel to prevent drying. Cover the pile of sheets again while working with one at a time.

Set eggplant in a colander and sprinkle with coarse or Kosher salt. Let it rest for 30 minutes, then drain.

Dredge veal with flour; set aside. In a skillet large enough to hold all the veal in 1 layer, heat butter and 1 tablespoon oil. Add the veal and sauté until meat loses its pinkness. Add garlic, and salt and pepper to taste; stir. With a slotted spoon remove veal to a platter. Add onion to the skillet and sauté until translucent. Return veal to skillet, add the wine, and let it evaporate over medium heat. Add tomatoes and basil, cover, and simmer for 25 min-utes, or until meat is tender. With a slotted spoon remove mixture to the bowl of a food processor, or to a blender, and chop fine. Set aside.

In the same skillet in which the veal was cooked, heat remaining oil and sauté the eggplant cubes. You may need additional oil. Stir often. Add parsley at the end; set aside. In a mixing bowl combine 1 tablespoon flour, the yogurt, and beaten eggs. Add chopped meat and the eggplant cubes.

Butter a 10-inch pie pan. Preheat oven to 375°F. Line the prepared pan with 1 sheet of phyllo; brush with melted butter. Top with 3 more sheets, each one brushed with butter. Let dough hang over the edge of the pan. Spoon meat mixture in and smooth top. Cover with remaining phyllo sheets, each one brushed with melted butter. Turn in overhanging pastry and brush again with butter. Bake for 35 to 40 minutes, until top is crisp and nicely browned.

KREATOPITTA KEFALLINIAS *(GREECE)*
Cephalonian Spicy Meat Pie

12 SQUARES

This is a traditional pie from the island of Cephalonia in the Ionian Sea. It is prepared for two occasions: the Feast of the Ascension and the last day of Carnival before the beginning of Lent.

DOUGH

16 phyllo sheets	4 ounces (1 stick) butter, melted

FILLING

1 leg of lamb, 4 pounds, boned (reserve bones)	3 cups cooked rice
½ cup lemon juice	1 cup crumbled Feta cheese
2 onions	½ cup chopped parsley
1 small carrot	4 leaves of fresh mint, chopped
1 celery rib	pinch of orégano
1 parsley sprig	1 garlic clove, slivered
1 dill sprig	pinch of ground cinnamon
4 peppercorns	peel of 1 lemon, shredded
3 medium-size potatoes	salt and pepper
1 large carrot	2 tablespoons tomato paste
¼ cup oil	3 hard-cooked eggs, sliced

Cut lamb into small cubes, place cubes in a bowl, and pour in lemon juice. Toss to mix and set aside. Place lamb bones in a kettle. Cut a cross in the base of 1 onion and add to the kettle. Also add the small carrot, the celery, parsley, dill, and peppercorns. Cover with cold water and simmer for 1 hour. Strain, and reserve 1 cup of the broth.

Meanwhile, parboil the potatoes and the large carrot, peel them, and dice them. Chop the second onion. Heat the oil in a skillet. Add chopped onion and sauté until translucent. Add lamb cubes and cook until brown; do not overcook. Remove lamb and onion to a mixing bowl, and add potatoes, carrots, rice, cheese, herbs, garlic, cinnamon, and shredded lemon peel. Season with salt and pepper to taste. Stir the tomato paste into ½ cup of the reserved lamb broth, and pour into the lamb mixture; mix well. If the mixture seems dry, pour on some more broth.

Unroll phyllo sheets on a working surface. Cover them with a sheet of wax paper, then with a damp cloth towel, to prevent drying. Cover the pile again while working with 1 sheet at a time.

Generously butter a pie pan 9 x 12 x 3 inches and set aside.

Preheat oven to 350°F. Lay 1 phyllo sheet in the prepared pan. Brush with melted butter. Top with 7 more sheets, each brushed with butter. Make sure the dough fits properly in the pan. Spoon the meat mixture in, and smooth top. Place the sliced eggs across the top. Cover with the remaining phyllo sheets, brushing each one with butter. Fold in the dough hanging over the sides. Using a razor or a sharp knife, score the top into diamonds or squares. Do not cut through. Bake for 40 to 50 minutes, reducing heat to 325°F. during the last 10 minutes.

Let the pie stand for 15 minutes before cutting through.

VARIATIONS: Other meats such as pork or veal can be substituted for lamb.

In season, fresh tender artichokes, quartered and braised in oil and garlic, are added to the filling.

WINE: Red Samos

BADEMJAN BI LAHMA   (I R A N)
Lamb, Cheese, Eggplant, and Tomato Pie
SERVES 8

I like to bake this pie in a springform pan with decorated bottom and sides. When it is unmolded, it looks like a glorious cake. However, it is better not to unmold it, because the juices running at the bottom will dampen the crispness of the dough, which is the essence of this dish. Sometimes, after removing the ring of the pan, I put the pie back in the oven if the sides look damp, but it is not always necessary to do so.

DOUGH

18 phyllo sheets

6 ounces butter (1½ sticks), melted

FILLING

1 ounce (2 tablespoons) butter

1 large onion, chopped

¼ cup olive oil

1 medium-size eggplant

¼ teaspoon poultry seasoning

1 pound boneless lamb, cubed

salt and pepper

1½ tablespoons tomato paste

1 cup lamb broth

¼ teaspoon ground turmeric

1 large egg, beaten

½ cup cottage cheese, drained

3 tablespoons bread crumbs

½ cup chopped fresh parsley

1 cup Béchamel Sauce made with 1 tablespoon butter, 2 tablespoons flour, 1 cup milk, and ¼ cup cream (see method p. 17)

1 cup shredded mild cheese (mozzarella, Munster, Gouda, etc.)

1 large tomato, peeled, sliced, and drained

10 to 12 cherry tomatoes

Unroll the phyllo sheets on a flat surface. Cover them with a sheet of wax paper, then with a damp towel to prevent drying. Cover the pile of sheets again while working with one at a time.

Heat 1 tablespoon butter in a skillet. Add the onion, cover, and cook over low heat until onion is very soft. Remove onion with a slotted spoon to a mixing bowl. Reserve skillet. Preheat oven to 350°F. Pour 2 tablespoons oil into a baking sheet (11 x 16 inches), with sides, and coat the bottom. Peel eggplant and cut into ¼-inch slices. Place eggplant slices in a single layer on the sheet and turn once, so that both sides are coated with oil. Sprinkle with poultry seasoning. Bake eggplant for 15 to 20 minutes, until the slices are soft when pierced with a fork. Do not overcook. (The eggplant slices can be sautéed in a skillet but I feel that they absorb too much oil that way.) Cool eggplants and dice. Add to the bowl with the onion. Set aside.

Heat remaining butter and oil in the skillet in which you cooked the onion. Sauté lamb cubes over high heat until brown. Sprinkle with salt and pepper. Remove lamb from skillet and chop it. (This can be done in a food processor.) Return meat to skillet. Stir tomato paste into the broth and add broth to lamb. Cover and simmer until liquid is absorbed. Add turmeric, mix well, and let the meat mixture cool.

Add the egg to the bowl with onion and eggplant; mix. Add cottage cheese, bread crumbs, parsley, and cooked lamb, mixing after each addition. Stir in the béchamel sauce. Taste for seasoning. Butter a 9-inch springform pan. Preheat oven to 375°F.

Brush 1 phyllo sheet with melted butter and line bottom and sides of buttered pan. Repeat with 5 more sheets, brushing each one with butter. Let dough hang over the edges of the pan. Pour half of the filling into the pan, smooth the top, and scatter half of the shredded cheese over all. Cover with 6 more phyllo sheets, brushing each one with butter. Add the rest of the filling, scatter remaining cheese on top, and place tomato slices over the cheese. Cover with remaining phyllo sheets, brushing each one with butter. Fold in the overhanging dough and brush again with butter (you may need additional melted butter). Bake for 45 to 50 minutes, until top is crisp and nicely browned.

Serve hot, decorated with cherry tomatoes.

SFEEHA

Lamb Pies

(LEBANON)

18 PIES

These little pies are sold in Lebanon the same way pizza and hot dogs are sold in the United States. They make wonderful appetizers. Also they can be prepared in advance.

DOUGH

1 package active dry yeast
1¾ cups lukewarm water (105° to 115°F.)
4 cups all-purpose flour

1 teaspoon salt
¼ cup olive oil
oil for baking sheet

FILLING

1 tablespoon oil
⅓ cup pine nuts (pignoli)
1 pound boneless lamb from the shoulder, coarsely ground
1 cup minced onions
1 cup chopped, peeled, and seeded tomatoes
⅓ cup minced fresh parsley

3 tablespoons minced fresh mint
1 green pepper, trimmed and finely chopped
salt
¼ teaspoon cayenne pepper
¼ teaspoon black pepper
¼ teaspoon ground allspice
yogurt (optional)

Dissolve the yeast in 1 cup of lukewarm water. Set in a warm place for 10 minutes.

In a mixing bowl combine flour and salt. Make a well in the center and add the yeast mixture and the oil. Stir in remaining water while gathering the ingredients into a dough. Turn onto a floured board and knead the dough until smooth and elastic. Form into a ball and place in a lightly oiled bowl. Cover and set in a warm place to let the dough rise until doubled in bulk, about 1 hour.

Heat the oil in a skillet and lightly sauté the pine nuts. Remove with a slotted spoon to a paper towel to drain. Combine all the ingredients of the filling in a mixing bowl and add the sautéed nuts. Set aside.

Punch down the dough and divide into 18 pieces. Form each piece into a ball. Cover with a bowl and let them rest for 20 minutes.

Preheat oven to 500°F. Lightly oil 2 baking sheets. Roll 1 ball at a time into a 4-inch circle. Spread 2 tablespoons of the meat mixture in the center of the circle. Bring the dough up in 4 corners, just to hold the filling, like a cup, without enclosing it. The middle should remain open. Place the circles on the prepared baking sheets and bake for 15 to 20 minutes, until dough is nicely browned.

Serve hot with yogurt. However, *sfeeha* can be eaten at room temperature or reheated.

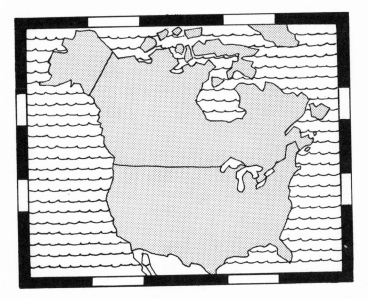

North America

United States · Canada

A real delight in food preparation and an appreciation of interesting cuisines has reached almost every section of the population in the United States. In the past, only the wealthy who floated across the Atlantic on deluxe ships experienced the sophisticated preparations of European chefs and the exotic fares of the East. It took some time before the rest of us (who in many cases were eating our own good food in our ethnic neighborhoods) had the curiosity or need to taste the new things. Although recipes for a variety of savory pies have appeared in the earliest cookbooks of this country, most of middle America fed on simple fare and variety was unimportant. Meat and potato was the preference. Corn breads, pancakes, and some meat pies of English origin were the nearest things to savory pies. Pizza came with the Italian immigrants. Pizza parlors mushroomed all over, as one can see traveling across country.

Meat pies became even more popular in the United States around the

199

early part of the century. Before this time, many Americans outside of the big cities were people of the land—farmers, cattlemen, and settlers. Although food was relatively abundant, the housewife had to help plant, harvest, slaughter, and grow the staples needed for the family. Her life was arduous; her job, as the cook of the household, was to supply sufficient food to feed everybody, including temporary harvest hands. She generally cooked in large quantity, to last for several days. She made bread but had little or no time for fancy dishes. The sauce or broth from meats was soaked up with hunks of bread broken from the loaf. Cakes and sweets were luxuries reserved for special occasions.

But by the late 1920s the rural population began to invade towns and cities, no longer content to stay on the farm. Urban women now bought most of the staples and could spend more hours cooking. Meat pies, also a vehicle for preserving and reusing meat, and cakes, were added to the menu.

In the early 1930s the Great Depression hit. Women were faced with the necessity of cooking only the food that was the cheapest and most filling. Potatoes, onions, flour, and beef fat were inexpensive. The beef fat could be browned, and flour was added together with water, salt, and pepper, to be cooked to the consistency of heavy cream. This was delicious and filling; a few boiled potatoes and onions mixed in made it even better. When topped with a bread cover—biscuits, dumplings, or piecrusts—the whole thing was even more filling and still cheap. If beef could be afforded, this was browned with the fat, and incorporated in the recipe, making the main-dish pie an important dish.

It is interesting to note that during the depression, many men who rode the rails across the country looking for work were fed and survived on this type of food, handed out by compassionate housewives through the back door of American homes.

America, being so open to new things, has in the last decade become so well acquainted with the French *quiche*, Greek *spanakopitta*, Turkish *börek*, and tarts of many kinds, that they have all been adopted here. Imaginative Americans have devised their own versions of these delectable specialties. The savory pies of today are adaptable for every occasion. Like wine from California, they can proudly cross the oceans with the imprint "made in U.S.A."

In this chapter there are many recipes invented by me or given to me by my friends. One can argue about their "American authenticity." I feel that since I live in this country and I use native or readily obtainable ingredients, these recipes belong to the U.S. cuisine, which is constantly being enriched by the output of new immigrants.

NEW ENGLAND CORN BREAD MARGUERITE
(UNITED STATES)
SERVES 6 TO 8

When Charles Dickens came across corn bread during his travels in America, he had this to say: "hot corn bread—almost as good for the digestion as a kneaded pin cushion." Well, in those days he might have been right. Nowadays, we have a much lighter way of mixing corn flour, or cornmeal, to permit the dough to rise and bake to a light and airy consistency. The result is pleasing and digestible.

A simple wedge of corn bread with a dollop of butter, a dribble of molasses, and a steaming cup of fresh coffee provides a delicious way to start or finish a day.

butter for pan	½ cup sugar
1 cup stone-ground cornmeal	2 eggs
2 cups all-purpose flour	1 ounce (2 tablespoons) butter,
¾ teaspoon salt	melted
1 tablespoon baking powder	1½ cups milk, warmed

Preheat oven to 450°F. Butter a 9-inch iron skillet. Combine all dry ingredients but sugar. In a mixing bowl beat the sugar and eggs together. Add the flour mixture and continue beating until well blended. Pour in the melted butter and the milk, and beat quickly for 5 minutes longer. Heat the skillet and pour the corn mixture in. Bake for about 30 minutes, or until a toothpick inserted in the middle of pan comes out clean.

NOTE: For a lighter corn bread use cake flour instead of all-purpose flour.

HERBED CORN BREAD. Reduce sugar to 2 tablespoons. Add ¼ cup minced fresh dill or dried dillweed, or ¼ cup minced parsley, and 2 tablespoons chopped pimiento.

CRACKLING CORN BREAD. Add 1 cup pork or chicken cracklings.

CARROT CORN BREAD. Add ½ cup grated carrot.

SHAKER HERB CAKES   *(UNITED STATES)*

12 TO 14 PIECES

1 cup hot milk
2 tablespoons sugar
¼ teaspoon salt
1 ounce (2 tablespoons) butter, at
    room temperature
1 package active dry yeast
1 egg, well beaten

1 tablespoon dried herb mixture
    (a blend of nutmeg, sage,
    rosemary, and caraway seed)
4 cups unsifted all-purpose flour,
    approximately

Pour the milk into a mixing bowl. Stir in the sugar, salt, and butter; cool to 105° to 115°F. Add the yeast. Stir until dissolved. Add the egg, herb mixture, and 2 cups of flour. Beat until smooth. Add enough of the remaining flour to make a stiff dough that will not stick to the bowl. Turn dough out on a floured board and knead until smooth and elastic. Gather into a ball and place in a greased bowl. Turn to grease the top. Let rise in a warm place, covered, until doubled in bulk, about 1 hour.

Punch dough down and shape into small flat rounds, or 1 large round. Place in a greased pan or pans. Cover and let rise again, for about 45 minutes.

Preheat oven to 425°F. Bake the cakes for about 15 minutes. Reduce heat to 375°F. and bake for 20 to 25 minutes longer, or until nice and crusty.

SOPAIPILLAS   *(UNITED STATES)*
Fried Bread Puffs

16 SQUARES

These crisp fried squares of dough never fail to please. I first discovered *sopaipillas* during one of the many journeys taken with my husband, Harold, and my cat, Salome, crossing the United States from East to West by car. The bread puffs were served to us as an appetizer with drinks in a very simple Tex-Mex restaurant in the town named after Buffalo Bill: Cody, Wyoming.

2 cups all-purpose flour
½ teaspoon salt
½ teaspoon baking powder
½ package active dry yeast
½ tablespoon vegetable shortening

2 tablespoons warm water
¼ cup lukewarm milk (105° to
  115°F.)
oil for deep-frying

Place the flour, salt, baking powder, yeast, and shortening in the bowl of a food processor. Turn the machine on and off a few times. Without a machine, mix by hand as you would a *pâte brisée* (p. 6). Add the water, and process briefly. With the machine running, pour the milk through the tube. Stop as soon as a ball forms on the blades. Remove dough from machine, cover it, and let stand for 10 minutes.

Divide dough into 2 parts. Keep one covered, and roll the other into a thin sheet. Cut into 3-inch squares. Roll and cut the second piece of dough.

Heat oil to the smoking point, 380°F. Stretch each piece of dough with your fingers, just before dropping it into the oil. This will give the *sopaipilla* a wavy shape. After *sopaipillas* have been in oil for about a minute, turn each pie immediately on the other side. Cook pieces, turning often, until golden brown. Drain on paper towels. Reheat oil for each new batch.

Serve hot, alone, or with cheese and sausages such as *chorizo* or Italian *salamino* (small salame).

NOTE: In Cody they told me that the *sopaipillas* should be dropped into the hot oil top first instead of bottom first. They tend to puff better.

SWEET POTATO BISCUIT (*UNITED STATES*)
10 TO 12 BISCUITS

1 cup flour
1 tablespoon baking powder
½ teaspoon salt

3 tablespoons shortening
1 cup mashed cooked sweet potato
½ cup milk

Preheat oven to 350°F. Sift flour, baking powder, and salt together into a mixing bowl. Chop in shortening; mix lightly. Add sweet potato. Gradually stir in the milk. Turn dough out on a floured board and roll out to a sheet ½ inch thick. Cut into 3-inch circles. Bake for 20 to 30 minutes. Serve hot.

YUKON PANCAKES   *(CANADA)*

SERVES 6 TO 8

James Beard includes pancakes in the bread family together with pizzas. For me pancakes are nothing but *pizzette*, or small pizzas, and the following are among the most interesting of the species. This is an adaptation of the famous sourdough pancakes so much loved by the early miners of the Yukon. The sour taste is mitigated in this version, but the time required to have the batter ready is the same—2 days. You do not have to work at it all the time, but you cannot forget it altogether.

2 potatoes, peeled and cubed
1 cup water
1 package active dry yeast
½ cup lukewarm water (105° to 115°F.)
2 tablespoons sugar

1 cup sifted flour
1 egg, beaten
2 tablespoons melted shortening
½ teaspoon baking soda
1 tablespoon hot water

Put potatoes and 1 cup water in a saucepan and boil for 25 minutes. Mash the potatoes in the cooking water until you have a smooth, thick liquid. Cool. Dissolve the yeast in the lukewarm water. Combine yeast with the potato mixture, add the sugar and flour, and mix. Turn into a bowl, cover, and let stand in a warm place for 24 hours. The mixture will ferment overnight.

Add the egg, shortening, and baking soda dissolved in the hot water, to the fermented batter. Mix well. Pour out spoons of batter to make pancakes of the desired size on a lightly greased frying pan. Brown on both sides. Serve with ham or bacon and syrup.

SONA KARA'S BÖREKS   *(UNITED STATES)*

18 BÖREKS

One of the delightful features of my friend Sona's elegant dinner parties are her little *böreks*. She usually serves them with cocktails while guests admire the sparkling Mondrian landscape of Roosevelt Island from her terrace, which hangs over the East River in Sutton Place. Ideal finger food, these triangles can be made in advance and they freeze extremely well. Just pop them in the oven directly from the freezer and they will come out crisp and crunchy as if they were just made.

DOUGH

12 phyllo sheets, about ½ pound   4 ounces (1 stick) butter, melted

FILLING

¼ pound Fontina cheese, shredded   1 large egg, lightly beaten
¼ pound Munster cheese, shredded   3 tablespoons minced fresh parsley
1½ cups cottage cheese   pepper

Unroll the phyllo sheets on your working counter; cover them with a sheet of wax paper, then with a damp towel to prevent drying. Cover the pile of sheets again while working with one at a time.

In a mixing bowl, combine cheeses, egg, parsley, and pepper to taste; mix well.

Spread out 1 phyllo sheet, brush with butter, cover with a second sheet, and cut these lengthwise into 3 strips. Place 1 teaspoon of the filling in a corner of each strip. Working with 1 strip at a time, fold the phyllo over the filling, enclosing it and forming a triangle, folding as you would a flag. Tuck the loose end in neatly. Place on a buttered baking sheet. Continue making triangles in the same manner until all phyllo is used.

Preheat oven to 375°F. Brush each *börek* with melted butter. Bake for about 20 minutes, or until pastry is crisp and golden.

Serve them hot.

VARIATION: Substitute ½ pound Feta cheese for the Fontina and Munster cheese. Add 3 ounces cream cheese and reduce cottage cheese to 1 cup.

HERB PUFFS   *(U N I T E D   S T A T E S)*
                                                    20 SMALL PUFFS

This dough is very versatile. One can make small puffs for cocktails, big puffs to be served as a first course, or the dough can be spooned in little mounds one next to the other, in a circular arrangement, until a cake pan is completely filled. In the first two cases the puffs are filled with herb cheese or tarragon filling. In the large "cake" the cheese in the dough is increased. It is served without filling, as a bread.

DOUGH

1 batch of Puff Shell Dough (p. 11) pinch of cayenne pepper
2 small sage leaves, minced, or ½
  teaspoon crumbled dried sage

HERB CHEESE FILLING

8 ounces cream cheese, at room ¼ teaspoon garlic powder
  temperature   1 tablespoon minced fresh parsley

Preheat oven to 425°F. Mix sage and cayenne into the dough. Fill a pastry bag with the dough and form small puffs on a baking sheet with nonstick coating. Space the puffs 2 inches apart. Bake for 15 to 20 minutes, or until puffs are golden. Remove pan from oven and turn puffs out on a rack. When cool enough to handle, make a slit on one side of each puff. Let them cool completely.

  In a small bowl, cream the cheese and add garlic powder and parsley; mix well. Fill the puffs with the cheese mixture.

8 BIG PUFFS

DOUGH

1 batch of Puff Shell Dough (p. 11) pinch of grated nutmeg
½ cup grated Gruyère cheese   pinch of Hungarian paprika
¼ cup grated Parmesan cheese

TARRAGON FILLING

½ cup fresh tarragon leaves   1½ cups milk
¼ cup dry vermouth   salt
2 ounces (½ stick) butter   white pepper
4 tablespoons flour   1½ teaspoons prepared mustard

Preheat oven to 425°F. Mix cheeses, nutmeg, and paprika into the dough. Fill a pastry bag with the dough and form 8 puffs on a baking sheet with nonstick coating. Space the puffs 2 inches apart. Bake for 20 to 25 minutes, or until golden. Remove pan from the oven and turn puffs out on a rack. When cool enough to handle, make a slit on one side of each puff. Let them cool completely.

  In a small enameled cast-iron saucepan, place the tarragon leaves and vermouth. Boil for a few minutes, then simmer very gently for 10 minutes. Remove from heat.

Heat 3 tablespoons of the butter in a saucepan. Add flour. As soon as butter and flour froth together, remove from heat and add the milk, a little at a time, stirring until sauce liquefies. Heat again and cook the sauce, stirring constantly, until it starts to puff. Remove from heat and stir remaining butter into the sauce. Strain the vermouth and tarragon mixture, pressing the leaves to extract as much liquid as possible. Add this liquid to the white sauce gradually so that it remains of the right consistency to fill puffs. Stir in salt, a pinch of white pepper, and the mustard. Cool the sauce to warm. I like these puffs with the filling still warm, so I fill them at the last minute. The sauce can be kept warm over a pot of hot water.

1 PUFF CAKE

1 batch of Puff Shell Dough (p. 11)

Preheat oven to 425°F. Butter a 10-inch springform pan. Prepare the dough as for the big puffs, but increase the quantity of Parmesan cheese to ½ cup and add a pinch of pepper. Spoon the dough in little mounds one next to the other in a circular pattern until the cake pan is completely filled. Bake for 25 to 30 minutes, or until cake is well puffed and golden. Remove from pan, and serve warm with soups or cheeses, or just as a bread.

RUSTIC TRUFFLE PUFF   *(UNITED STATES)*

SERVES 2 TO 4

2 eggs, lightly beaten
½ cup flour, sifted
½ cup milk
¼ cup grated sharp Cheddar cheese

2 to 3 teaspoons truffle paste
2 ounces (½ stick) butter

Preheat oven to 425°F. Mix together all ingredients except butter. Melt the butter in a 9-inch iron skillet and pour the batter in. Cook for 5 minutes, then put in the oven and bake for 15 to 20 minutes.

Serve immediately.

NOTE: 1 small fresh truffle can be used. If so, grate the truffle and mix into batter.

BERT GREENE'S RAPÉE ALSACE PIE
(UNITED STATES)
SERVES 6

This is Mr. Greene's adaptation of an Alsatian recipe. Bert Greene is an enthusiastic writer and researcher on American food. He is the author of two books on the subject, and at work on a third one called *Honest America Bert Greene*. He very kindly sent me this recipe, which he felt belonged in the "melting pot" of American cuisine.

6 slices of bacon
2 ounces (½ stick) butter
1 small onion, minced
4 eggs
½ garlic clove, crushed
2 tablespoons minced parsley
1¼ cups grated Swiss or Jarlsberg
    cheese

¾ cup heavy cream
good pinch of grated nutmeg
½ teaspoon salt
¼ teaspoon freshly ground pepper
3 large potatoes
chopped parsley for garnish

Preheat oven to 400°F. Fry bacon in a skillet until very crisp; drain on paper towel. Crumble bacon; reserve. Remove all but 2 tablespoons bacon fat from the skillet; add 1 ounce butter. Add the onion; sauté over low heat until soft but not brown.

In a mixing bowl beat the eggs. Add the garlic, parsley, 1 cup cheese, the cream, nutmeg, salt, and pepper. Stir in the onion.

Peel and chop or grate the potatoes, one at a time; squeeze out as much moisture as possible. Stir potatoes into the egg mixture. (Handle the potatoes quickly to prevent their turning brown.)

Grease an 11- or 12-inch baking dish with remaining 1 ounce butter; place in the oven until the butter foams. Spread half of the potato mixture in the dish; sprinkle with half of the reserved bacon. Repeat layers; sprinkle with remaining cheese. Bake until golden brown and puffed, about 35 minutes. Garnish with parsley.

AZTEC PIE (UNITED STATES)

SERVES 4

From the northwest corner of New Mexico comes this specialty; pies like this were made as far back as 1519.

DOUGH

8 large Tortillas (p. 249)

FILLING

6 ounces cream cheese, at room temperature

3 green peppers, roasted and peeled

salt

⅔ cup cream

Preheat oven to 350°F. Reserve 2 tortillas. In a deep baking dish, place alternate layers of remaining tortillas, cheese, and strips of peppers until all these ingredients are used. Add salt to the cream and pour it over mixture. Place the 2 reserved tortillas on top of pie. Bake for 20 to 25 minutes.

NOTE: Prepare the peppers by roasting them in the oven until the skins blister. Drop them in a paper bag. After 5 minutes, peppers can easily be peeled with the fingers. Discard seeds and ribs. Tear peppers lengthwise into strips. Instead of green peppers, one can use hot chiles. This way is more authentic, but *hot*.

FRESH CORN PIE (CANADA)

SERVES 6

DOUGH

1 tablespoon butter for pan

½ batch of Short Pastry (p. 9)

FILLING

2 eggs

2 cups cooked fresh corn kernels

salt and pepper

1 scant tablespoon flour

1 cup milk

4 ounces Canadian Cheddar cheese, shredded

fine dry bread crumbs

Preheat oven to 350°F. Butter a 9-inch pie pan. Roll out the dough to a circle large enough to line the pan. Fit dough into pan, turn over the edge all around, and crimp it. Break the eggs into a mixing bowl, and beat well. Add the corn, salt to taste, and grind in fresh pepper from the mill. Mix. Spoon flour into a mixer cup, and gradually pour in the milk, stirring to prevent lumps. Cover the cup and shake well. Pour into the corn mixture. Add cheese, and stir. Sprinkle a layer of bread crumbs on the dough, and pour in the filling. Sprinkle top with a light coating of bread crumbs. Bake for about 45 minutes, or until top is set, puffy, and golden brown.

TART CREOLE   (UNITED STATES)
SERVES 6 TO 8

DOUGH
1 batch of American Piecrust (p. 8)

FILLING

2 tablespoons oil	2½ tablespoons flour
4 tomatoes, skinned, coarsely chopped, and drained	½ cup broth or bouillon
½ cup chopped onion	¼ cup dry white wine
¾ cup diced green pepper	1 tablespoon Worcestershire sauce
1 cup sliced mushrooms	salt and pepper
1 ounce (2 tablespoons) butter	4 eggs
	1 tablespoon minced fresh parsley

Preheat oven to 375°F. Heat oil in a large skillet. Add tomatoes, onion, green pepper, and mushrooms. Cook until vegetables are soft but not mushy; most of the liquid should have evaporated. Set aside.

Melt the butter in a saucepan. Add flour and cook, stirring, until mixture just starts to color. Remove from heat and gradually add broth or bouillon and the wine. Cook stirring until the sauce thickens and starts to puff. Add Worcestershire sauce, and salt and pepper to taste. Pour this sauce into the vegetable mixture and stir to combine ingredients well.

Roll the dough out to a sheet large enough to line a deep 9-inch pie pan. Fit it into the pan and crimp the edges. Pour the filling into the dough-lined pan. Beat the eggs, season with salt and pepper, add the parsley, and mix. Pour egg mixture over the vegetables. Bake for about 45 minutes, or until top is nicely puffed and golden in color.

WINE: California Riesling

LENTIL POT PIE   *(U N I T E D   S T A T E S)*

SERVES 6

This recipe goes back to the year 1898. I found it in an old American volume, *Mrs. Rorer's Vegetable Cookery and Meat Substitutes.* It is a tasty and healthy dish and a good substitute for meat dishes.

DOUGH

1 batch of Short Pastry (p. 9)

FILLING

2 cups cooked lentils, drained	1 tablespoon minced fresh parsley
¼ cup fine-chopped Brazil nuts	pinch of marjoram
1 small onion, minced	salt and pepper
2 teaspoons peanut butter	1 bay leaf

Preheat oven to 375°F. Put lentils in a mixing bowl and add remaining ingredients except bay leaf. Toss to mix and taste for seasoning. Lightly oil a deep pie dish and turn the lentil mixture into it. Bury the bay leaf in the middle. Roll the dough out into a circle large enough to cover the pie, and fit it over the filling. Seal dough all around edges of pie dish. Make decorations with scraps of dough if you wish. Make 4 decorative vents on top of pie to allow steam to escape. Bake for about 40 minutes, or until top is golden brown.

CALIFORNIA TARTLETS   *(U N I T E D   S T A T E S)*

6 TARTLETS

DOUGH

butter for pans	1 egg white, lightly beaten
1 batch of Pâte Brisée I (p. 6)	

FILLING

½ pound Jerusalem artichokes	½ teaspoon prepared mustard
juice of 1 lemon	½ cup shredded crab meat
2 teaspoons salt	1 hard-cooked egg, sliced
1 cup mayonnaise	6 parsley sprigs
1 teaspoon minced parsley	

Butter 6 round tartlet tins, about 3½ inches across. On a floured board roll out the pâte brisée to a sheet ⅛ inch thick. Cut out 6 rounds, and use them to line the bottom and sides of the buttered tins. Trim excess dough with scissors and pierce the bottom of the dough with a fork. Chill for 30 minutes. Preheat oven to 400°F.

Line the dough with aluminum foil and fill with beans or rice to prevent dough rising unevenly. Bake for 10 minutes. Remove foil and reserve beans and rice for another use. Brush the dough with egg white and bake for 10 minutes longer. Remove from oven and cool.

Peel Jerusalem artichokes and drop them into a bowl of water mixed with half of the lemon juice. Bring 2 quarts water to a boil; add remaining lemon juice and the salt. Drop in the Jerusalem artichokes. As soon as water returns to a boil, drain vegetables. Refresh under cold water and drain. Dice vegetables.

In a mixing bowl, combine mayonnaise with parsley and mustard. Add the Jerusalem artichokes and the crab meat. Fill tartlet shells with the mixture. Decorate each tartlet with 1 slice of egg and a little sprig of parsley.

WINE: California Green Hungarian

GLORIA SAFFRON'S BELL PEPPER QUICHE
(UNITED STATES)
SERVES 6

DOUGH

butter for pan

1 batch of Pâte Brisée I (p. 6)

FILLING

1 to 2 ounces (2 to 4 tablespoons) butter or margarine

1 large onion, sliced

2 medium-size sweet red peppers, cut into strips

½ medium-size green pepper, cut into strips

1 garlic clove, minced

2 eggs, lightly beaten

2 slices of baked ham, ¼ inch thick, cut into small cubes

1 cup grated Parmesan cheese

¾ cup heavy cream

Preheat oven to 350°F. Butter a 9-inch pie pan. Roll the dough out into a circle large enough to cover the bottom and sides of prepared pan. Fit dough into pan, and trim excess dough with scissors. Flute edges, and pierce the bottom of the dough with a fork. Line with foil and fill with beans or rice to keep dough from rising unevenly. Bake for 15 to 20 minutes.

Melt butter or margarine in a skillet. Add onion and sauté until it turns gold, but not brown. Remove with slotted spoon to a bowl. Add more butter to pan if necessary and sauté red and green peppers until tender, adding the garlic after a couple of minutes so that it is sautéed but not browned. Set aside. Pour eggs into the bowl with the onion slices and add ham, cheese, and cream. Reserve a few red and green pepper strips for decoration. Add remainder to the bowl of filling. Stir well and pour mixture into the baked pie shell. Decorate with reserved pepper strips. Bake for about 30 minutes, or until a toothpick inserted in the middle comes out clean.

Serve at room temperature or slightly warm.

WINE: Cassis Rosé

ROARING BROOK GREEN TOMATO PIE KARA
(*U N I T E D   S T A T E S*)
SERVES 6

One day my friend Gisele Kara and I were exploring the autumnal garden of her lovely house in Roaring Brook Lake, New York, when she stopped in front of a vine bearing a bunch of shiny green tomatoes. "What can one do with those?" she said. "The weather has turned and they will not ripen." "Oh," I answered, "let's pick them and make a pie. We shall call it 'Roaring Brook Green Tomato Pie.'" And here it is!

DOUGH

butter for pan	1 batch of American Piecrust (p. 8)

FILLING

1½ ounces (3 tablespoons) butter	salt and pepper
1 large onion, sliced	8 to 10 green tomatoes, sliced
¼ cup Marsala wine or cream sherry	½ cup sugar
	pinch of ground allspice

Preheat oven to 425°F. Butter a 9-inch pie pan. Roll out half of the dough into a circle large enough to line bottom and sides of prepared pan. Fit dough into the pan, and pierce the bottom of the dough with a fork. Chill for 30 minutes.

Melt 2 tablespoons of the butter in a skillet. Add the onion and cook covered over very low heat for about 45 minutes. Stir occasionally. Add the Marsala wine or sherry, a little at a time, while cooking. Let the wine evaporate at the end. Season with salt and pepper to taste. Cool.

Place tomatoes in a colander and sprinkle with a little salt. Combine sugar and allspice. Dry tomatoes with paper towels and place in the dough-lined pan. Sprinkle with the sugar mixture and spread the cooked onion on the top. Dot with remaining butter. Roll out remaining dough and cover the pie. Trim excess dough with scissors. Seal edges all around in a decorative fashion. Make a funnel in the center of the pie to allow steam to escape. Bake for 15 minutes. Reduce temperature to 375°F. and continue to bake for 40 minutes longer. Cover pie loosely with aluminum foil if it starts to brown too much.

Cool before slicing.

CURLY QUICHE   *(UNITED STATES)*

SERVES 4 TO 6

I cannot resist a beautiful bunch of curly, crinkly chicory. The white parts at the bottom make a delicious salad; the green tops are ideal for a pie.

DOUGH

1 baked 9-inch tart shell, made of
    Pâte Brisée II (p. 7)

FILLING

1½ cups grated Gruyère cheese	8 strips of prosciutto, 1 inch wide
2 tomatoes, sliced	3 eggs
pinch of basil	½ cup milk
3 cups loosely packed blanched	½ cup light cream
curly chicory (green tops only)	salt and pepper

Preheat oven to 375°F. Sprinkle 1 cup of the cheese on the bottom of the pie shell. Arrange tomato slices on top, and sprinkle with basil. Arrange chicory all over. Place prosciutto over chicory like the spokes of a wheel. Beat eggs lightly. Add milk, cream, and salt and pepper to taste, and pour into the quiche. Bake for 25 to 30 minutes, or until top is puffed and nicely browned.

ROLLED TORTA RUSTICA ALLA JEAN HEWITT
(U N I T E D   S T A T E S)

SERVES 8 TO 10

Jean Hewitt doesn't need an introduction. She has been giving us her delicious and well-planned recipes from the pages of the *New York Times, Family Circle*, and her own books for quite some time. This is an adaptation of one of her recipes published in the *New York Times Magazine.* It is with her kind permission that I use her name and the recipe.

BATTER

2½ ounces (5 tablespoons) butter, plus butter for pan
½ cup flour
½ teaspoon salt
pinch of white pepper
2 cups milk
5 eggs, separated

FILLING

1 ounce (2 tablespoons) butter
4 shallots, finely chopped
4 medium-size fresh mushrooms, chopped
1 tablespoon dried mushrooms, soaked and chopped
1 cup chopped cooked spinach, squeezed rather dry
½ cup chopped cooked endive, squeezed rather dry
1 cup chopped ham
1 tablespoon prepared Dijon mustard
pinch of grated nutmeg
8 ounces cream cheese, at room temperature
salt and pepper

Preheat oven to 400°F. Butter a baking sheet or jelly-roll pan 10 x 15 inches, with sides, line with wax paper, and butter the paper. Sprinkle lightly with flour. Melt 2½ ounces butter in a saucepan. Blend in the flour, salt, and pepper. Cook briefly, stirring with a wire whisk. Remove from heat and gradually add the milk, stirring until sauce liquefies. Return to heat and cook sauce, stirring constantly, until it thickens and starts to boil. Let it puff 2 or 3 times. Beat the egg yolks just to break and mix. Add a little of the hot sauce, continue beating, and pour all of the egg mixture into the bulk of the sauce. Return to medium heat and cook, stirring, for 1 minute only. Do not boil. Set aside. Stir once in a while to cool.

Beat the egg whites until stiff but not dry and fold into the sauce. Pour the mixture into the prepared pan and smooth top with a spatula. Bake for 25 to 30 minutes, until well puffed and lightly browned.

While the sponge roll cooks, prepare the filling. Melt 1 ounce butter in a skillet. Add shallots and sauté until soft. Add fresh mushrooms and cook until they release their liquid. Add dried mushrooms, spinach, and endive. Cook briefly just to heat through. Add the ham, mustard, and nutmeg; stir, and cook briefly just to heat through; remove from heat. Stir in the cream cheese and season with salt and pepper to taste. Mix well.

Remove sponge roll from oven and immediately turn onto a clean towel. Peel off the wax paper. Spread the roll with filling. Roll with the aid of a towel, and slide the sponge, seam side down, onto a serving platter.

Serve hot.

NOTE: If necessary to reheat this, use a 300°F. oven.

QUICHE MICHELLE   (UNITED STATES)

SERVES 6

Michelle Cousin, in spite of her French name, is my English language mentor and a Francophile. I invented this quiche just for her.

DOUGH

butter for pan   1 batch of Pâte Brisée I (p. 6)

FILLING

1 tablespoon butter	2 tablespoons milk
1 tablespoon oil	1 tablespoon bread crumbs
1 cup chopped fresh mushrooms	1 tablespoon minced fresh parsley
2 tablespoons vermouth	2 cups cauliflowerets, blanched
salt and pepper	½ cup Béchamel Sauce (p. 17)
½ cup chopped smoked mozzarella cheese	¼ cup heavy cream
	4 tablespoons grated Parmesan cheese
½ cup chopped prosciutto	1 jar (4 ounces) pimientos
2 eggs	

Preheat oven to 400°F. Butter a 9-inch quiche pan. Roll dough out into a circle large enough to line bottom and sides of prepared pan. Fit dough into pan, and trim excess dough with scissors. Pierce the bottom of the dough with a fork. Set aside.

Heat butter and oil in a skillet. Add mushrooms and cook until all liquid released by mushrooms has evaporated. Add vermouth and cook for 5 to 10 minutes longer. Season with salt and pepper to taste. Remove skillet from heat and cool. Stir in the mozzarella and prosciutto. Beat the eggs in a mixing bowl until frothy. Add the milk, bread crumbs, parsley, and mushroom mixture. Pour into the dough-lined pan. Arrange the cauliflowerets all over. Combine béchamel sauce with the cream and dribble it all over the quiche. Sprinkle with Parmesan cheese, and decorate with strips of red pimiento. Bake for 15 minutes. Reduce temperature to 350°F. and cook for 30 minutes longer.

Cool and serve.

WINE: Rosé d'Anjou

HORSE'S TEETH PIE   *(U N I T E D   S T A T E S)*

SERVES 6

A surprisingly delicate, delicious, and filling dish, this *pizza rustica* is always a success. Nobody guesses that the light, almost spongy filling is made with a small type of pasta called "horse's teeth." It also looks beautiful when cut.

DOUGH

butter for pan

1 batch of Pasta Frolla Semplice (p. 9)

FILLING

1 cup "horse's teeth" pasta, or any small pasta

2 eggs, lightly beaten

1 cup grated Parmesan cheese

salt and pepper

2 pounds fresh asparagus, blanched and drained

1 tablespoon butter, plus butter for dotting

4 ounces smoked mozzarella cheese, shredded

4 tablespoons chopped prosciutto

Preheat oven to 400°F. Butter a 10- to 11-inch pie pan. Divide the dough into 3 parts. Roll 1 part out to a round sheet as thin as possible, and line the prepared pan; trim excess dough. Chill the pie shell. Keep remaining dough covered.

Cook pasta in salted boiling water, but keep it very *al dente*. Drain pasta and pour into a mixing bowl. Reserve 2 tablespoons of the beaten egg in a cup. Stir remaining eggs into pasta. Add 2 to 3 tablespoons Parmesan and salt and pepper to taste; stir and set aside.

Cut the tender parts of the asparagus into ½-inch pieces. Melt 1 tablespoon butter in a skillet, add asparagus, and cook very briefly, just to heat through; set aside.

Assemble the pie: Pour half of the pasta mixture into the chilled shell. Scatter half of the asparagus pieces all over, then half of the mozzarella and prosciutto; sprinkle with some of the Parmesan. Roll out another piece of dough into a thin round, and top the pasta mixture with it. Sprinkle with Parmesan, and dot with butter. Pour in remaining pasta, smooth the top, and add remaining asparagus, mozzarella, prosciutto, and Parmesan as before.

Roll out the last piece of dough and top the pie with it. Trim excess dough. Moisten edges of pie and pinch dough all around in a decorative edge. Decorate pie with scraps of dough. Pierce top and brush with reserved beaten egg. Bake for 20 to 25 minutes.

Cool for 10 minutes before slicing.

WINE: Chianti

FISH PIZZETTE DANNY AND JOSEPH
(UNITED STATES)
12 PIZZETTE

It was on the last day of a wonderful weekend at Eddy and Elly Green's house in Montauk that, with the help of two skeptical children, I invented this dish. Determined, as usual, not to waste the leftovers from the previous evening's barbecue feast of the fish Eddy caught, I started to sort all the good flesh from bones and heads of what had been a huge half-finished bluefish, some porgies and, if I am not wrong, a piece of eel or two. Enter the children: The conversation that followed was of the usual banal "yuck" and "gosh" and "I won't eat" which goes with leftover food all over the civilized world. However, they volunteered to go and pick the parsley and thyme from the garden and a bay leaf from the tree. Joseph even mashed the potatoes. Danny, who usually eats anything I cook with an enthusiasm rare for a teen-ager, finally said he would taste it, "just to please me." To make a long story short we grown-ups had to share two of the *pizzette*, fighting tooth and fork because the reluctant pair would not stop eating them.

3 cups barbecued fish, flaked

2 potatoes, boiled and mashed

1 onion, finely chopped

2 tablespoons chopped fresh
    parsley

leaves from a small sprig of thyme,
    cnopped

1 bay leaf, chopped

2 eggs

salt and pepper

bread crumbs

1 ounce (2 tablespoons) butter

4 tablespoons oil

In a mixing bowl combine all ingredients but bread crumbs, butter, and oil. Mix well and shape into 3-inch round ¾-inch-thick patties, or *pizzette*. Coat with bread crumbs. Heat butter and oil in a skillet and fry the *pizzette* on both sides, just enough for them to brown lightly.

Serve hot with lemon.

NEW ORLEANS SEAFOOD PIE
(UNITED STATES)
SERVES 6

DOUGH

butter for pan

1 batch of Pasta Frolla Semplice
    (p. 9)

FILLING

2 chicken bouillon cubes

2 cups hot water

1 pound firm white fish (cod,
    haddock, etc.)

½ pound scallops

12 oysters, shucked

2½ ounces (5 tablespoons) butter

¼ cup chopped onion

¼ cup minced celery

4 tablespoons all-purpose flour

1 cup diced cooked crab meat

¼ cup dry sherry

salt and pepper

Dissolve chicken bouillon cubes in 2 cups hot water and bring to a boil. Poach fish in this broth for 10 minutes, or until fish flakes easily when pierced with a fork. Add scallops and oysters. Cook only until broth returns to a boil. Remove from heat and cool uncovered for at least 20 minutes. Remove fish; flake the large pieces. Cut scallops into 4 pieces, oysters into 2 pieces. Strain the broth and reserve it.

Melt butter in a small skillet over medium heat, and sauté onion and celery. Stir in flour. Slowly add reserved broth, and cook and stir until sauce is thickened. Add fish, scallops, oysters, crab meat, and sherry. Season with salt and pepper to taste. Mix well and cool.

Preheat oven to 375°F. Butter a 10-inch pie pan. Divide dough into 2 parts. On a floured board roll out 1 piece into a circle large enough to line bottom and sides of prepared pie pan. Fit the dough into the pan, and pierce the bottom with a fork. Pour in the seafood mixture. Roll out the second piece of dough and top pie. Cut excess dough with scissors, and seal pie all around in a decorative fashion. Cut a few vents on top of pie to allow steam to escape. Bake for 30 minutes, or until top is golden brown.

Cool a little before slicing.

VARIATION: This pie can be made with just oysters, to be precise, 1 pint. Do not poach them. Prebake the bottom shell, lined with foil filled with beans, in a preheated 400°F. oven for 15 minutes. In preparing the filling, use 2 tablespoons lemon juice and a dash of Worcestershire sauce instead of sherry. Cover with a thin layer of dough, pierce top, and bake just until top is lightly browned.

WINE: California Chablis

TEXAS LOBSTER PIE   (U N I T E D   S T A T E S)

SERVES 6

Ideal for a luncheon or brunch, this elegant pie can be assembled at the last minute, and takes only a short time to cook. By the time you make the Bloody Marys, it is done.

DOUGH

1 baked 9-inch pie shell, made of
    Pâte Brisée I (p. 6)

FILLING

1 ounce (2 tablespoons) butter	6 poached eggs, drained
1½ tablespoons flour	1 cup diced lobster (from spiny
salt and pepper	lobster)
1 scant cup of milk	¼ cup freshly grated Parmesan
pinch of grated nutmeg	cheese

Preheat oven to 325°F. Melt the butter in a saucepan. Add the flour and a little salt and pepper. Cook, mixing, for a few minutes. Remove from heat and gradually add the milk, stirring, until sauce is completely liquefied and smooth. Return to heat and cook, stirring constantly, until sauce thickens. Let it boil for a few seconds, remove from heat, and add nutmeg. Cool, and stir every once in a while.

When ready to serve, arrange the poached eggs in the baked shell. Add lobster, pour sauce over evenly, and sprinkle with cheese. Bake for 15 minutes, or until top is set.

NOTE: I have used leftover scrambled eggs instead of poached eggs with excellent results. Cooked mushrooms can also be added or substituted for the eggs.

WINE: Emerald Riesling

CLAM POT PIE (UNITED STATES)

SERVES 6

DOUGH
1 batch of Short Pastry (p. 9)

FILLING

1 thick slice of ham, about 4 ounces, diced

3 onions, chopped

4 carrots, diced

½ cup dry vermouth

2 cups clam juice (canned if fresh is not available)

4 potatoes, peeled and diced

3 tablespoons minced fresh parsley

1 garlic clove, minced

2 bay leaves

2½ dozen shucked clams, coarsely chopped

good pinch of pepper

1 tablespoon cornstarch

In a saucepan, combine ham, onions, and carrots. Cook over medium heat, stirring frequently, for 10 minutes. Add the vermouth, clam juice, and potatoes, and cook over low heat for 15 minutes. Add the parsley, garlic, bay leaves, clams, and pepper. Dilute the cornstarch with a little water and add, stirring steadily until the boiling point is reached. Remove the bay leaves. Pour into a buttered 2-quart casserole.

Preheat oven to 375°F. On a lightly floured board roll out the dough to fit the top of the casserole. Place the dough on top of the filling and seal the edges well. Pierce the dough with a fork in several places. Bake for 30 minutes, or until top is browned.

Serve hot.

CLAM AND CHICKEN POT PIE. After cooking vegetable mixture and before adding the vermouth, a small (about 3-pound) chicken, cut up, with wing tips and back removed, can be added to the saucepan. Cook until brown and add vermouth. Let vermouth evaporate and add clam juice and potatoes. Cook over low heat for 25 to 30 minutes, or until chicken is tender. Follow the remainder of the main recipe. For baking, use a larger casserole; the dough will be sufficient to top pie.

NEPTUNE'S PIE SYLVIA O'BRIAN
(UNITED STATES)
SERVES 6

In spite of her busy schedule, playing the mother in the Broadway hit *Da*, Sylvia still had the time to entertain her friends with lovely little dinner parties. This quiche of hers is one of my favorites.

DOUGH

butter for pan   1 batch of American Piecrust (p. 8)

FILLING

2 ounces (½ stick) butter or   1 cup milk
    margarine   2 eggs, lightly beaten
1 small onion, minced   ½ teaspoon dillweed
¼ cup flour   1 cup cooked peas
1 teaspoon salt   ½ cup cottage cheese
¼ teaspoon pepper
1 pound canned salmon, with liquid
    from can

Preheat oven to 400°F. Butter a 9-inch pie pan. On a floured board roll the dough out into a circle large enough to line the bottom and sides of the prepared pan. Fit the dough into the pan, trim excess dough with scissors, and flute the edges.

Melt the butter or margarine in a saucepan. Add onion and sauté for 2 to 3 minutes. Blend in the flour, salt, and pepper. Drain liquid from salmon and mix with milk. Gradually add to the onion mixture, stirring until sauce thickens. Cool. Pour cooled sauce into the beaten eggs, mixing well. Flake salmon and add to the sauce, together with remaining ingredients. Pour into the dough-lined pan. Bake for 30 minutes, or until top is firm and brown.

Let stand for 10 minutes before cutting.

NOTE: This pie can also be made with tuna.

WINE: Lake Niagara

CLAM PIE MISS LESLIE   *(UNITED STATES)*
SERVES 6

Miss Leslie's New Receipts for Cooking was published in 1854. Eliza Leslie was a very well-known writer during the nineteenth century, together with Lydia Maria Child *(The American Frugal Housewife)*, and her cookbooks were well received. Her popularity declined toward the end of the century because she could not accept change and expected people to cook in fireplaces forever. Her recipes were especially planned for the bountiful, indigenous food of her time. When I discovered the following recipe I soon realized how well American steaks married clams. This was some time ago when I also found out that "receipt," a word I used frequently then, didn't quite mean what I meant; everybody thought I was getting my cooking instruction from my doctor. You see, "receipt" sounds very similar to my Italian *ricetta*, which is used equally well and without confusion either in the kitchen or the pharmacy.

DOUGH

butter for pan   1 batch of Pâte Brisée II (p. 7)

FILLING

3 dozen fresh clams, washed and   good grinding of pepper
    scrubbed clean   1½ ounces (3 tablespoons) butter, at
½ pound filet mignon, cut into thin   room temperature
    slices   1 tablespoon flour
salt   2 hard-cooked eggs, chopped
pinch of grated mace

Butter a 9- to 10-inch pie pan. Preheat oven to 375°F. On a floured board roll out half of the dough into a rather thick circle large enough to line bottom and sides of prepared pan. Fit pastry into pan and chill.

Place all the clams in a large skillet set over medium heat. Shake pan once in a while to distribute clams evenly. Remove each clam as soon as it opens. Reserve mollusks on a dish and the clam liquor in a bowl; discard shells.

Line the prepared pastry with the thin slices of beef, overlapping them a little. Sprinkle lightly with salt. Place clams over the beef. Add a pinch of mace and a good grinding of pepper.

Filter the clam liquor through a double thickness of cheesecloth to remove sand. Place butter and flour in a bowl and blend with fingers while adding the clam liquor. Add this to pie, and scatter the chopped eggs on top.

Roll out remaining dough into a circle, the same thickness as the one used at the bottom, and top pie with it. Cut excess dough with scissors and seal edges well. Pierce top with fork and decorate with scraps of dough, if desired.

Bake for 45 to 50 minutes, or until top is browned. Serve warm.

SWEETBREAD AND OYSTER PIE
(UNITED STATES)
SERVES 8

This recipe comes from the 1831 edition of Mrs. Mary Randolph's *The Virginia Housewife* cookbook. As usual, in those days and in the times of my grandmother, there are no measurements for the ingredients but the mere suggestion of "take this or take that," more or less at random. However, Mrs. Randolph, at the beginning of the recipe, recommends using puff pastry and concludes her instructions with a laconic "put a Paste on the Top and bake it." She then declares, "This is the most delicious pie that can be made."

I have re-created this pie according to her instructions and I hope you will agree with her statement; I did.

DOUGH
butter for pan
1 batch of Classic Puff Pastry (p. 11)
    or Quick Puff Pastry (p. 12)

FILLING

2 pairs of sweetbreads, poached and
  trimmed (p. 59)
1½ ounces (3 tablespoons) butter
1 tablespoon oil
3 tablespoons flour

1 cup cream
salt and pepper
lemon juice
½ pint shucked oysters
2 egg yolks, slightly beaten

Dice poached sweetbreads. Place 1 tablespoon butter and the oil in a sauce-pan. Sauté sweetbreads over medium heat until slightly browned. Remove with a slotted spoon and set aside.

Add remaining butter to the saucepan and stir in the flour. Cook briefly and remove from heat. Slowly add the cream to the flour mixture, stirring constantly until sauce liquefies. Cook over medium heat, stirring constantly, until sauce thickens and starts to boil. Remove from heat; add salt and pepper to taste, lemon juice to taste, the oysters and their liquor, and the egg yolks. Mix well and set aside.

Preheat oven to 425°F. Butter a 10-inch pie pan. On a lightly floured board, roll out half of the dough into a circle large enough to line the bottom and sides of prepared pan. Line the pan with dough, letting it hang over the edge. Pierce bottom with fork. Spoon half of the oyster mixture on the bottom of the pie; top with diced sweetbreads. Spoon in remaining oyster mixture and smooth the top.

Roll out remaining dough and top pie with it. Trim excess dough with scissors. Pinch edges all around in a decorative fashion to seal pie. Pierce on the top in several places to allow steam to escape. Bake for about 30 min-utes, or until top is nicely browned.

GLORY OF SALMON LUTÈCE
(UNITED STATES)
SERVES 6 TO 8

My friend Gloria Saffron told me all about a *saumon en croûte* she had eaten at Lutèce, the famed New York restaurant. She later offered me the recipe, which she got at a demonstration given by the great master, André Soltner, himself. Gloria, and her writer husband Bob, made it once for me and it was so delicious I decided to include it in this book. It is a somewhat adapted version, only in the fact that the ingredients are more readily available than those in the original and I made the preparation easier by using a food processor.

DOUGH

1 batch of Classic Puff Pastry
    (p. 11), ready to use
butter for pan

1 egg
2 tablespoons water

FILLING

1 salmon or salmon trout, 3 pounds,
    head and bones removed
2 tablespoons minced fresh parsley
1 sprig of tarragon, chopped, or ½
    teaspoon dried tarragon

salt
2 cups mousseline of pike

MOUSSELINE OF PIKE

1 pound fillets of pike or sole, cut
    into pieces
2 eggs
juice of ½ lemon

salt
freshly ground pepper
pinch of grated nutmeg
1 cup heavy cream

Prepare the mousseline first: Place fish, eggs, lemon juice, and seasoning to taste in the bowl of a food processor, and purée. Add cream through the tube in a steady stream, and process until smooth. Set aside.

If you do not have a fish poacher, set salmon on a long piece of cheesecloth. Holding the fish by the ends of the cheesecloth, immerse the fish in boiling water for 30 seconds, or until skin can be pulled away easily. Place fish on a dry cloth and remove the skin. Open the fish like a book; pick out and discard all visible bones. Sprinkle fish with parsley, tarragon, and a touch of salt. Spread the mousseline to cover one side of the fish. Fold over other side.

Roll out dough into 2 rectangles the length of the fish. Butter a baking sheet, and place 1 rectangle of dough on it. Place the fish on that sheet of dough and cover with the second. Cut the dough in the shape of the fish, leaving 1 inch extra all around. Mix the egg with 2 tablespoons water. Wet the bare inch of the pastry with this egg wash. Fold over the inch of dough and seal securely all around. Make notches with the dull side of a knife all around the edge. Decorate the top by imitating scales which can be drawn on the dough in overlapping circles made with the large opening of the metal nozzle of a pastry bag. Chill for 30 minutes.

Preheat oven to 425°F. Bake the pie for 20 minutes. Reduce heat to 375°F., and cook for 20 minutes longer. Cover with foil if top tends to get too brown.

Cool for 15 minutes before slicing.

NOTE: This pie can be served cold with a good homemade mayonnaise.

WINE: Cassis Rosé

CHICKEN PIE   (CANADA)

SERVES 6 TO 8

DOUGH

2 cups flour	2 tablespoons shortening
1 tablespoon baking powder	¾ to 1 cup milk
pinch of salt	butter for casserole

FILLING

1 stewing chicken (fowl), 4 pounds	8 ounces mushrooms, sliced
1 ounce (2 tablespoons) butter	3 tablespoons minced fresh parsley
1 tablespoon oil	3 tablespoons flour
1 onion, sliced	2 cups chicken stock (p. 19)
2 celery ribs, diced	1 hard-boiled egg, sliced
1 small carrot, diced	

For the dough: In the bowl of a food processor combine flour, baking powder, and salt. Turn the machine on and off 2 or 3 times. Add shortening, turn machine on, and pour in milk a little at a time. Stop as soon as a dough forms on the blades. Wrap and chill until ready to use. Butter a 2-quart ovenproof casserole.

For the chicken: Cook chicken according to the recipe on page 19. Remove chicken from stock, separate meat from bones, discard the skin, reserve meat.

In a saucepan place butter, oil, and onion. Cook over medium heat, stirring often, for about 5 minutes; add celery and carrot and cook until vegetables are almost soft. Add mushrooms and continue cooking for 10 more minutes. Add parsley, and sprinkle vegetable mixture with flour while stirring to blend well. Add stock, a little at a time, bring to a boil, and turn mixture into the buttered casserole. Add the cooked chicken meat. Cover with egg slices; set aside. Preheat oven to 425°F.

On a lightly floured board, roll out dough ½ inch thick and cut into rounds 2 to 3 inches in diameter. Arrange rounds on top of casserole and bake for 20 to 25 minutes.

NOTE: Peas or fresh corn can be substituted for mushrooms.

COUNTRY CAPTAIN PIE   (UNITED STATES)

"Country Captain" was the sobriquet for an officer of the Sepoys, the native troops of India in the service of England. The exotic recipe was probably introduced first in England by one of these officers. So explains the sapient Miss Leslie in her book Miss Leslie's New Cookery Book, published in 1857, with which she introduced the recipe to our shores. The following recipe is my free adaptation from Miss Leslie's book, whose charming instruction would, nowadays, leave a few people perplexed. So instead of "having well boiled a fine full brown fowl" as she suggests, let us use a nice tender frying chicken that does not need that extra step.

FILLING

1 frying chicken, 2½ to 3 pounds,
   cut into serving pieces
3 tablespoons flour
salt and pepper
1 teaspoon curry powder
4 tablespoons lard, or 2 tablespoons
   butter and 2 tablespoons oil

2 medium-size onions, sliced
1 garlic clove, minced
¼ cup wine or broth
8 ounces canned tomato sauce

TOPPING

2 cups cooked rice

1 egg, beaten

Wash the chicken and pat dry. Combine flour, salt and pepper to taste, and curry powder. Sprinkle the chicken pieces with this mixture. In a large skillet melt the lard, or butter and oil, and add the chicken. Brown pieces on all sides. Add the onions and garlic and pour in the wine. Cook over medium-high heat until chicken is tender. If mixture tends to become dry, add a little more wine or water.

Preheat oven to 375°F. Pour the chicken mixture into a 2½-quart casserole. Add ½ cup of the tomato sauce. Mix the rice with the beaten egg, and spoon over the chicken mixture, covering it. Dilute remaining tomato sauce with 2 to 3 tablespoons of water and pour over rice. Season with a touch of salt and pepper. Bake for about 30 minutes, or until top is nice and crusty.

TEX-MEX CHICKEN TURNOVERS
(UNITED STATES)
10 TO 12 TURNOVERS

These chicken and cheese turnovers are delicious warm or cold, and ideal to take along on a picnic.

DOUGH

1 batch of Cream Cheese Pastry
    (p. 10)

melted butter

FILLING

4 ounces cream cheese, at room
    temperature
1 tablespoon milk
1 cup chopped cooked chicken
1 cup shredded Cheddar cheese
2 ounces canned green chiles,
    chopped

1 cup sliced scallions, green part
    included
1 small garlic clove, minced
pinch of cuminseed
salt and pepper

Preheat oven to 400°F. In a mixing bowl cream the cheese with the milk. Add the other filling ingredients, with seasoning to taste, and set aside.

On a floured board roll out the dough into a rectangle 12 x 18 inches. Cut it into 6-inch squares. Divide the filling among the squares. Dampen edges of dough all around and fold into triangles. Seal edges securely, pressing with a fork to make a decorative edge. Brush with melted butter. Bake for 25 to 30 minutes, or until golden brown.

Serve cooled.

TATTERED PIE

This pie owes its name to a near disaster. When I made it the first time, I was not accustomed to working with phyllo dough, and the last sheet, which was supposed to cover the pie, got very dry and I couldn't manage it. Infuriated, I tore the dough apart and threw pieces of it on the top of the pie. All at once it began to look nice. When I brought it to the table the effect was spectacular: While baking, the pieces of dough had curled up like the petals of a large chrysanthemum.

DOUGH

5 phyllo sheets
1½ ounces (3 tablespoons) butter or
     margarine, melted

FILLING

2 eggs
2 cups chopped cooked chicken
1 cup chopped cooked endive or
     escarole
2 slices of prosciutto or ham,
     chopped

4 ounces mozzarella cheese,
     shredded
2 tablespoons grated Parmesan
     cheese
1 tablespoon chopped fresh parsley
salt and pepper

Unroll phyllo sheets on a working surface. Cover them with a sheet of wax paper, then with a damp cloth towel to prevent drying. Cover the pile again while working with 1 sheet at a time.

Preheat oven to 375°F. Beat the eggs in a mixing bowl. Add all other filling ingredients, with seasoning to taste, and mix well. Set aside. Butter a 9-inch pie plate from which you can serve. Fold 1 phyllo sheet in half, and line the pan with it. Let the dough hang over the edge of the pan. Brush with some of the melted butter or margarine. Place 3 more folded phyllo sheets in the pan, one at a time, brushing each one as before. Fill the pastry with the filling. Fold over the loose ends of the dough. Do not worry if it breaks. Tear the remaining sheet of dough into tattered pieces and cover the pie with them. Dot with remaining butter or margarine. Bake for 35 to 40 minutes, until top is puffed and crisp.

Serve hot.

TURKEY POT PIE (UNITED STATES)

SERVES 6

No need to go "cold turkey" the day after the feast. This recipe, and the following one, are just right to present the bird a second time in a completely different way, with new flavors.

DOUGH

¾ cup all-purpose flour
½ cup cornmeal
1½ teaspoons sage, crumbled
salt and pepper

4 tablespoons lard or vegetable shortening
½ cup cold water, approximately

FILLING

3 ounces (¾ stick) butter
1 onion, sliced
1 garlic clove
4 tablespoons flour
1½ cups chicken broth or stock, made with turkey bones

1 cup light cream
2½ cups cooked turkey, diced
salt and pepper
pinch of sage
1 tablespoon lemon juice

Place all dough ingredients except water in the bowl of a food processor fitted with the steel blade. Turn the machine on and off 2 or 3 times, or process until the mixture resembles coarse meal. Slowly add the water; stop as soon as a ball of dough forms on the blades. Chill while preparing filling.

Melt the butter in a saucepan. Add onion and cook over low heat until soft. Add garlic and cook briefly. With a slotted spoon remove onion and garlic to a mixing bowl. Add flour to saucepan and cook briefly, stirring all the while. Remove pan from heat. Combine broth or stock and cream and pour a little at a time into the butter and flour mixture, stirring to a smooth and liquid consistency. Replace saucepan over heat and cook, stirring constantly, until mixture thickens and starts to bubble. Pour into the bowl with the onion and garlic, which should be chopped. Add turkey, seasonings, and the lemon juice. Turn mixture into an ovenproof 6-cup casserole. Set aside.

Preheat oven to 425°F. Roll out dough ⅛ inch thick, shaping it to the size of the casserole. Top casserole with dough and seal edges all around. Cut a hole in the center and insert a funnel to allow steam to escape. Bake for 15 minutes. Reduce heat to 350°F. and continue baking for 10 more minutes, or until top is nicely browned.

NOTE: If you have a bread or cornmeal stuffing, you can use 1 cup of it and eliminate flour in the sauce. The sauce will be a little coarse, but quite tasty.

WINE: California Cabernet Sauvignon

TURKEY PIE WITH ALMONDS
(UNITED STATES)

SERVES 8

DOUGH

butter for pan

1 batch of American Piecrust (p. 8)

FILLING

1 cup shredded cheese (Swiss, mozzarella, or provolone)

1 tablespoon flour

1 cup blanched almonds, lightly toasted

3 cups chopped cooked turkey

4 tender celery ribs, sliced very thin

1 tablespoon lemon juice

1 cup mayonnaise

½ teaspoon poultry seasoning

salt

good pinch of freshly ground pepper

Preheat oven to 400°F. Butter a 10-inch pie or quiche pan. On a floured board roll out the dough to a circle large enough to line the bottom and sides of prepared pan. Fit dough into the pan and trim excess dough with scissors. Pierce the bottom of the dough with a fork. Flute edges all around. Chill.

Place the cheese in a mixing bowl. Sprinkle with flour and toss to coat pieces well. Add remaining ingredients and mix well. Spoon into dough-lined pan and smooth the top. Bake for 30 to 35 minutes.

RABBIT AND CHICKEN PIE   (*C A N A D A*)

SERVES 6 TO 8

DOUGH

butter for pan   1 batch of Very Short Pastry (p. 10)

FILLING

2 tablespoons chopped dried   pinch of rosemary
   mushrooms   pinch of thyme
¼ cup tepid water   pinch of ground cloves
1½ ounces (3 tablespoons) butter salt and pepper
2 celery ribs, minced   1 cup chicken broth
1 onion, minced   3 cups boneless cooked chicken,
1 tablespoon minced fresh parsley   cubed
2 tablespoons flour   3 cups boneless cooked rabbit,
pinch of savory   cubed

Soak the mushrooms in the tepid water for 10 minutes. Heat the butter in a saucepan over low heat. Add celery, onion, and parsley, and cook until soft. Add mushrooms and liquid in which they were soaked. Combine flour with the herbs, cloves, and salt and pepper to taste. Add to the vegetable mixture, stirring, and cook for a few minutes. Add the broth, a little at a time. Cook, stirring, until mixture thickens and starts to bubble. Add the meats and heat through.

    Preheat oven to 400°F. Butter a 10-inch springform pan. On a floured board roll out half of the dough into a circle large enough to line the bottom and sides of the buttered pan. Fit dough into the pan, and pierce the bottom with a fork. Spoon filling into the dough-lined pan. Roll out remaining dough and top the pie. Trim excess dough with scissors, and pinch edges together in a decorative fashion to seal well. Decorate pie with dough scraps. Bake for 20 minutes. Reduce temperature to 350°F. Cover pie loosely with foil if it tends to brown too much. Bake for 20 minutes longer.

NOTE: Turkey may be substituted for chicken.

CHINATOWN DOGGIE BAG PIE
(UNITED STATES)
SERVES 8 TO 10

What you are thinking is absolutely true. The same tidbits that were so appetizing the night before, but you couldn't finish, do not look so appealing out of the doggie bag the day after. Yet the beef was filet mignon, the chicken the tenderest morsel, the shrimps plump and juicy, and the vegetables green and dewy. All right, do not look any more. Stick everything in a pie and see! You can even get fancy and use Chinese spring-roll squares, which are sold in Chinese shops and in many supermarkets. I do that sometimes, but since this recipe is not the type one can plan in advance, let's use a few sheets of phyllo dough. One should always keep them in the refrigerator for their many uses.

It doesn't matter if you have a little more or a little less of some ingredients. Six cups should be the right amount to fill this pie. If you have less, use a smaller pie pan; if you have more make it into a strudel. This amount will make two 12-inch-long strudels.

DOUGH

12 sheets of phyllo	¼ cup vegetable oil
butter for pan	2 tablespoons sesame oil

FILLING

2 cups cooked meats or shellfish or a combination of both	1 garlic clove, minced
	2 tablespoons minced fresh parsley
1 cup mixed Chinese vegetables	3 tablespoons bread crumbs
1 large egg, separated	1 tablespoon margarine
2 cups cooked rice	1 tablespoon flour
½ teaspoon ground ginger	1 cup bouillon, hot

Combine all of the leftovers in a mixing bowl. Dice the larger pieces of meat, shellfish, and vegetables. Add the egg white, rice, ginger, garlic, and parsley. Mix well. Add the bread crumbs and mix again. Melt the margarine in a saucepan. Stir in the flour and cook briefly. Remove from heat and gradually add the bouillon, stirring until sauce liquefies. Heat again, stirring constantly, until sauce starts to boil. Remove, cool, and add the egg yolk.

Unroll phyllo sheets on a working surface. Cover them with a sheet of wax paper, then with a damp cloth towel to prevent drying. Cover the pile again while working with 1 sheet at a time.

Preheat oven to 400°F. Butter a 9- to 10-inch pie pan. Line the prepared pan with 1 sheet of phyllo dough. Mix vegetable and sesame oils. Brush the dough with the oil, and top with 4 more sheets, each brushed with oil as before. Spoon in half of the filling. Top with 4 more sheets of phyllo, each brushed with oil. Pour in remaining filling. Top with remaining sheets of phyllo, each sheet brushed with oil. Fold in the overhanging dough. Do not worry if it breaks. Dribble remaining oil over the pastry. Bake for about 10 minutes. Reduce the temperature to 375°F., and bake for 30 minutes longer, or until top is crisp and nicely browned.

Cool for about 15 minutes before slicing.

SWEETBREADS IN PUFF PASTRY
(UNITED STATES)
SERVES 6 TO 8

In Texas this pie is served as a first course. Texans either titillate you with little morsels or they fill you up totally with their bounteous offering; the dinner becomes an afterthought. I suggest serving this dish as an entrée with a large vegetable salad.

DOUGH

butter and flour for baking sheet	1 egg
1 batch of Quick Puff Pastry (p. 12)	2 tablespoons water

FILLING

2 pounds veal sweetbreads	1 cup fresh mushrooms, coarsely
3 cups thick Béchamel Sauce (p. 17)	chopped
¼ teaspoon cayenne pepper	24 blanched almonds, slivered

Soak and blanch the sweetbreads (procedure p. 59). Make the sauce, and season it with cayenne. Cut the sweetbreads into ¾-inch cubes. Add sweetbreads, mushrooms, and almonds to the sauce.

Butter and flour a baking sheet. On a floured board, roll the dough out into a rectangle 16 x 10 inches. Spread filling on half of the rectangle, leaving a 1-inch border free of filling on the 3 open sides of the dough. Brush edges with water. Fold second half of dough over on top of the filling. Press edges together to seal well. Trim excess dough with a toothed wheel. With the dull part of a knife, press all around to make a decorative edge. Place on the baking sheet. Cut a vent in the top of pastry and decorate with dough scraps. Mix egg with 2 tablespoons water and brush this egg wash all over the top of the pastry; do not let any drip down the sides, as it would keep the pastry from puffing during baking. Chill for 30 minutes before baking.

Preheat oven to 425°F. Bake for 35 to 40 minutes, or until top is puffed and well colored.

WINE: Moselle-Saar-Ruwer

BROCCOLI POTATO PIE VIVIAN
(UNITED STATES)
SERVES 6

It all began one weekend in our niece's and nephew's house in Spencertown. For our Sunday lunch we were left with a little bit of this and a little bit of that and, apart from the salad, not enough to make a decent portion for 4 people and a dog. So we put everything together and made this pie which was surprisingly good. We picked some fresh lettuce from the garden and had a scrumptious lunch. Here is the recipe which serves 4 people and, yes, one hungry dog.

½ cup mayonnaise
½ cup plain yogurt
3 tablespoons cider vinegar
1 teaspoon salt

2 pounds potatoes, cooked, peeled, and sliced (4 cups)
½ cup sliced scallions
1 tablespoon chopped parsley

butter for pan
bread crumbs
1 cup cooked broccoli
½ cup chopped cooked meat

2 eggs, beaten
¾ cup grated Parmesan cheese
2 tablespoons soy sauce
pepper

In a large bowl stir together the first 4 ingredients. Add potatoes and scallions; toss to coat well. Sprinkle with chopped parsley. Cover, and chill.

Preheat oven to 375°F. Butter a 9-inch pie pan and sprinkle with bread crumbs. Place the potato mixture in a mixing bowl and mash as much as you can. Add all other ingredients. Spoon everything into the prepared pan. Sprinkle with bread crumbs. Bake for 45 minutes.

VEAL POT PIE PICAYUNE   (U N I T E D   S T A T E S)
SERVES 8

This is a famous recipe from the South passed from generation to generation of Creole families.

DOUGH

butter for pan   1 batch of American Piecrust (p. 8)

FILLING

2 pounds shoulder of veal, boned   2 or 3 carrots
2 thick slices of ham, about ¼   1 garlic clove
    pound   2 or 3 sprigs of fresh parsley
1 tablespoon butter   1½ tablespoons flour
1 tablespoon oil   1½ cups water
salt   8 ounces canned tomato sauce
cayenne pepper   1 teaspoon tomato paste
2 to 3 tablespoons wine vinegar   1 bay leaf
2 onions

Preheat oven to 375°F. Butter a 10-inch pie pan. Divide dough into 2 parts. On a floured board roll out 1 part into a circle large enough to line bottom and sides of prepared pan. Fit dough into buttered pan, and pierce bottom with a fork. Line with aluminum foil, fill with beans or rice, and bake for 20 minutes. Remove foil, reserve rice or beans for another pie, and cool the pie shell.

Cut veal into small cubes; dice ham. Heat butter and oil in a large skillet. Add the veal and sauté over high heat until brown. Season with salt and cayenne to taste, and sprinkle with vinegar. Let vinegar evaporate and add ham.

Chop onions, carrots, garlic, and parsley, by hand or in the bowl of a food processor fitted with the steel blade. Add vegetables to skillet, stir, and sprinkle with flour.

Combine water, tomato sauce, and tomato paste; stir into veal mixture. Add the bay leaf, cover, and continue cooking until meat and vegetables are quite tender and sauce is reduced. Regulate the heat according to the liquid in the pan. Cool. Pour veal mixture into prepared pie shell.

Roll out remaining dough into a circle large enough to cover top of pie. Place over the filling and cut excess dough with scissors; seal edges all around. Cut a vent in the center and insert a funnel to allow steam to escape. Decorate with scraps of dough if desired.

Bake at 375°F. for 30 to 35 minutes, or until top is browned. Serve warm.

MINCEMEAT PIE   (UNITED STATES)
8 QUARTS

Mincemeat pies, the way modern cookbooks and magazines describe them today, have not seen a speck of real meat in centuries. They have remained, nevertheless, a bastion of Christmas tradition whenever the tradition goes back to British or Irish ancestry. A product of the Crusaders who wanted to use the spices brought back from the Orient, a pie of that era actually contained one capon, one pheasant, two rabbits, two pigeons, two partridges, eggs, mushrooms, and a liberal amount of exotic spices. With all that abundance inside, the cook's fancy began to take flight when it came to the outside, or the "coffin" as the crust was then called, molding it with sculptured figures. By the time of the Puritans, one pie made in the shape of a crèche sporting a Baby Jesus cradled on top of it caused an outrage. Fortunately for us the British bakers stuck to their ovens. Today mincemeat pies can still be enjoyed with or without meat, and decorated as you will. The following recipe is adapted from Mrs. F. L. Gillette's and Hugo Ziemans's *The White House Cook Book*, published in 1894. It appears that the meat has indeed been retained in American and Canadian recipes, while in England it has been replaced by a surprise: a penny or a ring which is buried in the mixture. The one who finds the surprise will be lucky for the year to come.

To obtain a full-flavored mixture, mincemeat cannot be made in small quantities. However, tightly packed in a crock and set in a cool place it keeps for several months. Mincemeat can also be used to fill omelets; when wrapped in the ubiquitous phyllo dough it becomes an easy and delicious dessert. Just be sure to remember that the filling of mincemeat must age or steep for 1 month before using.

DOUGH

1 batch of Short Pastry (p. 9), made with lemon juice instead of water

butter for pan
milk for glazing

FILLING

2 cups mincemeat

MINCEMEAT

2 pounds lean beef
1 medium-size onion
2 cloves
1 celery rib, cut into 2 pieces
1 carrot, quartered
1 parsley sprig
3½ cups water
1 tablespoon coarse salt
10 peppercorns
1 pound suet
3 pounds tart green apples
1 pound dried currants
3 pounds raisins
¼ pound citron, chopped

¼ pound candied orange peel, chopped
1 tablespoon salt
1 tablespoon pepper
1 teaspoon grated mace
1 teaspoon ground allspice
1 teaspoon grated nutmeg
1 tablespoon ground cinnamon
1 cup brown sugar
1 cup molasses
3 tablespoons lemon juice
2 cups dry cider
2 cups brandy or Cognac
1 cup Madeira wine

For the mincemeat: In a kettle place the beef, the onion with the 2 cloves stuck in it, the celery, carrot, parsley, water, salt, and peppercorns. Bring to a boil, and cook at a steady simmer for 2 hours or until meat is tender. Remove meat and strain the broth. Measure 1½ cups of broth, and set aside. Reserve remaining broth and vegetables for a soup. Rinse the kettle and set aside.

Cut stewed beef and suet into chunks, chop coarsely in a food processor, and return the mixture to the kettle in which the meat was cooked. Peel apples, slice, and chop them coarsely in a food processor. Add to kettle together with the currants, raisins, citron, orange peel, salt, pepper, all the spices, sugar, molasses, and the 1½ cups of broth. Bring to a boil and simmer for 1 hour, stirring often. Add lemon juice and cider during the last 5 minutes. Remove from heat.

When mixture is almost cool, add brandy or Cognac and the Madeira. Turn into an earthenware crock, cover tightly with several thicknesses of wax paper, and fasten with a rubber band or cord. Place in a cool place. Stir every 8 days, and let the mincemeat steep for 1 month before using.

For the pie: Preheat oven to 350°F. Butter a 9- to 10-inch pie pan. On a floured board roll out half of the dough into a circle large enough to cover the bottom and sides of the pan. Fit dough into pan, leaving 1 extra inch to hang over the side. Spoon in filling, and smooth the top. Roll out remaining dough and cover pie with it. Trim excess dough with scissors, fold overhanging dough in, and seal, making a decorative rim all around. Pierce top with fork in several places to allow steam to escape. Brush top with a little milk. Bake for about 1 hour.

SHEPHERD'S PIE (UNITED STATES)

SERVES 6

TOPPING

3 medium-size potatoes
salt
1 ounce (2 tablespoons) butter
1 egg, lightly beaten

2 tablespoons grated Parmesan
　　cheese (optional)
butter for casserole

FILLING

3 tablespoons oil
1 onion, chopped
2 pounds lean lamb, cubed
salt and pepper
pinch of dried thyme

½ cup dry red wine
1 tablespoon flour
¼ cup water
1½ cups mixed cooked vegetables,
　　e.g., lima beans, peas, carrots

Boil potatoes until tender. Heat the oil in a skillet and add the onion. Cook until onion is soft. Add lamb, and brown over high heat. Add salt and pepper to taste and thyme, and pour in the wine. Cook until wine is almost evaporated. Sprinkle with flour, mix well, add water, cover, and simmer until meat is tender. Add a little more water if juices tend to dry; mixture should be moist. Stir in the vegetables and remove from heat.

Peel potatoes, mash, and combine with all remaining ingredients of the topping. Mix well.

Preheat oven to 425°F. Butter a 2½-quart ovenproof casserole. Pour meat mixture into it. Spoon potato mixture on top and smooth nicely. Bake for 20 to 25 minutes, or until top is browned.

LOU-ANN'S OLD-FASHIONED MEAT PIE
(UNITED STATES)
SERVES 8

The old-fashioned meat pie is closely related to the "pyes" of colonial times. The recipe came from England with the Pilgrims and it contained all sorts of ingredients from birds, like rooks, to plovers' eggs, and was well flavored with herbs and spices. Sometimes the pies included exotic fruits like dates. My friend Dr. Lou-Ann Pilkington has somewhat modernized her family recipe, using easy-to-find meat instead of a rook, and we are all glad for this.

DOUGH

1 batch of American Piecrust (p. 8)   2 tablespoons water or milk
1 egg (optional)   (optional)

FILLING

1½ pounds lean beef (if chuck is   1 bouillon cube
    used, trim fat)   1 bay leaf
flour   4 medium-size potatoes, cubed
salt and pepper   6 medium-size carrots, cubed
¼ cup oil or vegetable shortening   3 medium-size onions, chopped
pinch each of thyme and marjoram

Cut beef into ½-inch cubes. Roll cubes in flour and sprinkle with salt and pepper. Heat the oil or vegetable shortening in a heavy skillet. Add beef and brown well on all sides. Add thyme and marjoram; pour in enough water to cover meat. Add the bouillon cube and the bay leaf. Bring to a boil, reduce heat, and simmer until meat is nearly done, stirring now and then. Add potatoes, carrots, and onions, and continue cooking until vegetables are a little soft, about 25 minutes. Stir occasionally. Remove pan from heat, but make sure that the sauce has the consistency of cream. If it is too thick, add a little water.

Preheat oven to 425°F. Spoon the stew into an ovenproof 2-quart casserole from which you can serve. On a lightly floured board, roll the dough out to a sheet ¼ inch thick and large enough to cover the casserole. Top casserole with dough and seal all around. Cut a hole in the center to allow steam to escape. If desired, brush top with egg wash made by beating an egg with 2 tablespoons of water or milk. Bake for 15 minutes. Reduce temperature to 350°F. and bake for 30 minutes longer, or until crust is golden brown.

Serve a wedge of crust and some of the stew together.

VARIATIONS: Fresh or frozen peas can be added just before topping the casserole with dough. Sautéed mushrooms can be added instead of peas. After brushing crust with egg wash, grated Parmesan cheese can be sprinkled on.

WINE: California Mountain Burgundy

CANADIAN SAUSAGE PIE

SERVES 8

DOUGH

1 batch of Short Pastry (p. 9)	butter for pan

FILLING

6 Italian-style sausages, about 1½ pounds, cooked and cut into rounds	1 package (9 ounces) frozen peas, defrosted
	1 tablespoon minced parsley

SAUCE

1 tablespoon butter	3 eggs
1 tablespoon oil	¾ cup heavy cream
2 or 3 shallots, minced	good pinch of pepper
1 tablespoon flour	pinch of grated nutmeg
1 cup milk	

Make the pastry and roll it out to a circle large enough to fill a 10-inch pan. Butter the pan and fit in the pastry. Trim edges.

Preheat oven to 450°F. Heat the butter and oil in a saucepan; add shallots and sauté until soft and translucent. Add flour and cook, stirring, until mixture is lightly colored. Remove from heat and add the milk, a little at a time, stirring constantly until sauce liquefies. Place saucepan over medium heat and cook the sauce, stirring constantly, until thick. Let it "puff" once or twice. Remove from heat and cool. Beat eggs, cream, pepper, and nutmeg together. Stir the cooled sauce, a little at a time, into the egg mixture and mix well.

Pierce the bottom of the pastry with a fork. Arrange sausages on the bottom, scatter the peas over sausage, and sprinkle with parsley. Pour the sauce over. Bake for 20 to 25 minutes or until custard is set.

Serve hot.

TAMALE PIE   (UNITED STATES)

SERVES 8

A favorite dish from the Southwest.

1 tablespoon oil	salt
¼ pound salt pork, diced	¾ teaspoon chili powder
1 onion, chopped	4 ounces canned hominy grits
2 cups canned peeled tomatoes	½ cup olive oil
2 cups fresh or canned corn	butter for pan
½ cup yellow cornmeal	bread crumbs

TOPPING

½ cup pitted olives, cut into rounds	2 eggs
2 cooked sausages, about ½ pound, cut into rounds	½ cup milk
	pepper

Place the oil and salt pork in a casserole; brown lightly over medium heat. Add onion, cover, and cook until onion is translucent. Drain tomato juice into a bowl and set aside. Purée peeled tomatoes through a food mill to remove seeds. Add purée to salt pork mixture. Bring to a boil and simmer very gently for about 10 minutes. Add corn.

Pour the cornmeal in a steady stream into the reserved tomato juice. If mixture is too thick, add a little water; the consistency should be soupy. Stir into casserole. Add salt to taste, chili powder, hominy, and olive oil. Cook, stirring for 5 to 10 minutes. Remove from heat and cool.

Preheat oven to 350°F. Butter a 2½-quart ovenproof casserole. Sprinkle with bread crumbs. Turn cooled mixture into casserole, and smooth the top. Arrange the olive slices and sausages on the top in a decorative fashion.

Beat the eggs and milk together, add pepper and salt to taste, and pour into the pie. Bake for about 1 hour.

VENISON PIE   *(UNITED STATES)*
SERVES 6

This is an adaptation of an old Virginian recipe. The original is published in that little treasure of a book called *The Williamsburg Art of Cookery* by Mrs. Helen Bullock.

DOUGH
butter for pan
1 batch of Classic Puff Pastry (p. 11)
    or Quick Puff Pastry (p. 12)

FILLING

1 ounce (2 tablespoons) butter	pinch of dried rosemary
1 tablespoon oil	pinch of dried thyme
4 pounds lean venison (leg or shoulder), cubed	3 bay leaves
	pinch of grated mace
1½ tablespoons flour	salt and pepper
2 cups Chicken or Beef Broth (p. 19)	2 tablespoons chopped walnuts (optional)
1 large onion	4 ounces Madeira or sherry wine

Heat butter and oil in a heavy casserole, brown venison on all sides. Sprinkle with flour and cook, stirring until flour is quite brown. Add broth, a little at a time, while stirring and scraping bottom of casserole.

Cut a cross at the bottom of the onion and set it in the middle of the stew. Add all herbs, mace, and salt and pepper to taste. Cover casserole and cook at a simmer for 1 hour or more. Meat should be tender and sauce quite thick. Add walnuts, if used, and Madeira or sherry. Bring to a boil and remove from heat. Discard onion and bay leaves.

Preheat oven to 400°F. Butter a 2½-quart casserole. Pour stew into it. On a floured board roll out the dough into a circle large enough to top casserole. Place dough over the filling and trim excess dough with scissors; seal all around rim. Pierce top in several places to allow steam to escape. Decorate pie with scraps of dough if so desired.

Bake pie for 20 minutes. Reduce heat to 375°F., and bake for 40 minutes longer. If top tends to brown too much, cover loosely with foil.

TOURTIÈRE   *(CANADA)*

At Christmastime *tourtière* is as traditional in Canada as *Torta Pasqualina* is at Easter in Italy. They are both symbolic of the season. *Tourtière* is a hearty, warming, and filling winter dish, delicious to eat and a pleasure for the eye.

SAVORY PASTRY

2 ounces (½ stick) butter, plus
    butter for pan
4 tablespoons lard
1 egg, beaten
¼ teaspoon salt

½ teaspoon dried savory
2½ cups all-purpose flour
6 to 8 tablespoons cold water
1 egg, beaten with 2 tablespoons
    water

FILLING

1 ounce (2 tablespoons) butter
2 onions, chopped
1 garlic clove, minced
2½ pounds boneless pork shoulder,
    chopped
1 scant tablespoon cornstarch
¾ cup chicken stock or bouillon,
    hot

salt and pepper
½ teaspoon ground sage
¼ teaspoon ground mace
pinch of ground cloves
2 tablespoons minced celery leaves
4 to 5 tablespoons fine bread
    crumbs

Make the pastry: Cream butter and lard in a mixing bowl. Beat in egg, salt, and savory. Blend in flour until mixture resembles coarse meal. Sprinkle water, 1 tablespoon at a time, over flour mixture, mixing with a fork until dough is moistened and can be gathered into a ball. Refrigerate for at least 30 minutes.

Melt butter in a skillet. Add onions and garlic and sauté until tender. Add pork; continue to cook, breaking up the meat and stirring, until meat has lost its pink color. Sprinkle with cornstarch. Add stock, all the seasonings, and the celery leaves. Bring to a boil and simmer, uncovered, until meat is thoroughly cooked and excess liquid evaporated, 20 to 25 minutes. Cool.

Preheat oven to 400°F. Butter an 11-inch pie pan. Divide dough into 2 parts. Roll out 1 part into a circle large enough to line bottom and sides of prepared pan. Fit dough into pan, and pierce the bottom with a fork. Spoon filling into pastry. Sprinkle with bread crumbs. Roll out the second piece of dough into a circle and cover pie with it. Trim excess dough with scissors, and seal edges in a decorative fashion. Make a funnel in the middle. Decorate pastry with scraps of dough. Brush with the egg and water mixture. Bake for 10 to 15 minutes. Reduce temperature to 350°F., cover top of pie with foil, and cook for about 25 minutes longer, or until pastry is nicely golden in color.

Cool before slicing.

NOTE: The *tourtière* is usually baked 1 day ahead. It can be reheated in a 325°F. oven for 35 to 45 minutes.

WINE: Graves Blanc

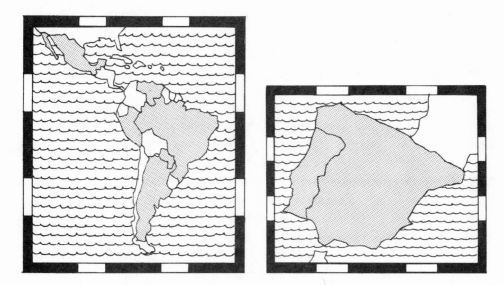

Latin Countries

Spain · Portugal · Latin America

*T*he cuisines of Spain and Portugal and that of the New World have very little in common. Although the roots were the same, the branches bore different fruits. The Conquistadors, like the North American colonists, had to learn to eat the indigenous food. Corn, a New World product, is the major ingredient in *empanadas* or pies, while on the other side of the Atlantic, wheat flour continues to be used. Flavorings and condiments are also quite dissimilar. Spain, according to a Mediterranean tradition, uses garlic with a fervor. Mexico is passionate about chiles.

Another marked difference between the two continents lies in the consumption of seafood. Today's Latin Americans are mostly meat eaters and think nothing of letting other nations fish their waters. This is especially true in Argentina, which has meat and vegetables of superior quality, thanks to the special soil and climate of the more fertile parts of the Pampas. The Iberians, instead, take full advantage of the offerings from the sea, and not

247

only in the coastal regions. Santiago de Compostela, for instance, is famous for its fish specialties. The scallop shell is identified with the city and is a symbol of devotion to the patron saint, James the Greater, Iago in Spanish. The *empanada* of scallops made here is a superb dish; this and the ubiquitous *empanadas gallega* are found all over Galicia and elsewhere in Spain.

The Iberians are imaginative when preparing fish, although the stress is on the freshness of the ingredients. The many elements of a *paella* seem discordant at first, but the sight of it is always reassuring. Invariably the taste is excellent as dictated by an educated palate. Even when pungent, the flavor is delicate and full of aroma.

The Portuguese love a touch of the exotic and have accepted with more readiness the use of certain spices from Mozambique, India, Brazil, and other places once part of a vast empire. After all, it was the need for spices which sent their famous navigator Vasco da Gama on the first voyage from western Europe around Africa and into the Indian Ocean.

Today the primitive dishes of the Conquistadors have become the most sought-out specialties. These dishes retain an earthy, natural quality. Corn is used not only for tasty *empanadas*, but also for *pasteles, tacos,* and *tortillas.* It is interesting to see the cunning food combinations, primarily dictated by the need to augment the protein content in a mostly vegetarian diet. The newcomers learned from the Indians that beans, peanuts, cashews, cacao, and other seeds were all rich in protein. Today one finds these used in many dishes.

The Indians showed many things to the new farmers. One was the tortilla, transformed by the Mexicans into the wafer-thin taco which they fill with beans and dress with a variety of sauces, just as a Neapolitan will do with pizza. Tortilla was born, like the unleavened bread of the Hebrew, out of necessity; a rapid, rustic bread whose principal element, corn flour, was too heavy to leaven. Freshly made and baked in the hearth, tortillas are delicious without any embellishment.

TORTILLAS   (M E X I C O)

The *tortilla*, another flat unadorned "cake of Elijah," becomes the foundation for a complete meal in Latin America. Tortillas are eaten plain or combined with an array of ingredients. Like pizza, a tortilla can be topped, stuffed, rolled, folded. The New World tortilla, which is a bread, must not be confused with that of Spain, which is a flat omelet. The best-known dishes made with tortillas are *tacos, enchiladas, tostadas,* and *quesadillas*. Every country in Latin America has its own variety.

It isn't easy to make a perfect tortilla without a tortilla press. But one can manage by using a rolling pin and flattening the dough between 2 layers of foil, or by patting them by hand as was done in ancient times and is still done in Indian villages.

2 cups *masa harina* (see Note)   1 to 1¼ cups warm water

Mix flour and 1 cup water in a large bowl; stir in enough of the remaining water to make a soft dough. Divide dough into 16 pieces; roll each piece into a ball. Place 1 ball between 2 sheets of wax paper in the center of a 6-inch tortilla press. Close press; push handle down firmly. Open press. Carefully peel paper from tortilla. Repeat with remaining dough.

Heat a small cast-iron skillet over medium-low heat. Place a tortilla in the hot pan and cook for 30 seconds. Invert tortilla and cook until brown, about 1 minute. Turn again, and cook first side until brown, about 30 seconds. Remove from skillet. Keep finished tortillas warm under a napkin.

NOTE: *Masa harina* (corn flour) is available in Mexican food stores, with directions for making tortillas on the package.

TORTILLAS DE HARINA   (M E X I C O)
Flour Tortillas

4 cups flour
1½ teaspoons salt
4 ounces (1 stick) butter, or ½ cup
    shortening
water

Sift the dry ingredients together. Chop in the butter or shortening and mix well. Add enough tepid water to form a soft dough. Turn onto a lightly floured board and knead a few times. Divide into 14 balls, each the size of an egg. Cover dough balls with a cloth, and let stand for about 20 minutes.

Roll out the balls into flat thin rounds. Cook in an ungreased iron skillet over moderate heat; turn each tortilla once.

TACOS   (M E X I C O)
Filled Tortillas

SERVES 6

Tacos are tortillas filled with fish, meat, or other tidbits. When the filling does not require cooking, a taco can be eaten just folded over. Otherwise it is rolled up and fried, grilled, or baked. There is no end to the variety of tacos one can improvise or devise. Just try making them once and you will be a master forever.

6 slices of Edam or Emmenthaler cheese
6 tortillas
¾ cup shortening
½ cup flour, or more
pinch of ground ginger
pinch of salt

pinch of pepper
1 egg, lightly beaten
1 medium-size onion, minced
2 tomatoes, peeled and chopped
hot chile pepper flakes, or ground chiles
1 cup bouillon

Place a slice of cheese on each tortilla. Roll and fasten with toothpicks. Reserve 2 tablespoons of the shortening and melt the rest in a skillet. Combine flour, ginger, salt, and pepper. Roll *tacos* in this mixture, dip into beaten egg, and sauté until golden. Set aside and keep warm.

Melt the reserved shortening in another skillet and cook onion until soft and transparent. Add the tomatoes and a few flakes of hot chile pepper or a pinch of ground chiles. Cook at a simmer for 10 minutes. Add the bouillon and continue to cook the sauce over medium heat until stock has been reduced and sauce is fairly thick. Check seasoning. Pour sauce over *tacos* and serve at once.

PAN DE MAÍZ Y VERDURA   *(U R U G U A Y)*
Corn Bread with Vegetables

SERVES 6 TO 8

3 tablespoons olive oil
3 onions, chopped
3 tomatoes, chopped
¾ cup stock, or 1 bouillon cube
    dissolved in ¾ cup water
1 teaspoon salt
butter for pan

2 cups cornmeal
1 teaspoon baking powder
½ pound cottage cheese
1½ ounces (3 tablespoons) butter,
    melted
1½ cups milk

Heat the olive oil in a saucepan. Add the onions and sauté, stirring frequently, for 5 minutes. Add the tomatoes and sauté, again stirring frequently, for 10 minutes. Add the stock and salt and cook over medium heat for 10 minutes. Preheat oven to 350°F. Butter a 9-inch pie pan.

Combine the cornmeal and baking powder together. Add the cottage cheese and butter, and mix well. Add the milk and beat until well blended. Combine with the tomato mixture. Pour into prepared pan. Bake for 1 hour, or until set. Turn out onto a platter and serve at once, cut into wedges.

CHEPA   *(P A R A G U A Y)*
Cheese Loaf

1 LOAF

⅔ cup shortening, at room
    temperature
2 eggs
1½ cups grated American or
    Cheddar cheese

2¼ cups cornmeal
¼ teaspoon salt
⅓ cup milk
butter for pan

Cream the shortening. Add the eggs and beat well. Add the cheese and mix until smooth. Combine the cornmeal and salt together and add to the cheese mixture, alternately with the milk, mixing steadily. Knead together with the hands until well blended. Preheat oven to 375°F. Butter a 9-inch loaf pan. Place the dough in prepared pan and cover with foil. Bake for 35 minutes, or until firm. Serve in slices.

TORTA DE PLÁTANO   (VENEZUELA)
Plantain Pie

SERVES 4

In Venezuela this *torta* is served as an accompaniment to meat dishes, especially pot roasts and stews.

2 very ripe plantains	3 tablespoons sugar
3½ ounces (7 tablespoons) butter, plus butter for pan	1 teaspoon ground cinnamon
2 cups grated queso blanco or Munster cheese	3 eggs, separated flour

Peel the plantains, cut into halves crosswise, and cut each half lengthwise into ¼-inch slices. Melt 3 tablespoons butter in a heavy skillet over moderate heat. Add sliced plantains and cook, turning frequently, until the slices are golden brown on both sides. Drain the plantains on a double thickness of paper towels.

In a small bowl, combine the grated cheese, sugar, and cinnamon; set aside. In a large bowl, beat the egg whites until stiff. In a separate bowl, beat the egg yolks until they are thick and lemon-colored. With a spatula gently fold the whites into the yolks.

Preheat oven to 350°F. Butter and flour a 1-quart baking dish or mold. Turn the dish over and rap it sharply to remove any excess flour. Spoon about a quarter of the egg mixture into the dish, and spread it evenly with the back of a spoon. Cover with a layer of plantains, using about one-third of the slices. Sprinkle with ⅔ cup of the cheese mixture and dot with 1 tablespoon butter. Repeat the layers 2 more times, ending with the egg mixture. Dot with remaining butter and place in the middle of the oven. Bake for 35 minutes.

NOTE: Plantains can be found in Spanish markets and wherever Caribbean people have settled. These fruits are starchy, like a potato, and double the size of a large banana. While ripe ones are used for this recipe, they can be cooked and eaten when still green.

QUEIJADAS DO SINTRA   *(P O R T U G A L)*
Cheese Pastries

DOUGH

butter for pans   1 batch of Pâte Brisée I (p. 6)

FILLING

3 egg yolks   ¼ cup pine nuts (pignoli), ground
⅔ cup grated Parmesan cheese   1 tablespoon flour
1½ cups pot cheese, sieved   cinnamon
¼ cup blanched almonds, ground

Drop egg yolks into a bowl with the Parmesan cheese and beat until the mixture is thick and lemon-colored. Beat in the pot cheese, the ground almonds and pine nuts, the flour, and a pinch of ground cinnamon. Butter 2 baking sheets 10 x 15 inches.

Preheat oven to 400°F. On a floured surface roll out the dough to a very thin sheet. Cut the dough into 4-inch squares. Put 2 tablespoons of the cheese mixture in the center of each square, turn up the edges of the squares, and pinch the corners of the squares together. Place the pastries on the buttered baking sheets. Bake for 15 to 20 minutes, or until pastries are golden brown.

Cool before serving.

BOLINHOS DE BACALHAU   *(P O R T U G A L)*
Codfish Cakes

Cod is the venerated fish of Portugal. To preserve the fish and have it at every season, it is salted and dried. To remove the salt, cod is soaked in water. The length of time needed for soaking depends on the kind of cure. Sides of cod that are as hard as shingles need to be soaked for 3 to 4 days, and the water should be changed several times during this period. But there are salt fish still flexible, and these require less time. Consult your fishmonger when you buy your cod; he will probably offer you a clutch of recipes as well as advice for soaking. At the end of this process the fish is like fresh again, with the addition of a delicate salty taste.

1 pound codfish, soaked and ready to use	1 mint leaf, minced, or a pinch of dried mint
2 cups hard bread, crumbled	2 tablespoons sweet paprika
½ cup olive oil	salt and pepper
1 tablespoon minced fresh parsley	¼ cup vegetable oil
¼ cup minced fresh coriander	2 garlic cloves, halved

Place cod in a saucepan, cover with water, bring to a boil, and simmer for about 20 minutes. Cool. In a mixing bowl combine crumbled bread, olive oil, herbs, and paprika. Mush the bread while mixing all ingredients. If mixture appears too dry, add a little more oil. Skin, bone, and flake the cod. Add to the mixing bowl together with salt and pepper to taste. Beat vigorously with a wooden spoon until mixture is well combined. Moisten your hands and shape into 6 flat cakes, 3 to 4 inches in diameter and ½ inch thick.

Heat the vegetable oil in a large skillet. Add garlic and fry until it starts to color. Remove and discard garlic. Add as many codfish cakes as possible without crowding them, and fry for a few minutes on each side, until golden. Drain on paper towels.

These cakes are often served topped with a poached egg.

TORTILLA DE MERLUZA AL HORNO   (S P A I N)
Fish Baked in Batter

SERVES 6

Merluza or whiting is a rather inexpensive fish in the United States. Its delicate flavor combines well with the airy batter in which the fish is baked in this recipe.

FILLING

2 pounds whitings, dressed	salt
1 onion, quartered	
1 celery rib, cut into 4 pieces	2 ounces (½ stick) butter, plus butter for pan
1 carrot, cut into 4 pieces	
1 bay leaf	1 large onion, chopped
2 tablespoons vinegar	1 tablespoon minced fresh parsley
4 or 5 peppercorns	1 tablespoon minced fresh dill

FISH VELOUTÉ

1 tablespoon butter

1 tablespoon flour

1 cup fish broth (from poaching
    fish)

1 teaspoon prepared mustard

salt and pepper

BATTER

1 ounce (2 tablespoons) butter,
    melted

1 cup flour

1 tablespoon grated cheese

1 teaspoon prepared mustard

pinch of pepper

pinch of ground allspice

salt

2 eggs

½ cup warm milk

1 cup Marinara Sauce (p. 17)

Place the fish in a large deep skillet. Add the quartered onion, the celery, carrot, bay leaf, vinegar, peppercorns, and salt to taste. Add water to cover. Bring to a boil and simmer for 15 minutes. Let fish cool in the broth, but remove 1 cup of the broth to make the velouté sauce.

Make the sauce: Melt the butter in a saucepan, add the flour, and cook stirring for a few minutes. Remove from heat and slowly add the fish broth. Stir until sauce liquefies. Return to the heat and cook, still stirring, until sauce thickens and starts to boil. Immediately remove from heat. Add mustard and seasoning to taste. Reserve.

Preheat oven to 375°F. Butter a 10-inch pie pan. Melt the 2 ounces butter in a skillet. Add the chopped onion and cook over low heat until onion is soft and translucent. Meanwhile, remove fish from its broth and bone completely. Add fish to the skillet and flake it while sautéing it for a few minutes. Stir in parsley, dill, and velouté sauce. Mix and remove from heat. Spoon mixture into the prepared pan, flatten the top, and set aside.

Make the batter: Place the melted butter in the bowl of a food processor, or the bowl of an electric mixer. Add all the dry ingredients with salt to taste; process briefly. Add the eggs, and gradually add the milk. Batter must be rather liquid; if it is too thick, add a little more milk. Pour batter over fish mixture. Bake for 25 to 30 minutes, until top is set. Do not let dry.

Serve with marinara sauce.

PASTÉIS DE CARANGUEJOS RECHEADOS
Crab Tartlets   *(B R A Z I L)*

12 TARTLETS

DOUGH

butter for tartlet tins
1 batch of Pâte Brisée II (p. 7)

1 raw egg yolk, beaten

FILLING

2½ pounds fresh crab meat
½ teaspoon ground dried chile
   pepper
¼ cup lemon juice
pepper
3 slices of white bread without
   crusts
¼ cup milk
2 ounces (½ stick) butter
1 cup chopped, seeded, peeled
   tomatoes

⅓ cup chopped onion
1 tablespoon minced fresh parsley
¼ cup clam broth
1 tablespoon flour
2 tablespoons water
3 hard-cooked egg yolks, chopped
salt
6 pitted black olives, halved

Place crab meat in a mixing bowl and sprinkle with chile pepper, lemon juice, and black pepper to taste. Let stand for 15 minutes. Put bread in a small bowl, add milk, and let bread soak; then chop coarsely and set aside. Heat butter in a large skillet over medium-low heat. Stir in tomatoes, onion, and parsley. Simmer uncovered until onion is tender, about 10 minutes. Stir in crab meat and soaked bread; simmer for 4 minutes. Add clam broth, and heat to boiling. Mix the tablespoon of flour with 2 tablespoons water and stir into the skillet. Cook, stirring occasionally, until thickened, about 15 minutes.

Preheat oven to 375°F. Butter 12 tartlet tins, each about ¾-cup size; set aside. On a floured board roll the dough out to a sheet ½ inch thick. Cut out 6-inch rounds of dough, or whatever size is large enough to line bottom and sides of the little tins, with enough extra to fold over. Line the tins, fold the edge over, and crimp all around. Pierce the bottom of the dough with a fork. Line each one with aluminum foil and fill with dried beans or rice. Bake for 10 minutes. Remove beans or rice and foil and set aside to cool.

Stir chopped egg yolks into the crab-meat mixture. Season with salt and black pepper to taste. Spoon mixture into prepared shells. Brush the edges of the pastry with beaten egg yolk. Garnish each one with an olive half. Bake for 35 minutes, until golden.

WINE: Dão Branco

EMPANADA DE SANTIAGO DE COMPOSTELA
Scallop Pie   *(S P A I N)*

SERVES 6 TO 8

This is my adaptation of the *empanada* special to the famous pilgrimage town. It is a delicate and tasty dish, to be served as the main course for an elegant lunch or supper.

DOUGH

butter for pan	1 batch of Pâte Brisée II (p. 7)

FILLING

1 ounce (2 tablespoons) butter	nutmeg
1 tablespoon finely chopped shallot	2 egg yolks
2 pounds fresh scallops	1 cup heavy cream
salt and pepper	flour
½ cup dry white wine	1 tablespoon minced fresh parsley

Butter a 9- to 10-inch pie pan. Preheat oven to 375°F. Heat 1 tablespoon of the butter in a skillet. Add the chopped shallot and cook briefly. Add the scallops and salt and pepper to taste. Cook over high heat for about 40 seconds. Add the dry white wine. Cook for about 1 minute. Remove the scallops with a slotted spoon. Reserve the liquid in the skillet. As the cooked scallops stand, liquid will accumulate. Add this, too, to the skillet. This liquid will be used in the sauce. Keep it warm. Place half of the scallops in the container of a food processor. Add salt and pepper to taste, a dash of nutmeg, and the egg yolks. Process the ingredients, with quick on and off turns. Gradually add the cream, and process to a creamy purée, about 1 minute. Pour the mixture into a mixing bowl and set aside.

Dice remaining scallops and combine with the puréed mixture. In a mixing cup combine ½ teaspoon butter with a scant tablespoon of flour. Add the juice from the scallops (you should have almost ½ cup or less) to the cup and mix until smooth. Add this thickening to the scallop mixture. Stir in the minced parsley, and mix well. Set aside.

On a floured board roll out two-thirds of the dough into a circle large enough to line the bottom and sides of the prepared pan. Fit the dough into the pan. Pierce the bottom of the dough with a fork. Let 1 inch of dough hang over the edge of the pan all around. Cut excess dough with scissors. Pour the scallop mixture into the dough-lined pan. Roll out remaining dough and cover top. Fold in the overhanging dough and pinch edges all around in a decorative fashion. Make 4 or 5 slashes in the top piece of dough to allow steam to escape. Bake for 45 minutes to 1 hour, or until top is golden brown.

Let cool 10 minutes before serving.

NOTE: This *empanada* reheats well.

WINE: Rioja Blanco

ENCHILADAS VERDES   (M E X I C O)
Chicken-Filled Tortillas with Green Tomato Sauce

12 ENCHILADAS

DOUGH

12 Tortillas (p. 249)

SALSA VERDE

6 to 7 green tomatoes, quartered	1 tablespoon oil
1 green pepper, cut in strips	1 tablespoon sugar
2 tablespoons butter	

In a food processor place tomatoes and pepper and puree. In a casserole place butter and oil. Add vegetable puree and sugar. Bring to a boil, simmer for 15 minutes, and cover.

FILLING

2 whole chicken breasts, each about ¾ pound	¾ cup finely chopped onions
1 cup chicken stock	2 tablespoons lard or vegetable shortening
6 ounces cream cheese	grated cheese
½ cup heavy cream	

Place the chicken breasts in a heavy saucepan, pour in the stock, cover, and bring to a boil over high heat. Reduce the heat and simmer chicken very gently for about 20 minutes, or until tender. Transfer chicken to a plate and reserve the stock.

When chicken is cool enough to handle, remove the skin and bones and shred the meat into small pieces. Place cream cheese in a large mixing bowl, and beat until smooth, then beat in the heavy cream, 3 tablespoons at a time. Stir in the onions and the shredded chicken, and mix thoroughly. Set aside while you make the sauce.

Preheat oven to 350°F. Melt the lard or shortening in a large heavy skillet over moderate heat until a light haze forms above the fat. Fry and fill the tortillas one at a time, as follows:

Dip a tortilla into the sauce, drop it into the skillet, and fry it for a minute or so on each side, or until limp. Transfer the tortilla from the pan to a plate and place 2 to 3 tablespoons of the chicken mixture in the center. Fold tortilla to enclose the filling. Place it, seam side down, in a buttered baking dish large enough to contain all tortillas in 1 layer. Fry and fill remaining tortillas. Pour remaining sauce over filled tortillas and sprinkle in grated cheese.

Bake for 15 minutes or so. Dish is ready when it starts to bubble.

NOTE: Chopped roast pork or beef can be substituted for the chicken.

EMPANADA GALLEGA DE GALLINA (*SPAIN*)
Galician Chicken Pie

SERVES 6 TO 8

One of the most famous specialties of Spain, this *empanada* comes from the city of Santiago de Compostela in Galicia. There are several types of *empanada gallega*; the Galicians are masters in the art of making these savory pies.

DOUGH

1 package active dry yeast
pinch of sugar
½ cup lukewarm water (105° to 115°F.)
3 cups flour
1 teaspoon salt

¼ cup warm milk
2 tablespoons olive oil
2 eggs, lightly beaten
1 tablespoon water
butter for pan

FILLING

1 frying chicken, 2 to 3 pounds, cut
    up
1 stack of celery, cut in 4 pieces
1 large onion, quartered
1 carrot, cut in 4 pieces
¼ cup olive oil
1 small onion, chopped

1 garlic clove, minced
1 red bell pepper, seeded and diced
3 medium-size tomatoes, peeled,
    seeded, and chopped
½ chopped serrano or prosciutto
    ham
salt and pepper

Dissolve yeast and sugar in the lukewarm water. Let it stand in a warm place for 10 minutes. Sift 2 cups of flour and the salt onto a pastry board. Make a well in the center and pour in the yeast mixture, the milk, oil, and 1 beaten egg. Beat with a fork to blend the flour into the liquid, and gather the mixture into a soft but consistent dough. Knead the dough for about 15 minutes, adding remaining flour if needed. Gather dough into a ball again and place it in a lightly oiled bowl. Cover, and set in a warm place to let dough rise until doubled in bulk, about 1½ hours. Punch dough down and let rise again for 45 minutes.

Place the chicken in a large saucepan. Add the quartered vegetables and enough water to cover. Bring to a boil, reduce heat, and cook chicken for 30 to 45 minutes. When chicken is cool enough to handle, remove skin and bones and cube the meat. Reserve vegetables for another use.

Heat the oil in a large skillet. Add chopped onion, garlic, and red pepper. Cook until vegetables are tender, about 10 minutes. Add the tomatoes and cook over medium-high heat for about 5 minutes. Add the ham, cubed chicken, and seasoning to taste. Continue to cook for 5 to 10 minutes longer. Make sure mixture is not too liquid. Cool to room temperature before assembling *empanada*.

To assemble, divide the dough into 2 parts. Roll each part into a circle, about 12 inches in diameter and ¼ inch thick. Butter a 12-inch pie pan. Place the first circle in the pan, and spread the filling over, leaving a 1½-inch rim all around. Cover with the second circle and seal, pinching edges all around in a decorative fashion. Let the pie rest in a warm place for 20 to 30 minutes.

Preheat oven to 400°F. Mix remaining beaten egg with the tablespoon of water to make egg wash, and brush the pie with the mixture. Bake for 45 minutes, until the top is lightly browned.

Let cool before slicing.

WINE: Rioja Tinto

PASTÉIS DO MADEIRA   *(P O R T U G A L)*
Madeira Turnovers

DOUGH
1 batch of Brioche Dough II (p. 14)

FILLING

1½ ounces (3 tablespoons) butter
1 medium-size onion, minced
¾ pound mushrooms, minced
½ cup bread crumbs
salt and pepper
thyme

1 egg, lightly beaten
1 tablespoon lemon juice
1 tablespoon minced scallion
3 whole large chicken breasts
2 cups minced raw broccoli
parsley sprigs for garnish

2 cups Madeira Sauce (p. 18)

Melt 1½ ounces butter in a skillet. Add onion and cook, covered, until onion is soft and translucent. Add mushrooms and cook, uncovered, until water released by mushrooms is evaporated. Add bread crumbs and salt, pepper, and thyme to taste. Set aside.

Reserve 2 tablespoons of the beaten egg and mix with 2 tablespoons water for egg wash. Place the rest of the egg in a mixing bowl and add remaining filling ingredients except chicken breasts and broccoli. Set mushroom mixture and broccoli near you. Skin the chicken breasts, split them and bone them, and place each piece between 2 sheets of wax paper. Pound them as thin as possible (they will never become as flattened as a veal scallop). Spread equal amounts of the broccoli on the 6 chicken cutlets and fold each cutlet over to enclose filling. Set aside.

Preheat oven to 375°F. Divide dough into 3 parts. On a lightly floured board, roll 1 piece of dough at a time into a rectangle 15 x 9 inches. Cut into halves and trim sides. Reserve scraps of dough. Spread each pastry rectangle with about 2 tablespoons of the mushroom mixture, leaving 2 inches empty all around the edge. Top each with a chicken roll. With a pastry brush, brush egg wash along pastry edges. Fold pastry over chicken, overlapping edges; press lightly to seal; tuck ends under to make a neat package. Continue until all dough pieces are rolled out and filled. Place the pastry packages on a baking sheet and refrigerate. Roll out scraps of dough, and cut into thin strips. Tie one strip around each pastry package, as you would a parcel. Make a decorative knot on the top of each. Brush pastry with remaining egg wash. Bake for 45 minutes, or until pastry is golden.

Present the chicken turnovers garnished with parsley sprigs. Serve Madeira sauce separately.

WINE: Monção Branco

TOSTADAS DE PAVO   (M E X I C O)
Turkey Tostadas

12 TOSTADAS

DOUGH

12 Tortillas (p. 249)   2 tablespoons oil

FILLING

2 tablespoons oil   1 avocado, sliced very thin

1 scallion, chopped   12 black olives, pitted

8 ounces canned tomatoes   ½ head of lettuce, shredded

2 cups chopped cooked turkey   (optional)

salt

4 radishes, peeled and sliced
     very thin

SAUCE

8 ounces canned tomato sauce   ½ tablespoon vinegar

1 hot chile pepper, fresh or canned,   pinch of orégano

     chopped (optional)   pinch of coriander

1 tablespoon oil   1 small scallion, minced

Heat half of the oil in a skillet. Add the scallion and sauté until soft and translucent. Add tomatoes and cook, stirring, for about 5 minutes. Add chopped turkey and stir well. Add salt to taste, cook briefly, and keep hot.

Sauté the tortillas in remaining 2 tablespoons oil. When golden, drain them on absorbent paper. Place all ingredients for the sauce in a saucepan. Bring to a boil, and cook at a simmer for 15 to 20 minutes. Working with 1 tortilla at a time, smear each one with 1 or 2 tablespoons of sauce. Add about 3 tablespoons of the turkey mixture. Place some radishes and avocado slices on top of turkey. Garnish with 1 black olive per tostada and a small amount of shredded lettuce. Serve at once.

EMPANADAS
Fried Pies

DOUGH

3½ cups all-purpose flour

1 teaspoon salt

4 ounces (½ cup) margarine

½ cup warm water

2 ounces (½ stick) butter, softened

oil for deep-frying

FILLING

2 tablespoons oil

1 pound tender beef (sirloin or
    tenderloin), cubed

2 medium-size onions, chopped

1 medium-size potato, cooked and
    cubed

2 hard-cooked eggs

½ cup raisins

10 green olives, pitted

1 teaspoon ground cloves

1 teaspoon paprika

cayenne pepper

salt and pepper

Combine flour and salt in a bowl. Chop in the margarine and add water; mix and gather into a ball. Turn dough out on a lightly floured board and knead for 15 minutes. Divide into 4 parts. Roll out each part, spread with a little bit of the butter, fold in half, and roll again. Spread with a little more butter, fold again, and refrigerate the 4 parts for 1 hour.

Make the filling: Heat the oil in a skillet. Add beef and onions and sauté until browned. Add ¾ cup water and simmer for 1 hour. Water should be completely absorbed; if not, let it boil until evaporated. Add the potato and cook briefly, just to warm through. Remove from heat. Add remaining filling ingredients with seasoning to taste, stir well, and cool.

Roll out the dough, 1 piece at a time, to a sheet ⅛ inch thick. Cut dough into 3-inch rounds. Put 1 heaping teaspoon of filling in the center, fold over, and crimp edges together. Deep-fry *empanadas* till brown on both sides.

EMPANADAS
Fried Pies

(V E N E Z U E L A)

In Venezuela, the dough for *empanadas* is completely different. It is made with a very fine cornmeal, available in specialty stores or Spanish groceries. Regular cornmeal will not do unless pulverized in a food processor. The dough must be mixed by hand. It takes a little practice to obtain a correct balance of meal and water.

DOUGH

½ pound very fine cornmeal   warm water

Place the cornmeal in a bowl and add just enough water to make a smooth ball. Dough must be flexible; if it is too thick, add a little more water; if too thin add a little more cornmeal. When the consistency is correct, pinch off a small ball of dough and pat it into a 3-inch round, ⅛ inch thick.

For the filling, omit the hard-cooked eggs and the potato. Add 2 to 3 tablespoons of capers to the meat mixture, and use a dash of Tabasco instead of paprika. Place 1 tablespoon of filling in the center of each prepared round and fold over. Crimp edges to seal, and deep-fry as in the Argentinian version above.

PASTEL DE CHOCLO   (ARGENTINA)
Corn Pie

SERVES 8

How many times have you been left with a batch of cooked ears of corn that you didn't know how to use up? I suggest you scrape the kernels off and make this pie.

4 ounces (1 stick) butter
2 onions, chopped
3 green peppers, cut into thin
    julienne strips
3 tomatoes, chopped
1½ pounds ground beef
2 tablespoons sugar
1½ teaspoons salt

⅛ teaspoon pepper
3 hard-cooked eggs, chopped
3 cups corn kernels, drained and
    ground
1 cup flour
1 cup milk
7 eggs, beaten

Butter a 2½-quart casserole. Melt 3 tablespoons of the butter in a saucepan. Add the onions and green peppers and sauté, stirring frequently, for 10 minutes. Add the tomatoes and cook over medium heat for 5 minutes. Add the meat, 1 tablespoon of the sugar, 1 teaspoon of the salt, and the pepper. Cook over medium heat, stirring occasionally, for 15 minutes. Add the eggs and mix well. Remove from the heat and set aside.

Melt remaining butter in a separate saucepan. Add the corn and stir.

Spoon flour into a bowl. Add milk and remaining sugar and salt, and mix to a smooth paste. Add to the corn, stirring constantly. Cook over low heat, stirring occasionally, for 10 minutes. Set aside to cool for 5 minutes.

Preheat oven to 375°F. Add the eggs to the corn mixture and beat well. Pour half of the corn mixture into the prepared casserole. Pour the meat mixture on top and cover with the remaining corn mixture. Bake for 30 minutes, or until eggs are set.

Serve hot, directly from the casserole.

PASTEL DE FRIJOLES Y MAÍZ   (P E R U)
Bean Tamale Pie

SERVES 6 TO 8

DOUGH

butter for casserole	1 teaspoon salt
1 cup cornmeal	¼ cup grated Parmesan cheese
4 cups water	

FILLING

2 tablespoons oil	1 teaspoon sugar
1 large onion, chopped	4 cups canned peeled tomatoes,
1 pound ground beef	drained
salt	2 tablespoons tomato paste
1 tablespoon chili powder	½ cup sliced ripe olives
½ teaspoon orégano	3 cups cooked pinto beans, freshly
½ teaspoon basil	cooked or canned, drained

Butter a 2½-quart casserole. Heat oil in a skillet. Add onion and sauté until tender. Add ground beef and cook until brown, breaking meat apart with a fork. Add salt to taste, chili powder, orégano, basil, sugar, drained canned tomatoes, tomato paste, olives, and drained beans. Simmer for 1 hour.

Preheat oven to 350°F. Combine cornmeal with ½ cup water. Bring remaining 3½ cups water to a boil. Add salt and moistened cornmeal. Cook for 10 minutes, stirring. Spread half of cornmeal in the bottom of the prepared casserole. Add bean mixture. Spread remaining cornmeal on top. Sprinkle with Parmesan cheese. Bake for 30 minutes.

Let the pie cool for 10 to 15 minutes before serving.

TORTILLAS A LA GUARANI   (PARAGUAY)
Baked Filled Tortillas

SERVES 6

The Guarani are the people of Bolivia, Paraguay, and southern Brazil. Their language has given us several food words, cashew for example.

DOUGH

12 corn Tortillas (p. 249)

FILLING

1 pound boneless cooked meat (pork or veal), chopped	pinch of black pepper
2 tablespoons chopped cashews	pinch of cayenne pepper
1 tablespoon raisins	1 tablespoon vegetable fat, butter,
pinch of sugar	or margarine (the Indians use
pinch of salt	beef fat), at room temperature

In a mixing bowl combine all ingredients for the filling except fat. Spread filling on 6 tortillas, and top with remaining 6. Brush each one with softened fat. Bake in a preheated 375°F. oven for 15 minutes.

BUÑUELITOS DE JAMÓN   (SPAIN)
Ham Puffs

10 TO 12 PUFFS

3 tablespoons flour
2 eggs, separated
1 cup milk
½ pound ham, chopped
oil for deep-frying

Combine flour and egg yolks in a mixing bowl. Gradually add the milk. Stir in the ham. Stir until batter is smooth. Beat egg whites until stiff and fold into the batter.

Heat the oil and drop in a tablespoon of the batter at a time. Turn puffs as they fry, and fry them until golden in color. Drain on paper towels.

These delicious fritters can be served hot or cold.

VARIATION: Substitute cheese, cooked fish, shellfish, sausages, etc., for the ham.

EMPANADA GALLEGA DE PUERCO *(SPAIN)*
Galician Pork Pie

DOUGH

5 cups all-purpose flour

2 eggs

4 ounces (1 stick) butter, at room temperature, plus butter for pan

1 teaspoon baking powder

1 teaspoon salt

1 cup cold water

1 egg yolk

1 tablespoon water

pinch of ground saffron

FILLING

⅔ cup lard or vegetable shortening

4 medium-size onions, chopped

1 pound boneless pork, cubed

½ pound chorizo sausages, skinned and sliced

½ pound veal, cubed

½ pound ham, cubed

pinch of ground saffron

few flakes of dried chile pepper (optional)

salt and pepper

Place the flour on a pastry board, and make a well in the center. Break the 2 eggs into it and beat them. Add butter, baking powder, salt, and cold water, and blend in the flour. Gather the dough into a ball and knead until smooth, about 10 minutes. Use more flour if necessary. Let the dough rest, covered with a bowl, while preparing the filling.

Heat lard or vegetable shortening in a skillet. Add onions and cook until soft and translucent. Add pork cubes and chorizo slices and cook for 10 minutes. Add veal, and cook for 10 minutes longer. Add ham, saffron, and chile pepper if used. Season with salt and pepper to taste, cover, and cook until meats are done, about 25 minutes longer.

Preheat oven to 450°F. Butter a 12-inch pie pan. Roll out three-quarters of the dough into a circle large enough to cover bottom and sides of prepared pan. Fit dough into pan and trim excess dough with scissors. Spoon filling into dough-lined pan. Reserve liquid accumulated at bottom of skillet. Roll out remaining dough into a second circle and cover the filling. Press dough all around and crimp edges together to seal the pie. Cut a little cross in the center of the top to allow steam to escape. Decorate pie with scraps of dough. Mix egg yolk with 1 tablespoon water and a pinch of saffron to make egg wash. Brush top of pastry with this egg wash. Bake for 20 minutes, or until golden brown.

Remove pie from oven and pour 1 or 2 spoons of the reserved liquid into the vent. Serve hot or cold.

NOTE: When this specialty of Galicia is served in a home, the pie usually sports the initials of the host on top of the crust.

EMPANADILLAS A LA VALENCIANA   (S P A I N)
Valencia Turnovers

12 TURNOVERS

Small *empanadas* are found all over Spain. They are served at the beginning of a dinner, in between, and after. Ideal as a snack, especially when sitting out of doors in the shade of an ancient cathedral, sipping a glass of cooling wine. *Empanadillas* can be made with a variety of stuffings.

DOUGH

3 cups flour
1 teaspoon salt
½ cup olive oil
½ cup cold water

1 teaspoon anise liqueur, or pinch
    of ground aniseed
butter for pan
1 egg
2 tablespoons water

FILLING

2 tablespoons olive oil
1 large onion, chopped
2 tomatoes, peeled and chopped
1 garlic clove, minced

2 thick slices of country-cured ham
    or prosciutto, diced, about ½
    pound
2 hard-cooked eggs, mashed
salt and pepper

Combine flour and salt in a mixing bowl. Make a well in the center and pour in oil, water, and flavoring. Blend thoroughly with fork. Gather dough into a ball and turn out on a floured board. Knead lightly and refrigerate.

Heat olive oil in a skillet. Add onion and cook until soft. Add tomatoes and garlic and cook until liquid evaporates. Add ham and cook, stirring, for 4 or 5 minutes. Remove from heat and add eggs. Taste for seasoning. Cool.

Preheat oven to 425°F. Butter a baking sheet. Roll dough out to a sheet about ⅛ inch thick. Cut out twelve 5-inch circles. Fill half of each circle with some of the ham mixture. Moisten the edge and fold the other half over. Seal *empanadillas* in a decorative fashion. Mix egg with 2 tablespoons water to make egg wash. Brush the pastries all over with egg wash. Pierce tops with a fork. Bake for 25 to 30 minutes, or until golden brown.

WINE: Valepeñas Blanco

Supply Sources

Many of the ingredients used in the recipes in this book are available by mail order from the following stores.

ABBONDANZA
1647 Second Avenue
New York, N.Y. 10028
groceries, processed meats, special foods

APHRODISIA
28 Carmine Street
New York, N.Y. 10014
herbs and spices

BALDUCCI'S
424 Sixth Avenue
New York, N.Y. 10009
fresh vegetables, groceries, meat and fish

BREMEN HOUSE
220 East 86 Street
New York, N.Y. 10028
groceries, processed meats

BROADWAY PANHANDLER
520 Broadway
New York, N.Y. 10012
kitchen implements

CAPECCI & PERNICE PORK STORE
26 Carmine Street
New York, N.Y. 10014
pork products, groceries

IL CONTE DI SAVOIA
555 Roosevelt Road West
Chicago, Illinois 60607
cheeses, spices, sausages, cooking implements

THE COUNTRY STORE
Weston, Vermont 05161
groceries

DEAN & DELUCA
121 Prince Street
New York, N.Y. 10012
groceries, processed meats, special foods

DEMARTINO'S FISH & OYSTER MARKET
132 Eighth Avenue
New York, N.Y. 10011
fresh fish

DIPALO DAIRY STORES
206 Grand Street
New York, N.Y. 10013
dairy products

269

GREAT VALLEY MILLS
Quaker Town
Bucks County
Pennsylvania 19951
flour

JEFFERSON MARKET
455 Sixth Avenue
New York, N.Y. 10009
groceries, fish and meat

OTTOMANELLI'S MEAT
    MARKET
281 Bleecker Street
New York, N.Y. 10014
meat

PAPRIKAS WEISS
1546 Second Avenue
New York, N.Y. 10028
spices and herbs

H. ROTH & SON
1577 First Avenue
New York, N.Y. 10028
herbs and spices, flour

STAUBITZ MARKET
222 Court Street
Brooklyn, N.Y. 11201
groceries

TODARO BROTHERS
557 Second Avenue
New York, N.Y. 10016
imported and domestic foods

PAUL A. URBANI
130 Graf Avenue
P.O. Box 2054
Trenton, New Jersey
08638
truffles

WILLIAMS-SONOMA
576 Sutter Street
San Francisco, California
94102
cooking implements

WILLIAMS-SONOMA
438 North Rodeo Drive
Beverly Hills, California
90210
cooking implements

ZAMPOGNARO (LO)
262 Bleecker Street
New York, N.Y. 10014
*cheeses, herbs and spices,
processed meats*

Index